Teaching Children's Literature

"What an amazing, important, and 'tide-changing' book! Theoretically grounded yet very practical and engaging to read, it will help readers easily envision using children's literature in their own classrooms."

Prisca Martens, Towson University

"I believe this text has the potential to shift the way teachers and teacher educators work with children's literature. It invites them to consider the role of children's literature in developing critical understandings of important issues in the world."

Amy Seely Flint, Georgia State University

"This is cutting-edge work. It shows what critical literacy curriculum can look like in classrooms and highlights the major tenets that define this approach."

Kathryn Mitchell Pierce, Wydown Middle School, Missouri

"This book fills a HUGE gap in the field right now. The demonstrations and strategies the authors provide illustrate the rigor of the classrooms that value authentic engagement with texts, curriculum, and alternate ways of knowing."

Tasha Tropp Laman, University of South Carolina

This groundbreaking text offers a fresh perspective on how to implement children's literature into and across the curriculum in ways that are both effective and purposeful. Honed over years of experience and reflection in classroom settings and rich with real examples of teachers implementing critical pedagogy, it invites multiple ways of engaging with literature that extend beyond the genre-and-elements approach and also addresses potential problems or issues that teachers may confront.

The book is structured around three "mantras" that build on each other: Enjoy; Dig deeply; Take action. The practical strategies for taking a critical approach focus on issues that impact children's lives, building from students' personal experiences and cultural knowledge to using language to question the everyday world, analyze popular culture and media, understand how power relationships are socially constructed, and consider actions that can be taken to promote social justice. This is not a book of prescriptive strategies and does not try to "sell" teachers a program. Instead, it trusts teachers as professionals and talks to them as such. *Teaching Children's Literature: It's Critical!* teems with pedagogical purpose. It is smart, principled, and useful. Its freshness and currency will resonate with readers and inspire their teaching.

A Companion Website enriches and extends the text. Features include an annotated bibliography of children's literature with key words to enable electronic searching, suggested text sets, and other relevant materials.

Christine Leland, Mitzi Lewison, and **Jerome Harste** are professors in the department of Literacy, Culture and Language Education at the Indiana University School of Education in Bloomington and Indianapolis. They have a long history of teaching courses in reading and children's literature and have worked together for many years exploring the role critical literacy can play in creating curriculum for students at all levels.

Teaching Children's Literature
It's Critical!

Christine Leland
Mitzi Lewison
Jerome Harste

Routledge
Taylor & Francis Group

NEW YORK AND LONDON

First published 2013
by Routledge
711 Third Avenue, New York, NY 10017

Simultaneously published in the UK
by Routledge
2 Park Square, Milton Park, Abingdon, Oxon OX14 4RN

Routledge is an imprint of the Taylor & Francis Group, an informa business

Library of Congress Cataloging in Publication Data
Leland, Christine.
    Teaching children's literature : it's critical! / Christine Leland, Mitzi Lewison, Jerome Harste.
      p. cm.
    Includes bibliographical references and index.
  1. Children's literature—Study and teaching (Elementary)—United States. 2. Literature—Study and teaching (Elementary)—United States.
I. Lewison, Mitzi.   II. Harste, Jerome C. (Jerome Charles)   III. Title.

LB1575.5.U5L45 2012
372.64′044—dc23   2011046273

ISBN: 978-0-415-50866-7 (hbk)
ISBN: 978-0-415-50868-1 (pbk)
ISBN: 978-0-203-12531-1 (ebk)

Typeset in Minion Pro
by RefineCatch Limited, Bungay, Suffolk, UK

Printed and bound in the United States of America
by Edwards Brothers, Inc.

Contents

Preface vii

Acknowledgments xi

CHAPTER 1 — Introduction 3

CHAPTER 2 — Why Reading Aloud Is Crucial 17

CHAPTER 3 — Teaching Reading with Literature 37

CHAPTER 4 — Choosing Books: Diversity Counts 59

CHAPTER 5 — Supporting Literature Discussions 83

CHAPTER 6 — Inquiry into the World through Focused Studies 107

CHAPTER 7 — Multimodal Responses to Literature 125

CHAPTER 8 — Language Study: Lingering in Text 143

CHAPTER 9 — Challenging the Challengers 161

CHAPTER 10 — Literature Response Strategies 179

References: Children's and Adolescent Literature...203

References: Professional Publications 209

Index...219

Preface

Children's literature is taught in English departments in colleges of arts and science, in departments of library science, and in schools of education. As a result, there are many different kinds of children's literature textbooks. Our experience has been that many books with "children's literature" in their titles do a very different kind of work than what parents, elementary and middle school teachers, and teacher educators want to do with children's literature.

So let's be clear from the start. This book is primarily written for teachers and teacher educators—people who work in preparing teachers in the area of reading and language arts and who are responsible for the ongoing professional development of teachers in these areas.

Within this frame, children's literature takes on heightened significance. We argue that using and teaching children's literature is critical to the development of a sound elementary and middle school curriculum. We also argue that it is crucial that children's literature be presented in a socially conscious fashion so as to prepare a critically literate citizenry for the 21st century.

This volume builds from and extends the instructional model of critical literacy found in our earlier book, *Creating Critical Classrooms: K-8 Reading and Writing with an Edge* (Lewison, Leland, & Harste, 2008). The ability to think critically is more important now than it ever has been because our nation's system of public education is under attack from forces that seek to privatize it. While politicians and the media focus on standardization and test scores, this book argues that the future of our democracy depends on our collective ability to ensure that our children become enthusiastic and savvy readers, thinkers, and doers. To accomplish this goal, we argue for a new educational mantra that shifts the focus from raising test scores to raising readers. You will find this mantra, ***Enjoy! Dig deeply! Take action!***, as a unifying theme throughout the book.

How This Book Is Organized

There are many ways to use trade books in classrooms and at home. To provide a coherent plan for exploring such a complex subject, we have organized the chapters around the mantra described above.

The first chapter (Introduction) describes our goals for the book and articulates a conceptual framework for our thinking.

Chapters 2–4 focus on creating the conditions for learners to *enjoy* reading—*Why Reading Aloud Is Crucial, Teaching Reading with Literature*, and *Choosing Books: Diversity Counts*.

The theme running through chapters 5, 6, and 7 is the idea of preparing intellectually engaged readers who *dig deeply* regardless of the text on a page or screen—*Supporting Literature Discussions, Inquiry into the World through Focused Studies*, and *Multimodal Responses to Literature*.

Chapters 8, 9, and 10 offer numerous suggestions for using children's and adolescent literature to provide opportunities for students at all levels to *take action* on issues they see as important—*Language Study: Lingering in Text, Challenging the Challengers*, and *Literature Response Strategies*.

Features That Make This Book Special

Each chapter opens with three elements that are closely linked:

- *Vignettes*. These short narratives showcase individual teachers using children's literature in their classrooms for a variety of purposes; they invite conversations about how others might use trade books to address different topics or goals.
- *Key principles.* Following the opening vignette, the main theme of each chapter is elaborated via a set of key principles that are intended to connect theory to practice. Since these principles relate specifically to the content of each chapter, they go beyond the mantra described above. In other words, while each chapter connects broadly to one part of the mantra, the key principles will help you to zoom in more directly on what each chapter is about. Because curriculum is something we want to do *with* our students (not *to* our students) we want students as well as teachers to own these principles. Curricular principles are too important to be kept for oneself. They need to be shared with students, administrators, and parents. Our goal is to support everyone in keeping his or her eyes on what is truly important.
- *Related research.* In this section we cite research focusing primarily on key studies that clarify the topic and speak to its importance. These research citations can be used in building a case for why the topic of the chapter is an important component of curriculum.

At the end of each chapter, six short sections focus on areas that merit extra attention:

- *Key issues in implementation*. We know that implementing many of our recommendations will not be easy. Therefore, this section attempts to do two things. First, we describe some of the policies and practices that might make achieving the goals of the chapter difficult. Second, we explain how some teachers have worked around these issues and consider what other strategies we might employ.
- *Working with linguistically and culturally diverse students.* These sections provide suggestions for working with diverse populations, including students whose primary language is other than English, older readers who are less proficient, and students who

are seen as "different" for any number of reasons. Topics like inclusion, racism, and homophobia—that many teachers find challenging—might also be addressed in this section.

■ *Technology extensions and electronic resources*. This section in each chapter references Internet resources that teachers and students will find useful. While we know that technology is a moving target, we also believe that there are many sites that will assist teachers in getting more children's and adolescent literature into their classrooms.

■ *Assessment*. Since we know that everyone is concerned with knowing how to document growth, we include a section that deals with this subject in each chapter. These pieces provide an alternative approach to standardized testing and challenge the idea that teachers should not be an integral part of the assessment process in their classrooms.

■ *Invitations.* These student-focused engagements at the end of each chapter exemplify what the chapter is about and provide a way to put the content into practice. These strategies support enjoyment, digging deeply, and taking action. They were created, developed, and tried out with teachers in a wide variety of classroom settings. Invitations are open-ended, generative and collaborative activities that teachers can discuss with students and then leave for them to work on in small groups. Curricular strategies that appear in bold italic print in any of the chapters signal that the strategy is written up in more depth in Chapter 10. These are ones teachers have found particularly powerful.

■ *Ideas for professional development.* Each chapter ends with suggested professional development activities and annotations for related articles. These resources will be especially helpful when teachers want to work together in study groups. Articles might be read together and discussed as part of study group meetings.

Companion Website. The dedicated Companion Website for *Teaching Children's Literature: It's Critical!* (www.routledge.com/cw/leland) gives readers access to a large collection of annotated books, suggested text sets, and other relevant materials.

Our Goals in This Book

Our central goal is to create a critically thoughtful citizenry, hence the title of the book, *Teaching Children's Literature: It's Critical!* By now, you have probably recognized the double meaning we have embedded in the title of the book. First, we think it is *critical* (i.e. really important) to make trade books the centerpiece of any reading program. But we are also arguing for a *critical literacy* approach to teaching that can guide thought and action across the content areas as well as throughout life. Beginning with what students bring in terms of their personal experiences and cultural knowledge, a critical approach encourages them to use language to question the everyday world, interrogate the relationship between language and power, analyze popular culture and media, understand how power relationships are socially constructed, and consider actions that can be taken to promote social justice.

Literacy keeps changing and expanding. To be considered literate today, students need to be more literate than their parents and their grandparents. This book is meant to support parents, teachers and teacher educators in using children's and adolescent literature to live a curriculum that is both literate and supportive of leading a critically literate life.

Acknowledgments

We are grateful to the many amazing teachers we have worked with over the years and want to thank them for sharing their ideas and their classrooms with us on numerous occasions. We made a "wordle" to recognize the teachers who contributed ideas and vignettes for this book.

FIGURE 0.1. Thank You, Teachers!

Our process of writing this book was greatly facilitated by the anonymous feedback we received from experts in the field on some of our early chapters. We wish to thank Prisca Martens (Towson University, MD), Kathryn Mitchell Pierce (Wydown Middle School, Clayton, MO), Amy Seely Flint (Georgia State University), and Tasha Tropp Laman (University of South Carolina) for keeping us grounded while also encouraging us to push our approach to children's and adolescent literature in needed new directions.

We also wish to thank Naomi Silverman, our editor at Routledge, who helped us to think through the design of the manuscript and then answered endless questions about how to pull it all together. Her input was invaluable to the success of the project.

one
Introduction

Welcome to *Teaching Children's Literature: It's Critical!* We wrote this book to help educators and families provide the optimal conditions for raising *real readers*. Our view is that real readers not only know how to read, but also *enjoy* reading. In addition, we see real readers as people who *dig deeply* into what they are reading and are subsequently willing to *take action* to get things done in the world and advocate for equity. These three components form the mantra *Enjoy! Dig Deeply! Take Action!* that we use throughout the book to keep all of us centered on what matters most. While each piece of the mantra can stand alone, we see the convergence of all three as providing our best chance for growing the kind of readers needed to address the challenges of the 21st century.

Enjoy! When we talk about developing students who enjoy reading, we don't mean that they read assigned texts without complaining or that they occasionally pick up a book on their own. No, we are talking about the kind of reader who gets reprimanded for having an open book in her lap during math class. We are talking about a reader with a flashlight under the covers after lights out because he simply cannot sleep until he finishes the chapter—or maybe even the whole book. In other words, we are talking about voracious readers who choose to read because they find great enjoyment in it. We know we have succeeded when our young people echo the sentiment of Jim Trelease (2006), who said, "reading is so delicious I must have it every day of my life" (p. 9). The goal of helping our students see reading as something "delicious" is why our mantra begins with a focus on enjoyment. Real readers enjoy reading and pursue it relentlessly, whether they are holding a book or looking at a screen.

Dig Deeply! While enjoyment is our first goal, digging deeply follows close behind in terms of importance. This part of the mantra refers to active reading that raises questions about the assumptions that are built into every text. Digging deeply into text can also be described as taking a critical approach to reading. It is very different from understanding reading as a process of saying all the words correctly and delivering standard answers to the comprehension questions at the end of the story or chapter. Instead of buying into the assumption that there is one right answer to any question, critical readers make a special effort to look for multiple perspectives and explanations.

Reading critically means that we see texts as expressing assumptions or perspectives that we may or may not want to accept. As Hilary Janks (2010) so aptly points out, "texts have designs on you." By this, she means that authors write texts for the express purpose of getting readers to believe something or buy into specific cultural models. Readers who are able to size up the situation and draw their own conclusions become *agents of text* since they retain the power to make their own rational decisions about what to believe. Those who don't engage in critical reading are more likely to become *victims of text* since they tacitly accept assumptions that might not stand up under further scrutiny.

Consider, for example, our suggestion that the humorous rendition of an old fairy tale like *Red Riding Hood* (Marshall, 1993) might not be as innocent as we think. While this story is one that many in our culture read to young children, there are a number of underlying messages or assumptions in the story. Some of these are subtle and some are not. Students in one of our children's literature classes were able to identify the following implicit messages:

Girls should stay on the straight and narrow path.
Parents always know best.
Women are vulnerable and easily sweet-talked into doing dumb things.
Men need to save young girls and old women.
Wolves are bad.
Men are wolves.
Red is a seductive color. Women who wear it are asking for trouble.

(Harste, Leland, & Jackson, 2002)

We recommend that you try to unpack the assumptions in another "innocent" fairy tale. You might be surprised by the hidden messages you discover too!

Take Action! Once we have readers who love to read and know how to read critically, the third step is that they use what they learn to get things done in life, advocate for equity, and make the world a better place. While this may sound trite, we see it as the ultimate goal for all schooling in a democracy. If we end up with citizens who cannot work with others and are only concerned with their own needs and interests, we have failed to educate them.

The taking action part of the mantra can play out in different ways. At the most basic level, it could entail a reader changing his or her mind about something. This might lead to more obvious actions like taking a new stand on an issue or joining a group to push for certain actions. Within the context of reading this book, taking action might be accomplished through changes in your practice. It might be the decision to read aloud from a piece of children's or adolescent literature each and every day, no matter what, or the decision to put the basal readers on a back shelf and find novels for students to read instead. In both examples, action is taken to give literature—what some call "trade books"—a more central role in the reading curriculum.

Why Trade Books Matter

According to *The Literacy Dictionary* (Harris & Hodges, 1995), "trade books" are books "published for sale to the general public" or "commercial books, other than basal readers, that are used for reading instruction" (p. 258). Note that commercial basal reading programs are not trade books; rather, they are anthologies put together by publishing companies expressly for the purpose of teaching reading skills. Basal programs often are seen as a complete reading package. They come with workbooks, follow-up activities, and a teacher's edition delineating what questions you, the teacher, should ask students. These programs are based on what we see as three erroneous assumptions: (1) that learning to read requires a discrete set of skills that must be taught in a pre-determined order; (2) that all learners progress at the same rate and need the same kinds of support; and (3) that teachers are not capable of designing their own lessons and need to be told exactly what to do and say. In addition, basal readers don't even pretend to focus on motivating kids to want to read.

In contrast, pieces of children's literature are "writings specifically intended for children, or that children have made their own" (Harris & Hodges, 1995, p. 30). These books are designed to appeal to a wide audience. They are focused on stories, told with humor and unforgettable language. Stories are often emotional and provide readers with a lived-through experience they are not likely to forget. In addition to stories, there are numerous non-fiction trade books for children and adolescents. These texts are popular with many young readers who are fascinated by the information they provide.

We want to see literature used across the entire curriculum, from reading instruction to teaching in the content areas. As a first step we believe teachers need to make children's or adolescent literature the basis of their reading and writing programs. While children's literature is often highlighted in commercial reading programs, it's important to understand that the original stories found in trade books are frequently revised to fit the instructional plan of the basal. What these programs do is adapt pieces of literature to fit their skill scope and sequence charts. They do this by altering the wording or not using all of the illustrations found in the original texts. Croce, Martens, Martens, and Maderazo (2009) gave children the original and the basal version of several children's books to read. Children were appalled by the changes and said things like, "How could they do that [in reference to leaving out certain illustrations]?" "No wonder we had trouble understanding that page! The original story is so much better" (p. 158). By making these comparisons children also began to note what made texts work, including how they were written and illustrated. Croce and her colleagues asked children to think not only about the text and what it meant, but also about how the illustrations in the stories supported the development of particular ideas, moods, and impressions:

> The results of our study emphasize that when students are supported in learning to draw on cues in both the written and pictorial texts and helped to consider the meaning each offers, they expand and enhance their learning, thinking, and meaning-making as readers. (pp. 167–168)

Real reading vs. reading instruction. It is important to understand the difference between a critical literature-rich curriculum and basal reading programs that *use* stories from trade books to focus on the skills of reading. Succinctly, it's the difference between "reading"—by which we mean "real reading"—and "reading instruction." Lots of children have learned to hate reading by the very way it has been taught.

Frank Smith (1981) argues that in every language event there are a number of demonstrations to which participants can attend, based on their interest, experience, and focus. When you are reading a book aloud to your class for enjoyment, individual students may attend to any or all of the following demonstrations: the story itself, the particular ways things are said, the voices you use for the various characters in the text as you are reading it aloud, the parts of the story that are funny, how the pictures support (or fail to support) the text, how the story relates to the things that are happening in the classroom, stereotypes that are being refuted, new stereotypes that are being perpetuated, etc. These demonstrations are what we want students to attend to as they are reading.

If, however, book experiences focus more on reading instruction than reading enjoyment, learners may pay more attention to correctness and getting the right answers. Instead of understanding book experiences as a process of interacting with text and other readers to make meaning, students will follow their teachers' example and jump in to correct their fellow students whenever they miscue (what the authors of basal readers see as making a mistake that must be corrected immediately). Rather than attending to the implications of the story for making sense of their world, they might focus instead on remembering information they suspect will show up on their comprehension worksheet, or that they are sure you are going to ask once you finish the read aloud. In one classroom that used a basal reading program focusing on vocabulary, when the teacher asked students what they wanted to talk about, they all began identifying new vocabulary words – responses they were sure their teacher wanted because this is what typically happened every time she read to them. The teacher was following the teacher's manual that came with the program in an uncritical way and did not realize the limiting nature of this approach.

Programs that use snippets of literature to teach the skills of reading highlight demonstrations that relate more to decoding than the strategies real readers use to make meaning and find significance. The focus of these programs is quite different: Commercial basal programs stress practice; those built on authentic literature focus on use. Douglas Barnes (1992) puts it even more cogently: "How you teach is just as important as what you teach" (p.8). Basal reading programs make the mistake of focusing on developing reading skills instead of developing readers. How reading is taught can, and often does, determine the amount of enjoyment developing readers experience.

Charlotte Huck (1966) addresses the same issue when she warns that we are creating a nation of "aliterate literates" (p. 8). By this she means that we teach people to read but the readers we create fail to exercise this right once they leave the classroom. Kylene Beers (1996) describes aliteracy in terms of the voices of reluctant middle school readers: "No time, no interest, no way!" (p. 30). We want to change all that by talking about how to teach literature so that it is central to lifelong learning and responsible citizenship. This entails talking about books in terms of their contributions as well as their shortcomings. It includes the sheer enjoyment of books and an appreciation of what the author was trying to do as well as a critique of what was left undone. Books not only help us see ourselves more clearly. They also help us see new possibilities for interacting with others.

A Purist vs. a Critical Approach

Some advocates of a literature-rich approach to reading are what we call "purists." By this, we mean that they often treat literature as sacrosanct and authors as providing the world with moral guidance, lasting values, and truth. While books can and do demonstrate important values to readers, when texts are treated as exemplars of the best and highest forms of culture, other forms of knowing are diminished and we may inadvertently be teaching young people not to question texts or to feel guilty for not liking what Hirsch (2010) would call "the cultural classics" (p. 9). While these are widely known as some of the "Great Books of the Western World" (Hutchins, 1952) we don't think this means they should be shielded from a critical perspective. A basic question that needs to be asked of Hirsch's list of cultural classics and Hutchins' list of great books is, *Whose culture is being represented?* There are a lot of great books including newer titles that are not well represented on these lists and many of these will resonate with underserved groups in our schools.

Another problem with a purist approach is that it focuses too much attention on what are referred to as the elements of literature—plot, setting, characterization, theme, symbolism—or the critique of text for critique's sake. We have been in classrooms where the elements of literature were the framework through which every book was discussed. While talking about an element of literature might be helpful for responding to a particular text, each element ought to be introduced only when it is important to extend or clarify an ongoing conversation. For example, when Karen Smith's students were reading a book that took place on "the steppe" in Russia, she brought a globe with her to literature discussion and used it to talk about setting and why it was important in this novel. With help from the children, she located where this particular story took place. Students made predictions about the weather and shared what else they knew about this area of the world. Similarly, when a book follows lots of characters Karen often uses a time line to work out how each character's life trajectory fits into the overall plot structure of the book. These "lightly and at the right time" strategies are what Lucy Calkins (1994) calls "mini-lessons" and should take no more than a few minutes during literature discussions. Throughout *Teaching Children's Literature: It's Critical!* we present strategy lessons that focus on the elements of literature but are taught in such a way that they don't take over the curriculum or become a rigid framework that straitjackets conversation.

Don't get us wrong. We, too, believe in looking closely at text. But—and this is a big BUT—we are more interested in focusing on how authors get language to work for them, or as Barbara Comber (2001) has said, "how texts do the work they do" (p. 3). In other words, we want students to understand how texts position readers and glorify some perspectives while deprecating others. This does not mean that we never talk about the elements of literature, because we do, but only in service of students' deeper understanding of the story and how it impacts their world.

Rather than using literature to teach discrete skills or to focus on the elements of literature, we wish to create critical readers. We see this goal as an absolute necessity for education in the 21st century. Colin Lankshear and Michelle Knobel (2006) argue, "Truth no longer exists. What matters is what story gets spun" (p. 8). Given Jerome Bruner's thesis (1987) that story is the basic element of mind—i.e. that we don't think in terms of facts but in terms of stories—Lankshear and Knobel's argument takes on even more significance. According to Bruner, we are bombarded from birth to death by an ongoing stream of stimuli. To make sense of this continual input, we break it up into stories. Stories are chunks of stimuli that we see as cohering or belonging together. Given these insights, we argue that it behooves us to prepare readers who can unpack stories and who know how to read in between and beyond the lines of stories, not only to comprehend them but to create counter stories that illuminate alternate ways of being and acting in the world.

Our Conceptual Framework

For readers familiar with our work, this volume builds from and extends the instructional model of critical literacy found in *Creating Critical Classrooms: K-8: Reading and Writing with an Edge* (Lewison, Leland, & Harste, 2008). That model (see Figure 1.1) shows our understanding of critical literacy instruction as a transaction among three components that are represented by rings: First, the personal and cultural resources we bring; second, the critical social practices we enact; and third, the critical stance that we are able to demonstrate in the classroom and in the world. What follows is an abbreviated explanation of each of these rings with references in parentheses to the original wording in the model. Readers who wish to understand this model more fully are encouraged to consult the original text.

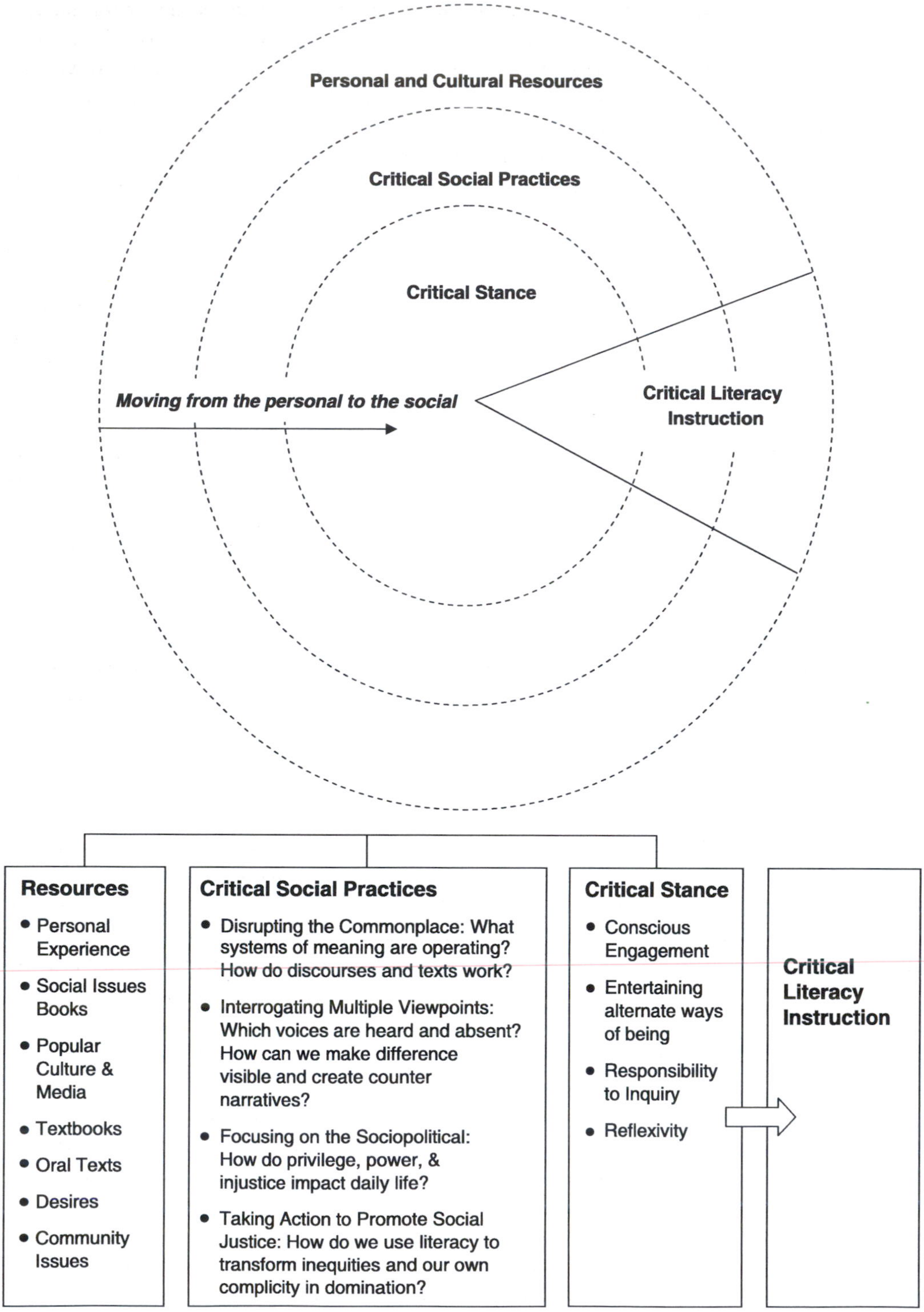

FIGURE 1.1.   Critical Literacy: A Theory of Instruction.

In literature-rich classrooms, children's and adolescent literature are *cultural resources* that permeate the entire curriculum. As books are chosen to connect with the personal and social interests of teachers, students and other stakeholders, they become the core of curriculum. The second ring of this model—*critical social practices*— includes the specific practices in which students and teachers engage as they create curriculum using literature as a resource. As part of reading and responding to literature critically, we want learners to question what has been taken for granted (disrupt the commonplace), see topics from multiple perspectives (interrogate multiple viewpoints), understand who the story benefits and who it disadvantages (focus on the sociopolitical), and do something as a response to the book and their discussion of the topic (take social action to promote social justice).

The inner ring—*critical stance*—consists of the attitudes and dispositions we want to develop in students as they interact with books and with life more generally. These include being thoughtful (consciously engaging), entertaining new ways of talking and acting (alternate ways of being), digging deeply and doing whatever research is needed (taking responsibility to inquire), and outgrowing old beliefs and old habits (being reflexive).

In addition, the model suggests that teachers begin using literature by talking with students in terms of the local—and their own lives and experiences—and only later tie into the global, or larger social issues. This move from "the local" to "the global" is important. Moving to a global perspective involves helping students identify the larger social forces that are at play in the local. When reading a book like *House on Mango Street* (Cisneros, 1984), teachers and students work together to understand the local experiences of Latino-American families in the early 1980s. Exploring the interplay between the local experiences Sandra Cisneros relates in the book and how these were seen in the larger culture helps readers begin to appreciate why the author grew up not liking her hair and not wanting to acknowledge the house she lived in nor, more broadly, the culture from which she came.

Turning Children and Adolescents on to Reading: The Basics

Let's talk basics. As noted in the first part of our mantra, enjoyment is the primary goal for language arts teachers. It is our job to turn our students on to reading. We also know that you will encounter individuals who never had the chance to experience enjoyment, or have been turned off to reading. Craig Larner, a prospective teacher in our program, is a good example since he remembers a time when he hated reading. This is somewhat surprising because earlier in his life, Craig reports that he "read voraciously." Nonetheless, he became increasingly disillusioned with reading as he moved into high school and was given books that were heavy on content but not very interesting to him. By the time he got to college he was "so sick of reading" that he did not want to pick up a book.

Craig was fortunate in finding his way back to reading the way many young people do—he found a book that seemed to reach out and pull him right into the story. "The first *Harry Potter* book (Rowling, 2009) is what did it for me" Craig reports. "And after the first one, I couldn't wait for the next one to come out." It's important to consider that during the decade from 2000–09, the *Harry Potter* volumes were the most frequently challenged books in the entire country (American Library Association, 2010). The series was challenged for being anti-family, promoting the occult, encouraging a problematic religious viewpoint, and being too violent. Although Craig read *Harry Potter* after he left K-12 classrooms, had he tried to read the books while still in the public school system (as many young people do), he might have been told that it was not appropriate reading for school. The very books that changed tens of thousands of non-reading young people into readers are often not on the shelves in classrooms.

While moving from feeling like a burned-out reader back to the enthusiastic reader he had been in elementary school, Craig was very persistent in his pursuit of *Harry Potter* books. When Rowling didn't write them fast enough for Craig, he went to a bookstore and asked what else they had. That's how he found other series books like *Pendragon* (MacHale, 2004) and *Eragon* (Paolini, 2008). Today Craig once again sees himself as a reader: "I get into the flow of the book and don't want to put it down," he said. "I have been known to read until my head literally drops." Teacher Donalyn Miller (Miller, 2009) says that she suffers from the same wonderful malady and sometimes stumbles into her class "bleary-eyed" because she stayed up reading too late. We agree with her conclusion that this is a good thing: "They (my class) may laugh but they also see that reading is something I value enough to lose sleep over" (p. 106).

Student book choice matters. Since we can never be sure that the same books will appeal to all readers, it's important to have a wide variety of books in every classroom—books we love, books we find troublesome, and books that challenge the status quo. They all hold a place on our shelves. Steve Krashen (2006) reports on a research study done by Daniel Fader who encouraged adolescent boys in reform school to read newspapers, magazines, and paperback books for pleasure and then talk about what they read in class. After one year, Fader said he "discovered the boys' reading comprehension scores on the Scholastic Achievement Test had increased by more than an entire grade level, or twice as much as the scores of those students who didn't read for pleasure" (p. 44). Fader went on to explain that he observed these reform-school boys reading in all kinds of places, "even in the bleachers at basketball games, instead of keeping their eyes on the action!" (Krashen, 2006, p.44).

When Mitzi and Chris were classroom teachers they used Daniel Fader's *Hooked on Books* (1981) as a trusted friend to remind them that the more books they had in their classrooms the more likely it was that all kids could find something they were passionate about reading, even if the books they chose weren't seen as "great" literature.

Are we creating passionate readers? One of the criteria we use in the early primary grades to judge whether or not our literature-rich curriculum is creating voracious, insatiable readers is to take note of when children have found a favorite book they wish to read (or hear us read) over and over again. Sometimes this takes extreme forms. We have had children who hid their favorite books in their desks so that others couldn't get them! We once watched a beginning reader read the same book 26 times. When we asked him what he had noticed after several of these readings, he always pointed out new things like the pictures or the repetitive structure of the text.

We use other criteria too. We like to note, for example, friends recommending books to each other. In one of the videotapes shot in Rise Reinier's classroom (Koshewa, 1992) a fifth grader runs up to her friends holding the book *Bridge to Terabithia* (Paterson, 1977) and says, "Hey, you guys. This book is so good. You are going to love it. I can hardly wait until you've read it."

We even like transgressive behavior, or behavior that kids think parents and teachers won't like. Transgressive behavior includes things like children reading novels when they are supposed to be listening to another lesson, and reading books that they have been told not to read. We think there is something quite powerful in an expression promoted by the American Library Association, "Everything I needed to know about life I learned from reading banned books;" we explore this topic in depth in Chapter 9. When a good book calls, we have even found children reading during recess or while waiting in line.

Almost without fail, avid readers can name a book they absolutely loved as a child. Kenneth Goodman (1990) tells the humorous story of a fourth grader who came home from school and told her mother that she had just finished reading *Stone Fox* (Gardiner, 1992). "Mother," she said, "the ending was so sad, I could hardly answer the comprehension questions." After laughing and thinking about this story, it dawns on you that the teacher didn't need a worksheet to check on comprehension given this child's emotional response to this text. In fact, an emotional response like this is evidence that you have created an engaged reader and that you have something really special to celebrate.

Why We Wrote This Book

We love reading and want to support you in your efforts to create readers who take delight in literature. Books offer stories about other people's lives and these stories help us to understand our own lives. We are drawn to books because they provide opportunities for conversations about what we think is important. Conversation allows us to hear what others have to say. While one person can read a story and make a specific connection to her own life, another can read the same story and make a totally different connection. Sharing these different connections and interpretations expands our knowing and helps build and deepen understanding.

We wrote this book to support teachers, administrators, and families in making children's and adolescent literature an important part of school and home learning. The good news is that there are books on every topic imaginable. Our goal is for all of our students to experience reading as something so powerful that they want to do it every day—both inside and outside of school.

We join others in arguing that students have to be more literate today than their parents or grandparents were before them. Literacy keeps changing and expanding (Myers, 1996). Gunter Kress (2003) sees the screen as overtaking the page as the major vehicle of communication. Rather than take what they read or hear at face value, today's citizens need to be able to unpack texts in order to understand and challenge the systems of meaning that are operating to position them in ways they may not wish to be positioned. Our central goal is to create a critically thoughtful citizenry.

What Makes This Book Special

We have organized the chapters according to three guiding principles. First, ***create readers***. Second, *create readers **who are savvy consumers of texts***. And third, *create readers who are savvy consumers of text and **who have the know-how to unpack texts for purposes of repositioning themselves and taking action***.

Guiding Principle One: Create readers. The first principle operating throughout this book is our belief that we as educators are committed to creating readers. We could add "first and foremost" or "who love to read," but these ends go without saying. When we hear politicians talking about "raising test scores," we respond by saying it's more important to focus on "raising readers." We want to immerse our students in books—all kinds of books. Not only fiction but also non-fiction, including the everyday texts that they encounter on a daily basis in their world. Regardless of the age of our students, we often begin by reading a favorite picture book and just enjoy the story and illustrations. Part of this enjoyment comes from relating to the book—talking about what things we really liked or didn't like and how the book connects with our life experiences. The chapter you are currently reading (Introduction) provides an overview of the book, identifies the three guiding principles, and explains how they are cumulative and build on each other.

Chapter 2 (Why Reading Aloud Is Crucial) focuses on creating readers by describing the important role that reading aloud plays both at home and in the classroom. In this chapter we explain why reading aloud is so important and how a good read aloud program gets students so interested in books that they don't want to stop reading. We want to help teachers find books they personally love as well as find books that children and adolescents love.

While Chapter 2 addresses the topic of opening up space for conversations about books through an ongoing read aloud program, Chapter 3 (Teaching Reading with Literature) focuses on teaching reading using trade books. In this chapter we discuss the reading process as well as instructional strategies that support learners in meaning making, attending to print, making predictions, and engaging in the underlying processes that proficient readers use to comprehend texts. A major emphasis of this chapter is the idea that anyone working with beginning or reluctant readers across the K-8 spectrum still needs to focus first and foremost on building a love of reading—in other words, creating readers!

Chapter 4 (Choosing Books: Diversity Counts) explains why it is so important to find, use, and introduce books that allow learners to see themselves in literacy. No one becomes literate without personally connecting to books. If books "other us" such that we cannot connect with what is being said, real reading isn't happening. The very first reader we need to be concerned with is ourself. This is true for us, as teachers, as well as for students. Chapter 4 focuses on the use of a wide array of literature, including social issues books, multicultural, and international literature. Two goals operate here. Give students opportunities to read *extensively* and support and encourage them in reading *intensively*. Given our ever-shrinking world, tomorrow's citizens need to do much more than simply tolerate diversity; they need to see diversity as a resource upon which they can build.

The theme running through these first four chapters is enjoyment. That is, in order to achieve guiding principle one—create readers—our first task as teachers is to get children and adolescents to take pleasure in books and value them. Our advice to teachers is that they begin by using books and activities that invite students into a memorable experience. Our goal as teachers is to help learners connect and relate to the ideas and concepts being read about.

Guiding Principle Two: Create readers who are savvy consumers of texts. Powerful readers do more than just enjoy books; they also question what books have to say by digging deeply and thinking broadly. In one sense they interrupt the assumed meaning by using what they already know or by finding new information that is pertinent to the topic being discussed. To start this process, readers need to go in depth, not only reading between the lines, but also learning to question the underlying assumptions on which the story is built.

Chapter 5 (Supporting Literature Discussions) includes numerous examples of how teachers implement literature study in their classrooms. In this chapter we explore a range of literature study strategies and consider how introducing a set of books around a particular topic like immigration provides opportunities for students to develop new perspectives. We focus particularly on instructional strategies that allow students to read broadly and to think deeply.

Chapter 6 (Inquiry into the World through Focused Studies) describes how teachers can support an inquiry-based program using trade books while building from the questions children and adolescents have about topics of interest. We want to create a knowledgeable citizenry— people who understand the value of multiple perspectives and who refuse to take what others might see as "common sense" at face value. Our goal is to create a literate population that not only understands the value of knowledge but also takes responsibility to inquire and question. To further these ends we advocate that teachers invite students to linger in text, take on challenging texts, and use well-selected text sets to open up new and important curricular spaces. This is done through involving learners in focused studies that address a broad variety of topics, authors, and genres.

Chapter 7 (Multimodal Responses to Literature) demonstrates how the arts might be used to support learners' access to literacy as well as to deepen, broaden, and extend meaning. And, we are not just talking about paper and pencil art activities. We are talking about using all forms of art as well as drama, dance, music and even mathematics to open up new curricular spaces and to support in-depth understanding.

The theme running through Chapters 5, 6, and 7 is the idea of digging deeply. This is meant to remind readers to attend to the questions they have as they are reading and to pay particular attention to anomalies or what doesn't quite make sense. These are signals that more information, and often more research, is needed. In many ways the questions we have and the anomalies we encounter drive the learning process. When we encounter something that doesn't fit or feel right, we have to start thinking anew, searching for what is wrong and thinking about how to fix it. This is what we mean by thoughtful readers who are "savvy consumers of text."

Guiding Principle Three: Create readers who are savvy consumers of text and have the know-how to unpack texts for purposes of repositioning themselves and taking action. Teaching children's and adolescent literature isn't simply a matter of knowing the "right books" to put into students' hands. Teachers also have to put in place the social practices needed to unpack any text that ends up in their hands or on their screens. We want readers who can talk about texts in terms of equality and justice and think about how to take action to effect positive change.

We agree with Sumara (2002) who says that curriculum at its best "disrupts normality" (p.1), by which he means that the best curricula disrupt what people see as typical or expected. Sumara argues that literature should involve "reformulating the already formulated, interrupting certainty, [and] making trouble" (p. 46). Rather than accept the taken-for-granted, we want students to attend to what doesn't make sense to them. We want them to question why the world portrayed in this story, this text, or this piece of literature is problematic and for whom.

The phrase "take action" is meant to suggest that reading isn't a spectator sport. Critically literate readers enjoy books, reflect thoughtfully about the issues raised, and then take action by repositioning themselves and figuring out how to talk and walk differently in the world. For example, *Willy and Hugh* (Browne, 2000) is a book about bullying and while it does good work in the sense of teaching readers that everyone has things to offer regardless of their size or physical prowess, it also perpetuates the stereotype that only boys are bullies. It is easy to read this book and not notice that it is boys—once again—who are being disruptive. While at first it may seem logical that Anthony Browne used boys to portray bullying, the problem is that the book perpetuates what many already think—that boys (not girls) are bullies. By being thoughtful and learning to dig deeply, below the surface structure of text, readers learn to unpack what is often taken-for-granted, even by well-meaning authors. These understandings, then, become the basis of social action. In the safe environment of the classroom, students can use these new insights to try out different ways of being in the world. From what they learn in the classroom, they can go on to reposition themselves in the larger world.

While language study permeates this book, Chapter 8 (Language Study: Lingering in Text) focuses specifically on how language does its work. We want to create a literate citizenry that has the best analytical skills we know to deconstruct texts. At one level, students already have the ability to talk analytically. They often declare that some situation or practice is not fair or "is just not right." In this chapter, however, we want to provide students with technical terms and techniques so that they might create more powerful texts themselves and then use them to take action.

Chapter 9 (Challenging the Challengers) furthers this theme by addressing issues related to censorship and what resources teachers have to combat ongoing attacks on books. We discuss the question of why advocating for open access to books is central to a more just and democratic world. Because the books we as teachers choose to use *or decide not to use* is a pervasive and subtle form of censorship, we encourage you to step out of what might be your current comfort zone.

We want critical literacy to go beyond the schoolhouse walls. We want students to implement new ways of being that allow them to talk and act differently in the world. One way to think about taking action is to see it as combining new ways of talking with new activities. For example, reading *Quick as a Cricket* (Wood, 1998) started Vivian Vasquez's kindergarten children on an inquiry about frogs, insects, habitats, and rain forests. The class moved to social action by writing letters to parents "asking them not to buy wood that's been harvested from rain forests" (Vasquez, 2004, p. 50). Similarly, after reading a series of books about child labor, David Nakai's seventh graders wrote letters to various shoe companies protesting their use of child labor and low wages (Vasquez, 2010). While it is hard to know if these actions led to visible change, it is important to remember that change, over time, does occur and often begins with the act of a dedicated group of people. The Civil Rights Movement is one example; as a result we now have members of previously under-represented groups playing major roles in business, education and government. The creation of Mothers Against Drunk Driving is another example; as a result of this group's work, much of the English-speaking world now parties more sanely than it did in the past. Protecting the environment and trying to become more "green" about our consumption is a third example and includes everything from the light bulbs we use to the food we eat and the cars we drive. While we still have miles to go in each of these areas, it is easy to argue that children and adults taking action have been instrumental in pushing all of them forward.

Critically literate citizens explore alternate ways of being in the world. What better place than school to take these risks and try on these alternate ways of talking and acting? Taking action entails creating counter texts (oral and written) that do a different kind of work, work that suggests how citizens might walk and talk differently in the world.

While these three guiding principles are interrelated and even overlap, each one pushes literacy in new, much needed, critical directions. To further this end, in Chapter 10 (Literature Response Strategies) we describe curricular strategies that support enjoyment, digging deeply, and taking action. These invitations were created, developed, and tried out with teachers in a wide variety of classroom settings. While we introduce instructional strategies in every chapter, Chapter 10 highlights the ones teachers have found particularly powerful. When you come across a strategy that appears in bold italic print in any of the chapters you are reading, it's a signal that the strategy is written up in more depth in Chapter 10. While some of the strategies in Chapter 10 are ongoing and only the resources change from week to week, most are meant to be curricular engagements that students can do with little or no guidance after being introduced in a whole-class session or walk-through. We have found that one secret to good classroom instruction is to change invitations often as this puts a new edge on learning.

After working through the invitations, we hope students and teachers will have ideas for new strategies and for creating new invitations. As we continue to develop and try out new strategies ourselves, we will put them on the companion website for this book www.routledge.com/cw/leland. We encourage you to do the same. In that way we can—each of us—collaboratively outgrow ourselves.

Why This Book and Your Beliefs Are Important

What you believe about reading makes a difference. *Teaching Children's Literature: It's Critical!* advocates a critical-transactive view of reading in which the reader transacts with text, generates new meaning, and repositions him or herself in the world. As such, theoretically we build from but extend Rosenblatt's (1987) view of reading. People who view reading as a critical transaction create meaning with text as well as argue with text to reread their world. The wonderful thing about literature is that it provides the meat and potatoes for a critically transactional reading experience.

The other side of the coin is what we see as a dysfunctional view. It happens when teachers and students understand reading as a sounding out or memorizing process. When reading is reduced to phonics and the teaching of isolated skills, it loses its allure and becomes boring. In cases like this, reading is taught via a transmission view of reading. The key belief here is that reading is a matter of transferring information from the page to the head of the reader. Since this is not how learning happens, we want to help you find a better way.

We started this chapter by saying how much we love children's and adolescent literature. We would like to see trade books permeating the curriculum. If you are like most of the hundreds of teachers with whom we have worked, you will find that the approach advocated in this book revitalizes both your teaching and your thinking more generally. Creating a critical literature-rich curriculum is not for wimps, but with this book and the resources that children's literature provides, it is within reach.

two

Why Reading Aloud Is Crucial

Kate Kuonen reads to her eighth graders every day even though most of them are accomplished readers on their own. When she read the final page of *Fox* (Wild, 2001) and put the book down, Makayla indignantly exclaimed, "That just *can't* be the ending!" She held out her hand to take the book from Kate and check for herself. Jasmin reached for the book at the same time. "I SO want to draw the fox's eyes," she said longingly as she flipped through the pages to find the illustration she wanted to emulate. Why were these eighth graders so drawn to what looks on the surface like a simple picture book? Jasmin was intrigued by how illustrator Ron Brooks drew the stylized animal characters and wanted to try out some of his techniques in her own art. For Makayla, the story of betrayal and lost friendship was painfully unresolved and she wanted to figure out why the characters acted as they did. She said that the story reminded her of a time when she had been "stabbed in the back" by someone she considered a true friend and wondered if there was any hope for salvaging the previously strong friendship between Bird and Dog. While different interests motivated the two girls, what they had in common was that both of them wanted to spend more time with the book.

We think of reading aloud as a type of advertising for literacy that gets listeners interested in topics, books, and reading in general. Reading aloud helps to set up the conditions for children and adolescents to follow in the footsteps of Kate's eighth graders and reach out for books so they can pursue their own interests and inquiries. Why is advertising necessary? Consider how we are all bombarded with ads for movies, video games, television shows and sports events. There's a lot of competition for how kids spend their time both inside and outside of school. Yet research from the past 30 years has shown over and over again that reading is the best way to become a better reader. For example, a seminal study by Gordon Wells (1986) followed the literacy development of 32 children from different backgrounds over five years. Wells found that conversation and growing up in a literate family environment where reading and writing occurred naturally gave children a big advantage over those who did not have this type of home environment. "And of all the activities that were characteristic of such homes, it was the sharing of stories" that was found to be the most important (p. 194). The child who scored the lowest on all of the tests was never read to; the child who scored the highest had experienced many stories and was already interested in books and written language more generally by age two (p. 181).

This is not to say that children who do not experience this particular type of literate home in their early years are doomed to failure. As Meier (2008) reminds us, children from homes with less written literacy often bring strong oral abilities because they have heard many stories being told. It does, however, underscore the necessity of including reading aloud in the school curriculum. Given the way schooling is currently constructed in terms of what is valued, it's true that some children will be perceived as having a lot of catching up to do. What's important to remember is that these kids will grow more quickly as readers when their teachers focus on reading aloud instead of directly teaching letter names and sounds. This connects to the first part of the mantra we described in Chapter 1. Success in getting kids to enjoy reading and books provides the foundation for literacy growth. It's also important to understand that what is traditionally valued is a subjective construction that can change over time and across cultural groups. We might imagine contexts in which oral literacy trumps written literacy and the whole paradigm gets turned upside down, but this doesn't appear to be on the near horizon.

There is nothing new about the power of reading aloud. Almost three decades ago, Jim Trelease, author of *The Read-Aloud Handbook* (1982) talked about the importance of motivating children to see reading as an activity that brings pleasure and fulfillment. He noted that lots of time and money were going into teaching children to read but something must be wrong because many of them end up *not* reading. Trelease's 2006 edition of *The Read-Aloud Handbook* makes many of the same points. Educators are concentrating too much emphasis on teaching children *how* to read, and not enough on setting the stage for them to *want* to read. His solution? Motivate and engage children through reading aloud to them. While this does not replace teaching them how to read (although we all know kids who *did* learn to read this way), it serves a purpose that is just as important: It gives them a reason for wanting to learn to read, and for keeping them reading after they know how.

No one is too young or too old, too good a reader, or too poor a reader to get something positive out of a well chosen and well prepared read aloud. Babies (even still in the womb) benefit from hearing the patterns of spoken language and come to associate the reading voice with security and comfort. We like to see reading aloud happening several times a day in classrooms—whether students have behaved well or not. Using books as threats and withholding them when children don't do what they have been asked to do is counterproductive at best, since it thwarts our efforts to motivate our students as readers and thinkers.

Principle 1: Good Books Lead to Good Conversations

Have you ever listened to a read aloud and wished that there would also be an opportunity to discuss the book? Sometimes the group is large or time is short and it seems impossible to work a discussion into the schedule. In either case, giving people a chance to turn to a neighbor and talk for two or three minutes can be very beneficial. Once we've had a conversation about a book or other text, our understanding is never the same because we have been introduced to new perspectives and alternate interpretations. Of course conversation also entails some degree of noise, and we can understand why letting lots of kids talk at the same time might be a little scary to a new teacher or someone reading to a large group. However, we see conversation as so powerful for enjoying books and building comprehension that we think the result is well worth the extra time and effort it takes.

Conversations about a book can take place throughout a read aloud or at the end. A simple question like "What were you thinking about as I read this book?" usually leads to a rich discussion. We often provide our own response to get things going. For example, after reading *Fox* in one of her classes, Chris told students that she had been anxious all through the book, thinking that Fox was going to kill Bird. At the end, Bird was alive but her friendship with Dog seemed to be dead—so she wondered if it was a book about death. This led to a lively discussion that was similar to the one Kate had with her eighth graders after they experienced *Fox* as a read aloud. Both conversations focused not only on friendship, but also on philosophy, metaphorical thinking, and stereotypes. In this case, the story served as a scaffold for helping both groups access a number of sophisticated concepts. They made personal connections to the book and compared the events with similar situations from their own lives. They discussed the overarching fire metaphor and analyzed the illustrations in terms of how they supported the underlying sense of fear. In both cases, the conversation was rich and multifaceted. What was most surprising was the extent to which participation in the event seemed to encourage both adults and adolescents to move from simply enjoying the book, to digging more deeply into issues it brought to the surface. How many of us have been guilty of brushing an old friend aside when a new friend seems more exciting or stylish? How many of us have acted foolishly and then regretted our hasty decisions? Making these connections through a book might also move us to take action in addressing past injustices.

Much research has focused on the effects of discussing books as part of the read aloud experience. For example, Beck and McKeown (2001) studied how the teacher's use of "text talk" could enhance children's comprehension of the stories being read to them. The text talk process included the use of intellectually challenging texts and open-ended questions that invited children to discuss and explain what was going on rather than expecting them to recall or retrieve specific words from text. Follow-up questions encouraged children to elaborate on initial ideas and develop them further. For example, when children were unable to answer an open-ended question about an important event in the story, the teacher reread that section and emphasized key words and phrases before rephrasing the question. The researchers concluded that in-depth and extensive experiences with this type of interaction positively affected children's ability to construct meaning. A similar approach called "dialogic reading" (Doyle & Bramwell, 2006) involves the teacher in creating engagements that are designed to "bring the children deeper into the meaning of the story" (p. 554). For example, after reading aloud a story about characters who cooperated to achieve something, the teacher in this study guided the children through an activity where each child had to "contribute for the task to be successful" (p. 557).

Quality conversations. Ralph Peterson and Maryann Eeds (1990) are advocates for "grand conversations" that people have around shared literature experiences. They note that different interpretations are common and disagreements about the "author's message" frequently occur. We have found this to be true in our own work as well. For example, we have an ongoing disagreement about how much of a critical perspective the book *Appearing tonight! Mary Heather Elizabeth Livingstone* (Dunrea, 2000) takes. This is the story of a child star who eats too many chocolates and literally "outgrows" her appeal as a dancer and entertainer. After losing her star status, she finds another job but still likes to sing and dance as she works. (She also keeps eating chocolates and maintains her ample size.) At the age of 82, she auditions for a dancing and singing role in the theater and gets it. Everybody cheers and she is a star once again. Jerry says the book has a happy ending so it isn't very critical in terms of focusing on difficult social issues that are not easily resolved. Chris and Mitzi say that waiting until you're 82 to be accepted for your physical appearance is not a happy ending because it reinforces social norms about weight. We love to argue about it and are not the least bit concerned that we never reach an agreement. What matters is that the grand conversations continue.

To ensure that quality conversations will follow a read aloud, we always have some appropriate open-ended questions ready. These might be as simple as:

What did you think of this book?
What's on your mind after hearing this story?
Has something like this ever happened to you?

We might also make note of any topics that we want to make sure get included, in the event the discussion goes in directions we did not anticipate. Our general rule of thumb is to assume that listeners have comprehended the text and to let them lead the conversation. Asking "test questions" does not lead to good conversations. To the contrary, it sends the message that the story is less important than our desire to evaluate the students' understanding of it. We define a "test question" as one that has a correct answer and the test or teacher knows what it is. When kids hear one of these questions, they instantly switch from thinking broadly (or grandly) to thinking narrowly. They know that this kind of question requires them to figure out what the teacher or test writer believes, not to pursue multiple possible responses. One strategy we use to keep our questions open-ended is to make a conscious effort to avoid asking any question for which we think we already have the answer. This is not as easy as it sounds since many of us had little experience with open-ended questions in our own schooling. It's easy to fall back into the type of literal questioning that we remember some of our own teachers doing. They always knew the answers and our job was to figure out what they were thinking.

Trina Parsons, a teacher in Toronto, uses open-ended questions when she reads aloud from the chapter book *Because of Winn Dixie* (DiCamillo, 2000). This book includes topics like alcoholism, single parent families, the death of a sibling, bullying, incarceration, sorrow and loneliness. When she first read the book, Trina wondered if some of these topics might be too controversial. But she also realized that many of her third graders were dealing with some of these issues and decided to read a chapter each day and take time to talk about these issues as they came up. She reports that her children bring up the issues they want to talk about with little direction from her.

Informal rehearsal and drama. After selecting a book, we think it's a good idea to rehearse reading it aloud on our own before sharing it with an audience. This gives us an opportunity to get used to the phrasing and rhythm of the text. We can think about how we will handle any dialogue and how we can change our voice or gestures to represent the different characters. If there are any words that we feel are inappropriate, we can pencil in a substitution or leave a post-it note so we won't have to hesitate when we get to that place in the text later. This is a good time to think about where we might pause in the reading or the conversation to ask a question or provide additional information about what might be a difficult word or concept. Vocabulary development is also something to consider during our preparation for a read aloud even though we won't be making a list of words to look up in the dictionary. During the read aloud experience, new words and concepts are presented in the context of the story or conversation and listeners are highly motivated to make sense of them. A study with eighth graders carried out by Nagy, Herman, and Anderson (1985) concluded that new words are learned incrementally, that meanings are often inferred from context, and reading is the best way to promote vocabulary growth.

Good conversations often get even better when some drama is added to the read aloud. We can do this by reading the book with expression and changing our tone of voice to fit what the different characters are saying. A read aloud is actually a dramatic performance in which the reader uses his or her voice to interpret the story orally. Using one's voice and gestures purposefully is also important if we decide to use storytelling as a way to connect with the rich oral traditions that many children bring to school with them. "By telling their own family stories and orally interpreting folklore from a range of cultures, teachers invite children to use storytelling as a form of oral authorship" (Short, Harste, w/ Burke, 1996, p. 175). These authors also recommend designating a special "author's chair" where the teacher sits to read aloud each day and where student authors sit when sharing their work (p. 174).

Drama activities also help to make the book come alive during a read aloud experience. For example, we might stop at several points during the story to ask how a character was feeling and ask students to respond by making a facial expression that shows how they think the character felt. "Thumbs up" and "thumbs down" can be invited to evaluate the actions of any of the characters. Students might be surprised to see that not everyone agrees. Getting alternate opinions out on the floor can be instructive and mind stretching for everyone. We might ask students what they think is going to happen next or how the book reminds them of something in their own lives. (See additional drama suggestions in Chapter 7.)

Principle 2: Reading Aloud Supports a "Readerly Identity"

Chris and Mitzi both remember how their fourth graders would reach for the box of tissues when they were reading aloud from *Where the Red Fern Grows* (Rawls, 1974). If the principal or other adult entered the room and looked worried to see so many kids openly weeping, one of them would say, "It's okay. She's reading *Where the Red Fern Grows*" and figure that no further explanation was needed. These kids were demonstrating what we have come to call a *readerly identity*. They were not embarrassed to be seen grabbing tissues because the classroom culture made it socially acceptable to get totally absorbed in a read aloud. By the time the book was finished, the students' *readerly identity* also manifested itself in the large number of fiction and non-fiction dog books and pieces of canine art that filled the classroom. While Mitzi and Chris contributed a few pieces, most of the additional material came from the kids. They showed their *readerly identity* not only through their dramatic emotional reactions but through their intellectual and artistic responses as well. A great read aloud story about some unforgettable dogs left them with a desire to keep reading and thinking about dogs.

Seeing yourself as a reader. Reading aloud is important because it encourages people—both young and old—to develop a *readerly identity* and to become a member of what Frank Smith refers to as the "Literacy Club" (1988). Members of this club know how to talk about what they are reading and how to share their perspectives with other readers who might respond differently. They begin to say things like, "Oh! I never thought of it *that* way" as they open their minds to multiple perspectives and possibilities. Enjoyment of a text being read aloud leads to people beginning to see themselves as individuals who are interested in reading and this, in turn, encourages them to read more often and to put more energy into their reading lives.

Picture book author Bill Martin Jr. (1987) credits his development as a reader to his fifth grade teacher who faithfully read aloud to her class three times each day and often kept reading on when the students begged her to continue after the allotted time had expired. She knew that "a good story refuses to be left alone. It keeps nagging one to continue. That kind of nagging is life's most pleasant reading instruction" (p. 17). Martin admits to being a non-reader at this time in his life and thanks this teacher for tuning his ears "to the literate language, to the voice of the text" (p. 16) so that he was finally able to attain a *readerly identity* and join the literacy club (Smith, 1988). We applaud the idea of reading aloud three times a day and urge other teachers to try it as well. One read aloud might be from a text that is familiar to the students; the second might be from a text or genre that is newer or more challenging; and the third might be a "free choice," a story specifically requested by one or more students. What a wonderful gift this would be—both for developing readers and for proficient readers who might be potential literacy club dropouts due to overdoses of skills instruction and meaningless busy work administered in the name of increasing test scores.

How does reading aloud encourage the development of a *readerly identity*? First and foremost, it provides broad demonstrations (Smith, 1982; Harste, Woodward, & Burke, 1984; Cambourne, 1988, 1995) of successful communication. When learners are read to, they see how language works, what it looks like in action, and how rewarding it can be to take part in language events. Through the demonstrations they see as part of a read aloud experience, students come to understand what a story is, how authors give life to their stories, and the role of text and picture in conveying meaning. When the teacher also points out that they can accept or reject an author's message, students begin to form the foundation for a critical perspective. Through the demonstrations in a read aloud, young people see both the mundane behaviors (like how to turn the pages in a book and how to hold the book) as well as more sophisticated behaviors (like reacting critically to a text). Reading is demonstrated as an active process that invites commentary and critique. An added bonus is that all of this knowledge about reading is delivered as a whole package. Students do not learn about turning pages on one day and responding to an author's message on another.

Developing a readerly identity with younger readers. Many beginning reading programs feature simplified *decodable* texts that include a limited number of phonemes and/or words. As a result the plot line is constrained and the final product lacks credibility as a real story. (Who really cares if a fat cat is sitting on a mat?) Reading aloud, on the other hand, provides demonstrations of complex texts. Meier (2008) argues that without access to texts read aloud to children, the early literacy curriculum would be "essentially devoid of any literary or intellectual substance" (p. 108). Meier goes on to argue that when simplified (decodable) texts constitute the majority of what children are exposed to in a classroom, then one can virtually guarantee poor outcomes for many of them. This is especially true for those who enter school with little prior experience with books. Meier points out that many in this group will be children who have experienced an active, playful tradition of oral literacy; most will be totally turned off by a written literacy that emphasizes boring questions and mindless routines. This author observed negative effects in classrooms where children had teachers who viewed "reading aloud to children as an 'extra' or 'bonus,' a pleasurable activity that provides a kind of balance to the serious literacy work that gets accomplished when children are doing phonics activities or sounding out words in their basal texts" (p. 108). While we certainly want reading aloud to be seen by the students as a pleasurable activity, we also want them to see it as something that is too important to leave out. For us, reading aloud is more like the main course of a meal than the dessert. See Textbox 2.1 for more suggestions on reading aloud to younger readers.

Textbox 2.1. Reading Aloud to Younger Readers

- Predictable books pull kids in.
- Conversation is important.
- Kids need opportunities to interact with the text.
- Using different voices brings the characters to life.

One way to provide engaging reading instruction for young readers is to encourage them to join in the reading of picture books with repeated or predictable text. For example, children and adults alike take great delight in calling out the amusing lines whenever we read *The Napping House* by Audrey Wood (1984). This story adds a new character (like "a snoring granny" and "a dreaming child") on each page and repeats the lines for the characters that have already been introduced. It doesn't take long for listeners to start giggling as they raptly watch the pictures to see what will happen next. Similarly, young children love to "read along" with patterned texts like Eric Carle's *From Head to Toe* (1997) and Bill Martin Jr.'s *Brown Bear, Brown Bear, What Do You See?* (1983). See Textbox 2.2 for a list of some of our favorite predictable books.

Predictable picture books have special value in that they help emergent readers to see themselves as capable readers. As Huck and Kerstetter (1987) note, "These are the books children can take home after a few days, show their parents, and say 'Now I can read!'" (p. 33). This is a great way to build their confidence and identity as developing readers. Rhodes (1983) contrasts predictable books with typical commercial instructional materials for beginning readers and concludes that trade books are more supportive due to the natural flow of language and the use of familiar topics. She notes that predictable books allow emergent readers to develop word recognition strategies while reading instead of teaching them new words before reading. This encourages a stance of reading for understanding right from the beginning.

Textbox 2.2. Our Favorite Predictable Books

Brown Bear, Brown Bear, What Do You See? (Martin, 1983)
The Napping House (Wood, 1984)
Alexander and the Terrible Horrible No Good Very Bad Day (Viorst, 1987)
Yo! Yes? (Raschka, 1998)
It Didn't Frighten Me (Goss & Harste, 1981)

Developing a readerly identity with older readers. Young adolescents (intermediate readers) usually don't have the problem of too much simplified text in their lives, but sometimes the opposite is true for them. Once they are plunged into content area textbooks, the writing becomes very dense in terms of introducing complex technical terms and concepts. As we learned with Craig's experiences in Chapter 1, older students often find it challenging to keep paying attention when there is no "story" to sustain their interest. If you ever sat in with a group of fifth graders reading aloud "round robin style" from a social studies or science textbook, you may have noticed how hard it was to stay focused. Reading aloud to older students from a riveting piece of historical fiction can provide human interest and work with the social studies text to support students in learning the new content. For example, reading aloud from a book like *My Brother Sam Is Dead* (Collier & Collier, 1985) can be very helpful preparation for students who will be going on to read a rather dry passage about how the American Revolution divided (and decimated) whole families. Experience with the fictionalized version encourages students to read the textbook more actively and critically. If they notice contradictions in the two renditions, they have to entertain alternate ways of being and take responsibility to inquire or engage in further inquiry (see Chapter 6). These actions are all components of taking a critical stance, as described in Chapter 1.

Older students also need to hear entertaining books that don't relate to anything they are formally studying in school. There is much adolescent fiction that focuses on the many difficult social issues that all teens encounter. Reading aloud for a few minutes each day from a book like *Keesha's House* (Frost, 2003), *Ironman* (Crutcher, 2004) or *Luna* (Peters, 2004) has been known to get middle school kids to class on time because they don't want to miss the next installment. They want to know what happens when Liam/Luna finally gets the courage to put on a dress and come out at school as a transgendered person—in this case a male who is becoming a female. They want to know what happens to Keesha's friend Carmen after she was arrested for drunk driving. While many of the students won't be experiencing the same problems as the characters in these books, they see those topics (teen pregnancy, gender identity, alcoholism, parents in prison, etc.) as real issues that are worth thinking about and talking about.

Reading aloud from graphic novels, horror fiction, and series books can also be effective ways to support older students in further development of a *readerly identity*. While some of this material might not be our first choice for our own reading tastes, it's important to remember that our students come from a different generation and different cultures. It's reasonable to expect they will also have different interests in reading material. We might not be willing to stand in line for hours in the middle of the night to buy the latest *Harry Potter* (Rowling, 2009) or *Twilight* (Meyer, 2005) series adventure, but that is just what lots of kids do each time a new book in these series becomes available. But surely we can learn something from the fact that over 20,000 reading fans (many in wizard or witch costumes) made history in the *Guinness Book of World Records* for the most spectators at a live reading of a book when Rowling appeared in the Toronto Skydome (Kooy, 2003, pp. 136–37). See Textbox 2.3 for more suggestions about reading aloud to older readers.

It's also important to note that popular teen books differ in terms of how easy or hard they are to read. As McGill-Franzen and Botzakis (2009) note, "The very redundancy of the language of series books supports inexperienced readers" (p. 111). These readers benefit from reading easier texts that give them practice and help them in becoming fluent. At the same time, many popular books introduce sophisticated vocabulary and concepts. Chris came across the word "ululation" while reading aloud to her university students from a trade book (*The Graveyard Book*, Gaiman, 2008) and used that as an opportunity to extend the read aloud into a demonstration of what good readers do when they come across challenging new words. After discussing the context of the word and making predictions, a student looked it up in an online dictionary and everyone took a turn howling and shrieking as they imagined how the character in the story might have sounded. Popular texts can also provide interesting contexts for modeling critical thinking during a read aloud. Questions focusing on the author's intent and what authors do to position readers in certain ways often lead to conversations that transcend what we might judge as the overall quality of the literature.

Why cross-age reading helps to develop a readerly identity in both older and younger readers. In many homes, the younger children in the family learn to read by following along as their older siblings read aloud to them. In schools, however, students are usually separated according to age and academic level with the result that older and younger children rarely get to interact, let alone read together. A cross-age reading approach brings children of different ages and ability levels together so that the older, more experienced readers can read aloud to the younger, less experienced readers in a cozy one-on-one setting. In a typical cross-age reading project (for example, Leland & Fitzpatrick, 1993) kids from a fourth or fifth grade classroom are paired with kindergarten or first grade students for a regularly scheduled read aloud experience. The older students get to choose and practice reading easy books that might be socially unacceptable if they were reading on their own. They don't mind being seen with these "baby books" if they can easily explain that they are just getting ready to read to their kindergarten partner, however. It works out well for everyone. The older kids get to feel like an expert (since they have had opportunities to practice reading and sound better than usual) and the younger children get to spend time hanging out with big kids they admire while also having positive literacy experiences that might be very motivational.

Textbox 2.3. Reading Aloud to Older Readers

Introduce graphic novels to lure developing readers into books.
Take advantage of the latest reading fad—vampires, werewolves, and the *undead*.
Use series books to span a wide range of reading ability.
Capitalize on the fact that social issues books address important problems in kids' lives.

Principle 3: Don't Apologize for Having Fun

The first part of our mantra and the foundation for this entire book is the idea that it is crucially important to enjoy reading. We decided to focus Chapter 2 on reading aloud because experiencing a read aloud is entertaining and fun. It's like watching a movie or listening in on someone's conversation without feeling guilty about it. We shouldn't worry that we're not doing our jobs as educators if our kids are having fun in school. Actually it's the exact opposite: Bringing joy into the classroom and helping students have fun are major parts of our job. If we don't succeed in showing them that books and reading are exciting things they want to pursue, then we have failed. A read aloud has the power to transport participants to new worlds and to introduce them to characters who are dealing with issues and problems that might be a lot like theirs or totally different. Either way, the power of a good story draws listeners in and they want to find out what happens to the characters. Kids who hear lots of good stories are very apt to see reading as an enjoyable activity that they want to keep doing on their own. Reading for fun provides more experience with text and that builds kids' *readerly identities* as well as their level of skill.

The National Assessment of Educational Progress (NAEP) is the only nationally representative and continuing assessment of what America's students know and can do in various subject areas. Assessments are conducted periodically in several core academic areas and results are reported in terms of "report cards." The 2004 Reading Report Card produced by NAEP concluded that kids who read "for fun" were better readers than those who didn't. Those who said they read for pleasure almost every day did better than those who said they never or hardly ever read for pleasure and this was true for students at all three age levels tested. In addition, this test showed a marked decline in reading for pleasure as students got older. While 54 percent of nine-year-olds read for pleasure, this figure dropped to 30 percent for thirteen-year-olds, and 22 percent for seventeen-year-olds (Petrie, Moran, & Lutkus, 2005, p. 55). The inescapable conclusion is that many students become less motivated to read for enjoyment as they grow older. Why does this happen? It might have something to do with the fact that many teachers of older students see no reason to keep reading aloud to them. Maybe they are thinking that these kids can read on their own now, so there's no need to keep advertising. (This seems like questionable reasoning since it's hard to imagine a fast food chain deciding that they don't need to gear ads to kids once they can eat on their own.) Other possible reasons are that students have less choice about what they read and less free time for reading. Finally, there's the fact that school days for adolescents are organized according to content areas that often have no connection to each other and that frequently rely on boring textbooks to present new material. While reading used to be entertaining, it suddenly becomes tedious and something to get through as quickly as possible.

Reading for fun during the school day. The title of Richard Allington's 1977 article asked an important question: "If They Don't Read Much, How They Ever Gonna Get Good?" Allington observed that struggling readers didn't actually read much when they were in school and made an argument for including more time for real reading in school. Revisiting this topic 30 years later, Allington (2009) says that the question is still important, even though "we have not sufficiently spelled out the nature of the most effective forms of reading practice" (p. 48). He concludes, however, by saying "I am convinced that developing readers need an enormous volume of high-success reading experience" (p. 49). One recommendation that ties in with both reading volume and reading for fun is to provide time for students to read for pleasure while they are in school. Steve Krashen (2006) calls it free voluntary reading or "reading because you want to" (p. 43) and urges teachers to include time for sustained silent reading (SSR) every day. This idea is implemented as DEAR (Drop Everything And Read) time in some schools but the underlying premise is the same: Simply that students get time at school to read something they choose. There are no questions to answer, no worksheets to complete, no tests to take—everyone just reads a text of his or her choice for enjoyment.

Reading aloud can play an important role in encouraging reading for fun since some kids will need help in deciding what they want to choose during SSR or DEAR time. Chris remembers a sixth grader in her class who couldn't seem to find a book that he could stick with and actually finish. Mark was always starting a new book and then putting it back because it "wasn't that interesting." He became quite animated, however, when Chris started reading aloud each day from *The House With a Clock in its Walls* (Bellairs, 1973). He remarked that the book was "really scary" and sometimes caused him to have trouble falling asleep at night. Soon after that, he approached Chris and asked if she had any other books by Bellairs that he could read during DEAR time. Chris said she had a copy of *The Figure in the Shadows* (Bellairs, 1975), but she was worried that it might be too scary. She said that she didn't want Mark's mother calling her to complain that she was giving Mark books that kept him awake at night. Mark responded that he was "tough" and would not get Chris into trouble by telling his mom that he couldn't sleep. They went back and forth for several days until Mark ended the debate by going to the public library and taking out his own copy of *The Figure in the Shadows*. When he triumphantly produced the book at DEAR time, Chris hid her smile and said she hoped it wouldn't keep him awake. The next day, Mark's best friend asked to borrow Chris's copy of *The Figure in the Shadows* so that he and Mark could read it together and compare notes about the scariest parts. Mark subsequently read the whole Bellairs series and his book-hopping behavior at DEAR time became a thing of the past. (As a footnote, when parent conference time came around, Mark's mother told Chris that he had ended up in his parents' bedroom a few times because his own room was "too lonely at night" but he made her promise not to blame the book or his teacher for these visits. She also noted that she was thrilled to see Mark choosing and reading entire books without being prodded and credited the practice of reading aloud in the classroom for this positive development.)

Key Issues in Implementation

Reading aloud to students seems like it should be an easy thing to do. After all, how hard can it be to pick up a book and start reading it to a classroom of students? Actually, pulling off a successful read aloud (as well as a successful read aloud program) takes some planning and knowledge of where problems might arise and how to handle them if and when they do. Thinking about some key issues in advance can make the process go more smoothly and this will lead to more reading aloud in the long run.

Selecting a book. Although it may sound simplistic, our advice is to choose books that will draw listeners in and keep their attention. Typically this involves stories that address universally significant topics and lay the foundation for rich conversations. Draw from a wide variety of written and oral literature including stories written by students in the classroom and professional authors. Include picture books, wordless picture books, chapter books (including graphic novels), historical fiction, poetry, and informational (nonfiction) books. (See Chapter 4 for more suggestions on selecting books.)

Reading nonfiction is sometimes referred to as "reading to learn" and is often contrasted with fiction that is seen as what needs to be used for "learning to read." While the distinction between learning to read and reading to learn can be helpful, it can also be misleading. It's easy to assume that children who are learning to read will focus primarily on narrative in the primary grades, and then advance to nonfiction and "read to learn" in the intermediate grades. The problem with this reasoning is that it leaves out early experiences with easy nonfiction that build students' ability and confidence to use this genre successfully. Harvey (1998) recommends reading nonfiction aloud to younger children as "a great way to fire kids up about the genre" (p. 69). A visit to Carole Damin's K-1 classroom to see the nonfiction books written by her children provides evidence for this claim. Joey's book on penguins and Sara's book on frogs showed that these children had researched their topics carefully and produced original texts that retained their own voices. When Chris asked to borrow Sara's and Joey's books to share with her university students, she learned that there were already waiting lists within the K-1 classroom for these publications. A five-year-old librarian politely suggested that she put her name on the list and come back in two weeks.

Reading aloud can be particularly interesting to kids when teachers choose to read books that are relevant to what's going on in their lives. For example, when teachers tell us they are having problems with bullying issues in their classrooms, we often recommend *Oliver Button is a Sissy* (De Paola, 1979), *The Sissy Duckling* (Fierstein, 2002), and *Willy and Hugh* (Browne, 2000) as read aloud choices because all of these books feature characters who are dealing with being bullied. Oliver Button is bullied because he is a dancer. Elmer is labeled a "sissy" because he doesn't like to do what boys are culturally expected to do. Willy is bullied because of his small size. After the class hears these books, it's easy to begin a discussion about bullying and what steps any of us might take to combat it. Teachers can also choose books that are particularly relevant to a few students but will also help their classmates to understand the situations of others and develop empathy. For example, many children are living with the reality of having a parent or sibling in prison. *Visiting Day* (Woodson, 2002) provides a nuanced look at the happy and sad feelings of a child as she travels with her grandmother to visit Daddy, who is "doing a little time." Choosing a book like this can open up spaces to talk about a difficult issue and to let children know that they aren't the only ones dealing with it.

How books position readers. It's important to be consciously aware that trade books, like all texts, are not neutral but are trying to get readers to believe something about life. Shannon (2002) reminds us to think about two sets of values when we select books to read aloud. First, there are the "values embedded in the author's representation of reality" (p. 8). For example, all of the books mentioned about bullying portray it as something negative since the bullies neither win nor end up looking good in any of these stories. Shannon suggests that the other values to consider are the ones you will assign to the text while reading aloud. We always expand and build on the negative image of bullying when we read *The Sissy Duckling* aloud because it fits with our personal values. But it's also possible to read this book and then make comments or ask questions that totally avoid the bullying issue. In practice, a potentially powerful message about the negative effects of bullying can be usurped if the teacher finishes reading this story and then focuses the discussion only on the clever things Elmer (the bullied duckling) was able to do after he was left in the forest for the winter. Of course this totally defeats the reason for choosing this book in the first place and is not something we recommend.

This is true for any story we read. We can read a Cinderella story and reinforce the dominant cultural interpretation if we smile at the end and comment about how lucky Cinderella was to find her Prince Charming and head off to "live happily ever after." The same story can be used to challenge this idea, however, if discussion following the reading encourages participants to talk back to the traditional interpretation that a woman has to wait around for some Prince Charming to come and rescue her. Shannon (2002) recommends *The Paper Bag Princess* (Munsch, 1983) as a read aloud since it turns the Cinderella tradition upside down by having the not-so-helpless Princess rescue the Prince and then cancel their engagement because he turns out to be a foolish snob. Not realizing that there are values embedded in every text doesn't make them go away. It just means that readers aren't aware of the values they might be unconsciously accepting.

Sometimes a book we choose because it highlights certain values turns out to challenge those values. For example, *Hooway for Wodney Wat* (Lester, 1999) features a character who is bullied at the beginning of the story but then shows some bullying behavior of his own once he gets some power. When Wodney turns the tables on a bossy new classmate, the audience is so busy cheering for him that they hardly notice how he is slipping into a bully role himself. Stopping to consider whether it's justifiable to *bully a bully* can lead to interesting conversations about fairness and getting along with others. Ann Mennonno's second and third graders loved the story but did not see any problem with the ending until she asked if Camilla (the original bully) was now being treated fairly by the hero. This led to a passionate discussion that ended with several children talking back to the book as they clarified what it means to take a stance against bullying. See Textbox 2.4 for one example.

Textbox 2.4. Talking Back to Books

"Wodney started out as a kid who was always getting bullied, but then he turned into a bully himself and picked on a new girl in his class. That just wasn't right!" (Emily, grade three)

What makes reading aloud difficult? The main issue with reading aloud in school is that it takes time. Many teachers say they value reading aloud and would love to do more of it, but they can't because they don't have time for it. Time constraints are often tied to administrative mandates designed to control teachers' use of time and their decisions about what gets taught. "I've had to drop my daily read aloud time," an elementary teacher announced in one of our graduate classes. "My principal says the most important thing for us to focus on this year is raising test scores. He wants us to concentrate on the basics, not on extra stuff like reading aloud." While on the one hand we sympathize with teachers who have to deal with this type of illogical reasoning, on the other hand we want to ask who gets to decide what is "basic" and what is "extra." In this case, the principal was reflecting *the discourse of testing.* This discourse (or way of seeing and being in the world) rests on the assumption that high test scores result when teachers frontload whatever is on the test into the curriculum. This is also known as *teaching to* *the test.* We encourage teachers to be familiar with research that supports literature-based approaches to reading instruction and to use it to "talk back" to the discourse of testing whenever they can. For example, studies by Wilson, Martens, and Arya (2005) and Arya, Martens, Wilson, Altwerger, Jin, Laster, and Long (2005) concluded that children taught with commercial phonics-based programs did not do better on tests of phonics use or comprehension than children taught with literature-based programs. In addition, children in literature programs were better at talking about stories and making sense of what was going on in them than children in phonics programs. Our experience has taught us that test scores do not define good readers and teaching to the test never pays off in the long run. We have also observed that good readers often do get good test scores, but not because they had teachers who taught to the test. More often, the best readers are the kids who love to read and read voraciously both in and out of school. These are the kids who can tell you about their favorite authors and the types of books they like to read. These are the kids who sometimes get reprimanded for keeping an open book on their desk and reading it "illegally" when they're supposed to be paying attention to the teacher.

Commercial influences on children's literature. Of course companies selling tests and associated preparatory materials have enjoyed getting bigger and bigger profits as *the discourse of testing* has worked its way into every public school in the country. So they have lobbied hard to sell a perception that students really aren't learning very much and we need to keep testing them so that schools and teachers can be held accountable. We want to argue that it's more important to focus on *raising readers* than *raising test scores*—and that reading aloud is an essential part of the equation for raising readers. This is because reading aloud sells kids on books and creates enthusiasm for independent reading. And kids who read more show more literacy development (Krashen, 2004).

We don't know how the teacher mentioned earlier was going to reallocate the time that she formerly used for reading aloud, but it wouldn't surprise us to learn that it would be used for more formal skill instruction. That's the most frequent response when educators are trying to raise test scores. Although it seems like common sense, this response actually causes more problems than it solves. Skill instruction rarely includes real reading or real texts and more often focuses kids on analyzing isolated sounds and words that they don't care about. While reading aloud is a pleasurable experience that leads to a desire to read more, a steady diet of skill exercises has the exact opposite effect. Instead of seeing reading as something they like to do and want to do, children come to see it as tedious work that offers no reward. Seen through this lens, reading becomes a boring *school activity* that has nothing to do with real life. The ephemeral promise of higher test scores might sell desperate principals and some teachers on more skill instruction, but kids are never fooled. They know what they like and will pursue it relentlessly. Similarly, they know what they don't like and avoid it at all costs. Instruction aimed at improving performance on discrete skills tasks might help students to perform those tasks more efficiently in isolated non-reading situations, but becoming a reader requires more than mastering a bunch of unconnected skills.

What happens when grand conversations get cut short? With the recent introduction of scripted lessons and skills-based reading programs in many classrooms, a growing number of teachers feel forced to shorten the amount of time they ordinarily devote to reading aloud. The teacher referred to at the beginning of this chapter was told to stop all reading aloud in her classroom, but many others have been advised to cut back. Copenhaver (2001) studied what happened when a first grade teacher who valued reading aloud discovered that others in her school did not see this activity as "real teaching." To comply with the new mandate for more direct skills instruction, this teacher starting cutting the amount of time she spent reading aloud. As the time for reading aloud in this classroom decreased, the researcher documented more and more examples of the teacher asking closed-ended questions, also known as I-R-E questions (Cazden, 1988) since the teacher Initiates a question, the student Responds by giving an answer and the teacher then Evaluates the answer. This type of "test question" is more suitable for getting children to show evidence of knowing simple facts like "Where was the dog?" than getting them to describe or explain something like "What might have caused the dog to run away?" So in this sense, shortened read aloud time negatively impacted the children's ability to construct meaning.

Copenhaver also noted that some children did not function as well with the increased amount of I-R-E questions because they had trouble following the new procedures. Previously, they had many opportunities to interact during story time; now they were expected to sit silently and listen. As opportunities to share their views decreased, they started calling out answers and engaging in inappropriate physical movement like wiggling around on the floor and poking at each other during the read aloud (p. 154). While they had been able to follow the rules of the more relaxed and conversational read aloud experience successfully, they were now identified as discipline problems. The surprising conclusion was that something as simple as changing the amount of time for reading aloud led to marginalization for children who did not "fit" the new curricular model. Over time, this type of marginalization can have a snowball effect. As children become more disengaged from the activity at hand, their behavior deteriorates and they are more apt to be removed from the group altogether. As a result, the borderline kids who need the most enrichment end up getting the least and continue on a downward spiral. Krashen (n.d.) lists "fewer discipline problems" as one of "88 Generalizations about Free Voluntary Reading" on his website—although he also notes that more research on this topic is needed. We want to make the same argument for not cutting the time for read alouds. There will be fewer discipline problems when kids get to participate in a truly interactive experience than when they are subjected to a type of test prep boot camp.

Working With Linguistically and Culturally Diverse Students

Children and adolescents who are learning English need to have many opportunities to interact with texts written in both their native language and the new language they are trying to learn. Many children's books are now available with two languages side by side on the pages. Teachers at the Center for Inquiry in Indianapolis involve students in creating dual language books for both their own library and for that of a school in Honduras where both the students and many of the teachers are learning English. Because they contain Spanish and English text, these books support second language learning in both schools.

If teachers are fluent in more than one language, it's important for them to alternate their use of those languages when they read aloud. Teachers who are not comfortable reading in any language other than English can invite others to read aloud from non-English books. These readers might be children within the class, students from other classes in the school or district, parents, family, or community members. Children who speak only English will benefit from experiencing a read aloud in another language and children who know that language will benefit from knowing that their native language is valued. A classroom that offers children frequent choices for hearing books in English or other languages is a good goal to have in mind. For example, the teacher might be reading a book in English while a parent is reading a book in Spanish at the other end of the room and children get to decide which group they will join that day.

Books featuring characters from different cultures are also needed so that children can see people like them in what they read. Students in the class who know only about the mainstream culture also benefit by learning about people who are different from them in some way. For example, Gloria Anzaldua's *Friends from the Other Side/Amigos del Otro Lado* (1995) addresses the thorny question of illegal immigration by highlighting the dilemmas faced by people on both sides of the border. *Amelia's Road/Camion de Amelia* (Altman, 1991) and *Tomás and the Library Lady /Tomás y la Senora de la Biblioteca* (Mora, 1997) focus on the challenges faced by the children of migrant workers.

Children and families seeking asylum from the ravages of war are featured in books like *Gleam and Glow* (Bunting, 2001) and *The Color of Home* (Hoffman, 2002). While the nationality of the family in Bunting's book is not specifically identified, the family portrayed in Hoffman's book is described as having fled from violence in Somalia. The author notes that the mother's decision to wear a hajab identifies her as a Muslim. This book also shows the strong role that the arts can play in literacy development. The main character, Hassan, is a child who can't speak any English when he arrives at his new school. He is, however, able to communicate through his art. Engaging both immigrant and non-immigrant children in conversations about families and the challenges they face is helpful for developing a sense of understanding all around. Instead of fearing or making fun of someone dressed differently, children come to see that different dress is "normal" in different cultures. Finally, a book like *Sami and the Time of the Troubles* (Heide & Gilliland, 1992) may help children to develop a better understanding of the long-standing conflict in the Middle East and how the people who live there face many challenges in their daily lives. Since the strife in this region of the world continues to be a frequent story in the news, it is important for children to be able to put these stories into a larger context that puts actual faces on the people who are so gravely affected by the ongoing violence.

Technology Extensions and Electronic Resources

A number of electronic extensions and resources are available to provide extra opportunities for kids to have read aloud experiences both at home and in the classroom. "Storyline Online" is a program of the Screen Actors Guild Foundation Book Pals. If you visit their website (http://www.storylineonline.net) you will be able to click on a title and follow along as a professional actor or actress reads aloud from a picture book. Some titles on this site include *Somebody Loves You, Mr. Hatch* (Spinelli, 1996) and *A Bad Case of Stripes* (Shannon, 1998). The main characters in both stories disrupt commonplace notions of how people should act by outgrowing their former selves as they pursue their own inquiries and dreams.

There are other opportunities to hear skillful reading aloud on a number of authors' websites. For example, if you go to Mem Fox's site (memfox.com) you can see and hear Mem reading many of her own books. There is also access to documents like "ten read-aloud commandments" and "do it like this" for those who want ideas for reading aloud with more style and panache. While sites like these are great for helping teachers and prospective teachers hone their read aloud skill, they might be even more important for kids and adults who need many opportunities to see and hear the language of books. Although a teacher or parent might tire of reading *Koala Lou* (Fox, 1989) after what seems like the hundredth time, the author is always ready online with an enthusiastic rendition of that or another favorite story.

Assessment

How will you know if you are achieving success with your read aloud efforts? It might seem strange to think about assessment before you get started, but knowing what you are aiming for will help you get there. The most common way to assess a program is to give students a pre- and post-test and compare the results. If the scores improve, then one can argue that the program is achieving success. We don't advocate testing for a read aloud program. Instead, we recommend that teachers look for changes in their students' actions and attitudes. For example, we think one sure sign of success is that kids are grabbing books out of our hands or even stealing them off the shelves. Another sign is that they beg to hear another chapter or book when we are reading aloud. Textbox 2.5 provides ideas for assessing the results of a read aloud program.

Textbox 2.5. Assessment

We know we are succeeding in getting kids turned on to books when they are:

- Grabbing books out of our hands and stealing them off our shelves.
- Totally engaged during read aloud time and begging to hear another chapter—then ONE more.
- Saying AMAZING things during literature discussions.
- Getting together in pairs or small groups to read the same books and talk about them.
- Complaining if we decide to skip a scheduled read aloud time.
- Suggesting new books for us to read aloud.

Invitation: Deconstructing Fairy Tales

Our sample teaching activity for this chapter (see Textbox 2.6) provides suggestions that can be used to help people of any age recognize the implicit messages in cultural texts that are rarely questioned.

Textbox 2.6. Invitation: Deconstructing Fairy Tales

Fairy tales are often positioned as cultural icons that teachers and parents accept without question. They are seen as timeless stories that all children should learn as part of their heritage. But are they innocent in terms of trying to get children to believe certain things? Or do they have clear messages about cultural norms and expectations? This activity focuses on making the messages of fairy tales explicit so that they can be identified and interrogated (Lewison et al., 2008).

Materials & Procedures

- Traditional fairy tales like "Little Red Riding Hood," "Cinderella," "Jack and the Beanstalk," and "Goldilocks and the Three Bears."
- A large sheet of plain paper for each group of children.
- Markers.

1. Form small groups and give each group markers and paper.
2. Choose a traditional fairy tale and begin reading it aloud. Invite students to sketch the main character someplace on their poster.

3. Pause periodically and invite students to add words and images that represent the messages the story is sending. For example, with "Jack and the Beanstalk," one message might be that it's okay to steal from someone judged to be bad—like the giant. With "Cinderella," one message might be that girls need help getting things done. Another might be that girls should wait around to be rescued by boys so that they can "live happily ever after."

4. Ask students to think about how each message positions different groups of people. Which characters come across as being smart or having power? Which are portrayed as helpless or clueless? Do they agree with these assumptions or want to argue with them?

5. Invite each group to share their ideas and keep a list of the major findings for the book that was read.

6. Students turn their posters over and work in groups to do the same process with a different fairy tale.

7. Share posters by hanging them up and moving in small groups to view and discuss them.

Other Notes

Bring in cartoons, songs, and poems that feature fairy tale characters and invite students to unpack them as well. One of our favorite cartoons shows the Big Bad Wolf with a disgusted look on his face walking away from the Three Little Pigs as he reads a newspaper headline about swine flu.

Professional Development

Reading aloud is a great topic for study groups of teachers and prospective teachers. Talking about the benefits reminds everyone of how important this seemingly simple activity is. Participating in discussions about key implementation issues is good preparation for dealing with problems when they arise. Textbox 2.7 provides some focusing questions that study groups might use to get started. Table 2.1 summarizes some key texts relating to the subject of reading aloud. Groups might choose some to investigate further.

Textbox 2.7. Small Group Discussion Questions

- What are some ways you can advocate for reading aloud at school and at home?
- What read aloud books do you remember from your childhood? Why are they memorable?
- Do you see yourself as having a *readerly identity*? Why or why not?

TABLE 2.1. Suggestions for Future Reading

Krashen, S. (2006) Free reading. *School Library Journal*, 52(9), 42–45.	Copenhaver, J. (2001) Running out of time: Rushed read-alouds in a primary classroom. *Language Arts*, 79(2), 148–158.	Trelease, J. (1982, 2006) *The read-aloud handbook*. New York: Penguin Books.
This piece begins with a provocative question and response: "If there were a surefire way to help kids become more literate, would you ignore it? Of course not. But that's exactly what's happening across much of our nation." Krashen goes on to argue that sustained silent reading (SSR) is the surefire way even though it has received little attention or support from the US Department of Education. This brief overview of SSR and its research base provides a good starting point for further discussion about kids, reading, and the role government has played in the debate about teaching methods.	The author describes what transpired in a first grade classroom when the teacher was pushed to cut back the amount of time for reading aloud so that the children would receive more direct instruction on reading skills. The article provides a fascinating analysis of how this seemingly minor curricular adjustment had wide-reaching consequences in terms of how individual children were positioned as successful learners or discipline problems in the classroom.	This is a useful and enlightening book for every parent and teacher who is interested in helping children to fall in love with reading. Trelease takes a hands-on, practical approach to the art of reading aloud to audiences of any age. The numerous success stories he shares provide encouragement and information for getting started and working with different age groups.

three
Teaching Reading With Literature

Paula Fischer teaches reading with children's literature. Her primary classroom is filled with bookcases, crates, and bins that are overflowing with picture books and other reading materials. Through the years, Paula has made a conscious effort to collect classroom sets of numerous texts with both fiction and non-fiction content. For many texts, she also has one enlarged copy, a **_Big Book_** version that she uses when she is working with the whole class. The big book sits on an easel where everyone can see as she and the children read the book and point out words, letters and pictures they want others to notice.

The day we visited, we were happy to see a big book version of _Night Noises_ (Fox, 1989) on the easel. As the children were discussing the title and the author, one of Paula's first graders noted that Mem Fox also wrote _A Particular Cow_ (Fox, 2006), a book they had read previously. This child further observed that both books had the same illustrator (Terry Denton) and the pictures in the cow book were funny, so she hoped this book had funny pictures too. While it might be hard to think of first graders as literary critics, we want to make the case that it's all a matter of experience. Children who read and discuss lots of books by different authors are positioned differently than children who only read school textbooks. While the textbooks might teach children the mechanics of "how to read," literature helps them to develop as real readers—people who enjoy reading, know what they like and are savvy consumers of what they read.

Paula identified Jack as the "pointer for today" and invited him to come up and point to the words while she and the children read the story together. After they read each page, Paula stopped to talk about any difficult words or concepts. For example, the first page contains the sentence: "Lily Laceby lived in an old cottage in the hills." Paula asked her students if anyone knew what a cottage was and one of them said, "It's a little house." Another child compared a cottage to a cabin. The next two pages described Lily Laceby and how she lived with her dog, Butch Aggie. After reading these pages, Paula asked the children to share one thing they now knew about Lily.

One child said that Lily's hair was "as wispy as cobwebs" and another said that her bones were "as creaky as floorboards at midnight." Paula invited her students to talk about those images. How can hair be like cobwebs? What does it mean to make a creaky sound? Some of the children made connections to people in their own families who had wispy hair or creaky knees.

This pattern was followed for every two pages that could be seen at the same time in the big book. The class read them together as Jack pointed to the words and then Paula asked them to share something they now knew. When Paula thought more discussion of a word or idea was needed, she asked, "What does that mean?" For example, when the text said, "Butch Aggie dozed at her feet," she asked what dozing meant and one child said it was like digging. Realizing that he was thinking of bulldozing, Paula suggested that they all look at the picture and think about what the dog was doing. The child immediately corrected himself and said, "Oh! Dozing is like sleeping."

After reading and enjoying the whole story, they looked at the dedication, which happened to be at the end of the book in this case, and noticed that it was "For Dorothy and her game leg." This led to a discussion of what a game leg might be and one child remembered that the pictures of Lily showed her with a bandage on one of her legs. Jack took them back through the book to check, and sure enough, it looked like Lily's right leg was bandaged in every picture. The children decided that a game leg must be one that has been hurt or is sore for some other reason—maybe even from playing too many games! Several children said they knew someone with a game leg and wanted to tell them about the story.

In Paula's classroom, students have the benefit of learning through being immersed in good literature, receiving feedback that helps them to connect the reading material to their own lives, and being welcomed as members of a reading community. They are learning to read, which is important, but they are also becoming independent readers who see themselves as capable of solving their own reading problems. While most children do learn to read, many do not become truly independent readers until later in life, and some never do and give up on reading. Since this negatively affects their future contributions as citizens in a democracy, we see it as an equity issue.

Principle #1: Not All Emergent Literacy Practices Are Equal

Years ago when Chris taught first grade, she did not follow a format like the one Paula used in the opening vignette. Instead, she followed the phonics and basal reading programs required by the district and did not question the teacher's guides that told her exactly what to do. The phonics program entailed spending a considerable amount of time each day introducing new sounds, using flash cards to review sounds previously taught, and demonstrating how to stretch the sounds out and come up with words. The basal reading program involved the children in reading simple stories that were written to give them practice with the sounds from the phonics program. The teacher's guide included a few literal questions for each story that she used to check comprehension. Chris evaluated each student frequently and noted that many (but not all) could identify the sounds they had been taught. They could also "sound out" new words that followed the phonics rules they had learned. Although some kids had big problems while reading orally, others made few errors. Chris concluded that even though she personally found both programs extremely boring, they seemed to be working for most of her students.

But then something happened that caused her to rethink her position. Joe was one of the children who always sounded great when he read aloud from the basal. One day while Chris was listening to him read a story about a dog, she went beyond the teacher's guide and asked him what he thought the dog would do next. (This was not the kind of question she usually asked.) Joe stared at her for a moment and then said, "What dog?" Chris felt a sudden chill. "You've been reading a story about a dog that got lost," she replied. "Don't you remember that?" Joe shrugged and looked back through the pictures. "Oh, yeah," he admitted. "I guess there was a dog but I didn't really notice." Chris was shocked. How could it be that this kid read flawlessly but had no idea of what the story was about? It didn't seem possible to her that he could say all the words but not be making any meaning from the text. She didn't want to believe that her instruction was turning out "word callers" instead of "readers." She wondered how many others were doing the same thing. The evidence suggested she was doing something wrong, but what?

As a brand new teacher, Chris had been happy to follow the programs that were handed to her because using commercial materials made lesson planning and teaching easier. Since the program focused first and foremost on phonics, the stories were written to reinforce the sounds being taught. So the story Joe read about the dog also included a frog and a hog—and of course they spent some time sitting on a log. All in all, it was a dumb story with little plot and she really couldn't blame Joe for not paying attention to it.

What was happening in this case was that the reading program was setting up a culture that focused on sounds and words instead of meaning and appreciation for literature. The fact that Chris was faithfully following the teacher's guide and using all the recommended materials didn't help and probably made things worse. In other words, even though she thought she was doing the right thing, she was inadvertently supporting a process that created good decoders, but not thoughtful readers. If she had known more about how kids learn to read and the role that real literature can play in creating a culture of reading to make meaning, she wouldn't have set Joe up for developing such a dysfunctional view of reading.

How do children become literate? This topic has received a great deal of attention over the years and continues to be debated by researchers, educators, and policy makers. In studies published in 1982 and 1983 that continue to be relevant today, Shirley Brice Heath concluded that "the means of making sense from books and relating their contents to knowledge about the real world . . . are as much a part of learned behavior as are ways of eating, sitting, playing games, and building houses" (1982, p. 49). In other words, children approach school literacy according to the models of literacy they bring from home. Heath's findings are based on her extensive observations of parents and young children in three diverse communities: A mainstream middle class community, a white working class community, and an African American working class community. Heath studied the practice of adults reading bedtime stories to children as a way to compare the introduction of books and reading in each of the three cultures.

Literacy learning in three communities. Children in mainstream families learned early on to talk about books, pay attention to books, and attend to the information that came out of them. They learned to expect someone to ask them questions about books, and they learned how to respond to both factual and open-ended questions. They came to see book activities as a form of entertainment. Heath found that the stories read and the social practices that surrounded books in the mainstream middle class community were similar to those found in many early childhood classrooms.

Parents in the white working class community did less bedtime reading than mainstream parents and put more emphasis on teaching letter names and letter sounds than on talking about stories and what they might mean. These parents tended to ask factual questions and rarely asked children to give an opinion or think beyond the literal text. Heath reported that children in this community were initially successful. They knew letter names and were good at "following orders and adhering to school norms" (1982, p. 64). These successes faded by the time children entered the fourth grade since students had no way of keeping up and thinking more broadly.

Heath reported that African American working class parents "do not simplify their language [or] label items or features of objects in either books or the environment at large" (1982, p. 68) although such practices are common in primary classrooms. In addition, stories in this community are often free flowing and lively. Children are encouraged to jump in and add to the story instead of waiting to be invited. When adults read aloud, they often do so in a group with one person reading and the others chiming in with their questions and opinions. While the model of having one person reading while everyone else listens quietly is not common in this community, it is almost universal in schools.

School practices support some children more than others. Heath's findings help to explain why children from mainstream middle class communities consistently achieve greater academic success than children from both working class communities. The close match between what happens at home and what counts in school gives mainstream children a considerable advantage over their non-mainstream peers who come to school with a different set of expectations. For example, children from the African American working class community come to school expecting to participate actively in story experiences. Some teachers might see them as disruptive when they "do not sit at their desks and complete reading workbook pages" or "tolerate questions about reading materials which are structured along the usual lesson format" (1982, p. 69). Heath's findings are important because they shine a light on why many non-mainstream children never seem to be "at home" in school. They urge us to think about how we might change school practices to fit children rather then expecting children to fit school practices.

How can teachers help children from diverse communities? Many of the students Chris taught during her first year came to school from homes with few books and the type of bedtime reading that focused on letter names and factual information about the books. Since her students had little opportunity for probing conversations about literature at home, she could have helped to fill the gap by reading lots of trade books to them and not spending so much time on the basal reader. Instead of just asking the mostly factual questions that came in her teacher's guide, she could have engaged them in conversations about why they thought characters acted as they did and what they would have done if they had been in the same situation. If she had been asking what they thought of the stories, she might have realized earlier that many of the stories in the basal program were of poor quality and she could have taken action to supplement them with better ones.

Teachers need to do everything they possibly can to insure all of their students' success. All children benefit from hearing many stories read aloud and having lots of conversations about books. Since some children might be accustomed to participating actively (calling out comments or repeating words or phrases) during a read aloud, it isn't productive for teachers to interpret their participation as annoying interruptions or bad manners. While teachers can engage children in conversations about the roles of audience members during read aloud experiences, they will likely gain more from taking an approach that accepts differences than from one that insists on uniformity. Teachers can also introduce more informal book discussion formats that draw on the strengths of children who are accustomed to chiming in with comments without being called on. Most adult book discussion groups use this model. There is no "teacher" and participants often interrupt each other in their enthusiasm to join the conversation.

Kathryn Au (2001) worked with children in Hawaii where the cultural norm was for children to interact with the storyteller as they were experiencing a story. By adopting a "talk-story" approach in her classroom—one in which the children were allowed to interact with each other and the teacher during read times—she was successful in supporting them in learning to read. She concluded that it is important both to pattern interaction in a manner responsive to students' cultural backgrounds and to encourage them to construct their own understandings of literacy.

Teachers do not have to be of the same ethnic background as their students to be effective. They can learn new styles of interaction if they are receptive to students, open to change, and willing to give priority to literacy learning rather than to conventional procedures. (p. 122)

Au's final point about literacy learning having priority over conventional procedures is especially important. It is often these conventions (like expecting children to sit quietly during story time) that position some children as not fitting in and, ultimately, not succeeding in school.

The question of how to give priority to literacy learning for all children is not a new one. After an extensive study of young children learning to read and write, Brian Cambourne (1988, 1995) identified seven conditions of learning. We think they apply across cultural groups and to older students as well.

Immersion: Learners need to be surrounded by an environment that is rich in spoken and written language. That's why bedtime reading and piles of books are important at any age. Teachers need to provide an environment in which language is used in authentic ways for authentic purposes

Demonstration: Learners need opportunities to experience written language in daily life. Teachers provide positive models when they engage in independent reading and writing with their students and talk about how they made sense of something they initially found difficult. Teachers should invite students to take risks and to try out strategies that have been demonstrated.

Responsibility: Learners learn best when they have opportunities for choice and when they are invited to take responsibility for their own learning. It is beneficial for learners to try reading and writing activities on their own. Teachers can be supportive by inviting children to read as much of a text as they can—as soon as they can. This is why predictable texts are so important.

Expectation: Learners succeed in an environment that positions them as capable readers and writers. The expectation is that they *will* achieve in reading and writing. Paper, pencils, and books are in the hands of learners from day one.

Use: Learners use reading and writing for functional purposes on a daily basis. Rather than read and write for the teacher, they have many opportunities to use literacy in personally relevant ways.

Approximation: Learners are free to use what they currently know about reading and writing, to take risks, and to experiment with using language to achieve different purposes. This means that adults are happy to accept invented spellings and less than word-perfect readings.

Response: Learners have opportunities to test their own hypotheses about how language works. Providing feedback entails valuing students as learners, celebrating what they can do, and supporting them in moving on. To facilitate learning, feedback must be specific and non-threatening, and encourage more risk taking.

Ensuring that these conditions have been satisfied can take any teacher a long way in providing the optimal conditions for literacy learning in his or her classroom. Since Cambourne's conditions highlight the importance of giving all students safe spaces to grow as literate people, we recommend that you use them to evaluate your own classroom reading program (see Textbox 3.1).

Identifying what good readers do. Many teachers think it's important for children to internalize "what good readers do" and spend time discussing this topic with students. For example, we noticed a chart in Ann Mennonno's classroom with "Good Readers" at the top and a list of things they do underneath. Ann said that her second and third graders had generated the list after several class discussions on the topic.

Good Readers. . .

- Understand what they read.
- Have books of their own and go to the library for more.
- Don't like to stop reading.
- Like the classroom quiet when they read.
- Take care of their books.
- Imagine they are in their book.
- Finish their book most of the time.
- Read to others.
- Can talk about what they have read.
- Write about what they have learned.

We think it's important to note that not everyone has to agree with every statement. If the list brings out disagreements, this would be a good time to talk about multiple perspectives and why conversations about our different views are more valuable than having everyone agree on everything.

Meeting Cambourne's conditions with adolescents. Teachers often perceive older students who are less proficient readers as a particularly challenging group. While these students need to have the same type of rich experiences with easy texts that their younger peers receive as a matter of course, they are often resistant to being seen reading "baby books." One way to support them is to set up a Buddy Reading program (see Chapter 2). This type of project happens when a teacher of older students (third grade and up) gets together with a teacher of younger children (kindergarten through second grade) and pairs the students up. After talking with their partners to see what they are interested in, the older students choose picture books they think their buddies will enjoy. They prepare for their buddy reading session by orally reading their book to a classmate or taking it home to read to their parents or a sibling. After each session students engage in debriefing on what went well and what problems they encountered. Often they identify and get a handle on a reading problem they themselves are having when they observe their partner having a similar problem. While buddy reading is one way to get easy books into older students' hands without attaching a social stigma, it is not the only way. Many adolescents enjoy reading graphic novels that have complex illustrations and relatively simple texts. Table 3.1 is the American Library Association's list of the best ten graphic novels for teens (Retrieved April 5, 2011 from http://www.ala.org/ala/mgrps/divs/yalsa/booklistsawards/greatgraphicnovels forteens/ggnt11_topten.cfm). In both contexts, what is most important for older readers is that they have choices about what they will read and that they get opportunities to use language in authentic ways.

Principle #2: A Critical Transactional Model Explains How Reading Works

During the past fifty years, reading researchers have attempted to answer the question of how reading works. What happens in our brains to make it possible for us to see marks on a page and take a message away from them? In searching for an answer, scholars have identified and explored what they often refer to as different systems of language: graphophonemics, syntax, semantics, and pragmatics. These systems of language are also known as cueing systems because they signal or "cue" readers to pay attention to specific elements of the text as they are reading.

TABLE 3.1.   ALA's List of Best Graphic Novels for Teens

Author	Title	Brief Synopsis
Neri, G. (Illus. by Randy Duburke)	*Yummy: The Last Days of the Southside Shorty*	The life, death and aftermath of an eleven-year-old gangbanger, based on a true tragedy.
Telgemeier, Raina	*Smile*	Brace yourself: Middle school plus orthodontia equals dental drama.
Aristophane (Trans. by Matt Madden)	*The Zabime Sisters*	Experience the first day of summer vacation with three sisters on their island home of Guadalupe.
Dayton, Brandon	*Green Monk*	A young monk with the most powerful blade of grass EVER wanders into battle with a fierce giant.
Iwaoka, Hisae	*Saturn Apartments*	Mitsu takes on his late father's dangerous job as a window washer on the space ship Saturn Apartments.
Kim, Susan & Klavan, Laurence (Illus. by Faith Erin Hicks)	*Brain Camp*	Two teens discover there is something far more sinister than nature hikes going on at their summer camp.
Layman, John (Illus. Rob Guillory)	*Chew Volume 1: Taster's Choice*	Tommy Chu is a detective with psychic powers which he gets from whatever he eats.
Shiga, Jason	*Meanwhile Pick Any Path. 3,856 Story Possibilities*	You get to choose your own adventure.
Tennapel, Doug	*Ghostopolis*	Garth Hale has gone to the other side, but he's not dead yet.
Weing, Drew	*Set to Sea*	A disillusioned poet discovers hardship and wisdom on the high seas.

The systems of language are interconnected and work simultaneously. However, since they have different roles to play and they cue us to think about different things, it is often easier to talk about them separately.

Figure 3.1 shows one theoretical model of how reading works. It consists of three rings with a wedge cutting through them. While an early version of this model (Goodman, Goodman, & Burke, 1978) showed three rings of equal size, we have given the rings different sizes to show the relative importance of each language system. The pragmatics system is not shown as a separate ring because we see it as the social context that surrounds and permeates the other systems. In some ways, it is the ether in which all of the language systems shown in the rings operate. We purposely made the rings with dotted lines (as opposed to solid lines) to suggest that the various systems of language are not distinct and often overlap. While a solid line would look like a distinct border, the dotted lines make it look like there are opportunities for systems to blend together at times. The wedge that cuts through all of the systems represents an instance of instruction that includes all of them. In short, reading happens when all of the systems are working in harmony. The social context supports the belief that every instance of instruction pays attention to all of the systems and meaning is always expected.

Semantics is all about making meaning. The semantic system is situated in the center of the model and takes up relatively more space than the other two rings because we believe this cueing system should be everyone's top priority. Semantics includes all the different ways people make

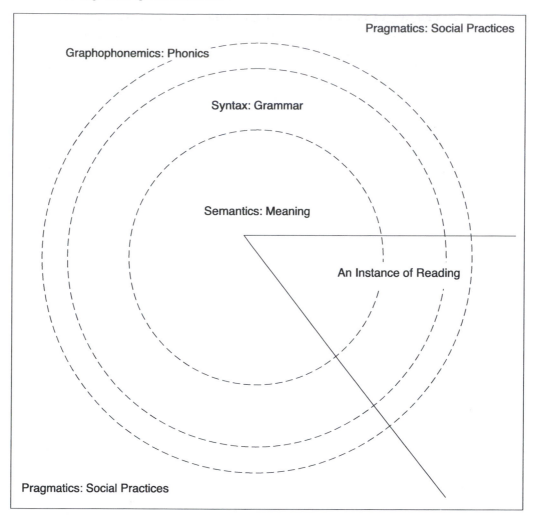

FIGURE 3.1.   Reading as Meaning-Making.

meaning from text. They might look at the pictures, talk to someone else, or think about the meaning of individual words and how they relate to each other. They might try to think of something in their own lives that connects with the text. These actions all relate to semantics. When working with students, we always want to keep meaning making at the center of our collective attention, just like it is in the model.

When a student gets stuck on a difficult word or concept, a good first question with a semantic focus is "What would make sense here?" For example, a first grader reading *Frog and Toad Together* (Lobel, 1972) comes to the sentence: "Toad put the list in his pocket" and stops at the last word. She makes the "p" sound a couple of times but goes no further. Her teacher keeps her focused on meaning by asking where Toad might want to put his list so that he can find it later. What would make sense here? He also suggests that the child look at the picture and think about what she sees there that might help her figure out the unknown word. With this support, the child says, "Well, he could put the list in his jacket" and keeps reading. At this point, making sense and continuing to read is more productive than getting the exact word.

Syntax connects to grammar and patterns of language. Syntax is the second ring in the model. This cueing system calls the reader's attention to the structure of the sentence and the kind of word he or she is looking for. When the child in our example reads, "Toad put the list in his _____" and gets stuck, her teacher will be providing a syntactic cue if he asks her to think about the kind of word that needs to go there. Is it a place (where you can put something) or an action? First, the reader has to realize that she is looking for some type of thing. It could be a jacket, a bag, or a sock, but it can't be a word like go or sing because "he put the list in his sing" does not sound like English. Syntax always works with semantics since the structure of language also has to fit with the meaning of the sentence. If the child decides that she can put something in a puddle, the teacher can agree that this sounds like English and is possible to do, but also ask what will happen to the list if he does that. Will Toad be able to read it later if it has been in a puddle? In this case, the syntax is appropriate, since a puddle is a thing and you can put something into it, but the semantics (meaning) suffers from that choice.

The graphophonemics cueing system refers to letters and sounds. Parents and teachers sometimes think that this must be the most important system because they can actually see letters on a page. There is an assumption that children need to learn letters and sounds before they learn anything else. But this assumption is challenged by children who learn to read without any formal instruction in phonics. One of our favorite videotapes of young children learning to read shows a group of first graders engaged in a conversation about three picture books that all make connections to the moon. This text set includes *Happy Birthday, Moon* (Asch, 1982); *Grandfather Twilight* (Berger, 1984); and *The Nightgown of the Sullen Moon* (Willard, 1983). In the video, the teacher sets up the expectation for a meaningful discussion by asking open-ended questions much like the ones Paula Fischer asked in the opening vignette: "What did you notice?" and "What do you think about that?" The conversation that follows shows how the children pick up on her cue and focus on issues that are important to them. They don't talk about letters or sounds but about why the illustrators drew the pictures as they did and whether the moons in the three stories are real or imaginary. One child states that she doesn't like stories about animals and another child reacts with amazement and pushes for an explanation. This is how real readers discuss books. If the teacher had started out by calling attention to the vowel sound in moon or reviewing the two consonant sounds in that word, we would not have seen such a rich conversation unfold.

We agree that children have to learn some letter/sound relationships but we don't see this system as more important than the others. Actually, we see it as less important and have therefore made the first ring quite thin. Long before children become consciously aware of letters and sounds, they become aware of reading as a meaningful activity. Therefore, we always want to teach sound/symbol correspondence within a meaningful context. To do this, we might occasionally stop when reading aloud, give the first letter of the next word, and invite kids to use the context and the letter to figure out what that word is. While reading a big book to a class of beginning readers, we might put a sticky note over some words so that just the first letter shows up. Students are encouraged to think about what will make sense there in addition to beginning with the letter they can see. This is one way to teach graphophonemics (phonics) in a meaningful way.

Pragmatics, the fourth cueing system, is concerned with the rules of language use in particular contexts or situations. In classrooms, teachers set up daily routines that affect how language is used. In classrooms where vocabulary is taught prior to reading a story, children have every right to expect that the new words will show up in the story they are about to read. Researchers have found that readers often substitute new vocabulary words while reading for words that look similar even though these substitutions don't make sense. In one study, researchers found children substituting "sound" (which was a new vocabulary word) for "should." While "sound" didn't make sense, the children were using the word they were expecting to see (Harste, 1978).

Another way to talk about pragmatics is to talk about language as social practice. When a third grade teacher says, "In this class we read aloud everyday—even when we're really busy" she is saying something about what is valued in that classroom. When another teacher tells her kindergartners "It's okay to pretend read and make up a story to go with the pictures" she is letting her children know that meaning is more important than getting all the words right. Pragmatics is also about social codes and being able to figure them out. When a teacher says, "I like how Jenny is thinking about what makes sense," she is really saying that she wishes all of her students would do more than say the sounds they see. Table 3.2 shows a list of social practices we recommend for implementation in your classroom.

Miscues demonstrate a reader's ability to use the cueing systems. One way to understand a reader's use of the different systems of language described above is to engage in the process of miscue analysis (Goodman & Burke, 1972). This process requires teachers to take a different perspective on the reading—to think about what cue systems were or were not being used as opposed to thinking in terms of the mistakes students make. Miscue analysis supports teachers in seeing readers' strengths rather than focusing on their weaknesses. For example, if the child reads the sentence "Toad put the list in his pocket" as "Toad put the list in his pack," a miscue analysis would identify this as a high quality miscue since it fits with the semantics, syntax and graphophonemics of the original sentence. If the student is using pack as an abbreviated version of backpack, then it makes good sense for Toad to put his list there. Pack is a noun, just like pocket, in the original. And many of the sounds are the same in both words. They both start with P and have a -ck cluster in them. This miscue suggests that the student is paying attention to semantics, syntax, graphophonemics, and pragmatics, in that meaning making is what is being highlighted via the social practices the teacher has put in place in this classroom.

TABLE 3.2. Social Practices We Recommend

Readers insist that their reading makes sense.

Readers see reading as time well spent.

Readers have a range of strategies to use when they come to something unknown.

Readers vary the strategies they use depending on what they are reading. (For example, reading poetry is not the same as reading a textbook.)

Readers read when they have extra time.

Readers love to talk about books.

Readers ask questions.

Readers believe reading isn't done until they have talked about the book with someone.

Readers question authors.

Readers often do research to find answers to their lingering questions after reading.

Readers know they don't have to finish every book they start.

Readers often go through stages where they read a lot of a certain genre, but this is not a concern as reading tastes almost always change over time.

Readers rethink, if not reread, books as a result of further reading or after talking with others about what they read.

When bombarded with print, readers know what is and is not important to read given their purposes at the time.

If, on the other hand, the student reads, "Toad put the list in his peeked," miscue analysis would identify this as a low quality miscue. Substituting a verb (peeked) for a noun (pocket) results in neither sounding like language nor making sense. Nonetheless, the student chose a word that matched the expected response both in length and in terms of some of the letters. Our analysis of this child's miscue provides useful information for how we might support her in growing as a reader. Since we always want to start with children's strengths, we should note that this child is demonstrating strength in her understanding of graphophonemics. While this is good, we now have to help her realign her priorities so that making sense becomes her first priority. In other words, while knowledge of sound/symbol correspondence can be identified as a strength, her dependence on graphophonemics alone isn't going to make her a successful reader. We want to help her rely more on semantics and syntax, not sounds. Once she knows what kind of word she is looking for (syntax) and is thinking about what would make sense (semantics), then the sounds can also be considered.

We encourage teachers to cultivate the social practice of listening to students with a miscue ear and tailoring their feedback according to the quality of the miscues they hear. (See **Developing a Miscue Ear** in the **Professional Development** section at the end of this chapter.) All of us make miscues when we read and most of the time we don't even notice because we have made high quality miscues that do not affect the meaning of the text. For example, a college student reading a story with the line "the boy said" read it as "said the boy" and was puzzled when a peer identified it as a miscue. Just as we saw that not all emergent literacy practices are equal, we can also conclude that not all miscues are equal. Sometimes they even improve a text.

We also see listening with a miscue ear as giving children a chance to figure out what a text is about before jumping in to tell them. Wayne, a second grader in Kittye Copeland's classroom, read an entire story about a man who made signs and the problems he had when he lost his glasses and couldn't do his job properly. Throughout the story (which Kittye taped), the boy paused when he came to the word "glasses" and then read on. He also paused when he came to the word, "building," skipped it, and read on. He never once said either word while reading. What a surprise Kittye got when she asked for a retelling of the story. He said, "Well, this story is about a man who lost his glasses and couldn't see where to put the signs. So he messed them all up." How could this happen? We can never know for sure, but because of the words he skipped, we suspect he believed that he couldn't read long words. The illustrations of glasses and buildings probably helped him, but he might have been too focused on letter sounds and word length to use them as he was reading. For the most part and as a general rule, extended text supports readers. The further a reader gets into a text, the more cues there are to figure out what the story means.

A critical transactional model pays attention to equity issues. While figuring out the words and making sense of them are important, good readers are also aware that "texts are social spaces" (Fairclough, 1995, p. 6) and are therefore never neutral. Luke and Freebody (1997) argue that readers in the 21st century need to develop a critical stance. They want readers to question who benefits from having this text written in this way and who is marginalized. They also argue that readers need to be able to identify the assumptions embedded in any text and challenge them. Taking a critical perspective on books means that children are learning to look at power issues, whose voice is being heard, and how different characters are positioned. They begin to ask questions like "What is this text trying to do to me? Which positions, voices, and interests are at play? Whose voices are silent or absent?" (Luke & Freebody, 1997, p. 214).

What does instruction from a critical perspective look like in the classroom? After reading a set of traditional "princess" fairy tales, Stevie Bruzas talked to her fourth graders about how to "unpack texts" and figure out how these texts portray characters as certain kinds of people. She then set them up in an online chat and invited them to talk about the stories they had read and what they might learn from them. Some examples of their conversation (with their original spelling preserved) are listed below:

- *They make the girls look soo preaty so the people can get more money for the supplies.*
- *Thats not right some people don't care about how they look they just care about there personallidy.*
- *Why are poeple doing this?* [trying to make girls look pretty] *i dont know why.*
- *It is a business. The people want to make money so that they can be rich! If they trick kids into thinking that princesses are cool and perfect then everyone will want to be like that and they'll make money!*
- *We unpacked that fairy tails make the princess and princes perfect with no zits or pimples. In real life to look like that you would need a lot of make up.*

In this exchange, we can see the children wrestling with questions about why the princesses and princes in fairy tales look so perfect. Their conclusion that selling makeup and other beauty supplies might be the reason demonstrates their growth in taking on a critical perspective. (For other ideas, see **Becoming a Text Analyst**, **Discourse Analysis for Kids**, and the **Language at Work** strategies in Chapter 10.)

Principle #3: Reading and Writing Go Together

Reading and writing are all around us. While we love to share books with children, we also believe there are benefits in working with environmental print. Signs, packaging, and advertisements contain words that children become familiar with at an early age. Research by Harste, Woodward, and Burke (1984) with children as young as three years old provides evidence of their ability to "read" the deeper meaning of this material even if they don't get all the words right. For example, children looking at a cup from a fast food restaurant identified it as saying things like "water," the appropriate restaurant name, and other fast food chains (p. 24). While every response was not technically accurate, they all made perfect sense and showed the children's understanding of print as communicating a message. These findings support the idea of using environmental print as reading material. Fortunately, there are many easy to read books that feature environmental print. Tana Hoban's *I Read Signs* (1983) and Zoran Milich's *City Signs* (2002) are two examples. The Read-Write-Think website hosted by the International Reading Association and the National Council of Teachers of English provides teachers with other ways they might use environmental print to support children new to reading (retrieved May 5, 2011 from http://www.readwritethink.org/classroom-resources/lesson-plans/stop-signs-mcdonald-cheerios-949.html). There are also several teacher guides available. One we particularly like is *Everyday Literacy: Environmental Print Activities for Children 3 to 8* (Mueller, 2005).

Children can be invited to make an **Environmental Print Book** after taking a walk around their school and identifying all the words they can read. These items can be collected in digital photos and made into a class booklet along with the children's illustrations of where the signs were found and what they said. Many early childhood and primary teachers start their year this way. By the end of the first day of school, children have a book they can read. Often these teachers follow up by inviting children to collect all of the environmental print (food labels, empty cereal boxes, flyers) they find at home that they can read. These too can be made into a reading booklet and shared with the class.

Nursery rhymes also make early easy reading materials. Children can make **Little Books** containing their favorite nursery rhymes and illustrations. By having children keep these books in the class library, even the very beginning readers in your room will have materials to read.

Using songs to support reading. Teachers who work with beginning readers need to know that the ear can guide the eye when it comes to reading. Even the easiest nursery rhymes can be used including songs such as *We're Going On a Bear Hunt* (Rosen, 2003), *Head, Shoulders, Knees, and Toes* (Kubler, 2002) and *Teddy Bear, Teddy Bear* (Hague, 1993). Amazon books lists several CDs on their website that teachers might use to download these and other jingles. *This Old Man* (Adams, 2000), *Mama Don't Allow* (Hurd, 1985) and *Zin, Zin, Zin, A Violin* (Moss, 1995) are more difficult songs, in that students won't already know all of the lyrics, but are natural extensions to the rhymes they already know. The secret is to keep raising the bar as they gain more and more confidence and skill.

Paula Fischer, an experienced primary teacher, recently told us that using music with her first graders is her newest strategy for teaching reading. She received an iPod as part of a professional development project and the only condition was that she had to use it in her teaching. So every week she finds a song that goes with something her class is learning about and they sing it several times. For example, when her students were learning about soil as part of their science curriculum, she found a song online called "Dirt Made My Lunch" recorded by the Banana Slug String Band (retrieved May 5, 2011 from http://www.ces.ncsu.edu/4hplantandsoils/Dirt%20Made%20My%20Lunch%20Song%20Lyrics.pdf). This song explains how dirt is the basis for growing all of the food we eat. Paula's strategy is to invite one of her students to be the leader and read each line, which is then repeated by the class in a kind of choral reading. She always stops to discuss potentially hard words—in this case plow, wheat, and flour—so children understand what they are reading. Then she turns on the music and lets them sing while following along with their song sheets. Paula sees music as providing a supportive framework for reading. She concluded by saying, "I've always wanted to use more music in my teaching but I wasn't sure how to do it. Now I know that it has to be part of my reading program."

Teachers of older reluctant readers also use song lyrics to reach their teen audiences. *The Lyric Book: Complete Lyrics for Over 1000 Songs from Tin Pan Alley to Today* (Hal Leonard Corporation, 2001) is a great resource. Songs range from Broadway to jazz to early rock 'n' roll. Titles include everything from *All You Need is Love* to *Lucy in the Sky with Diamonds*. Songs are presented alphabetically and the book includes an artist index, a songwriter index, and an index listing songs from musicals, movies, and television. As teachers who have worked with less proficient readers at various grade levels, we typically write the lyrics of songs and then use them as material for reading. We often begin by reading a piece chorally. The group's unified voice plus some knowledge of the song's text supports even those readers needing the most help. Depending on the students with whom you are working, you might also consider Celenza's *Gershwin's Rhapsody in Blue* (2006) and Giovanni's *Hip Hop Speaks to Children* (2008). (See Chapter 7 for more information on using music to teach reading.)

How reading books supports writing. A classroom literacy program based on environmental print and literature provides multiple opportunities for students to read and write. Sometimes students use writing to respond to books or other texts in terms of what they thought and why. For example, after reading *Night Noises* (Fox, 1989) Paula Fischer might extend the family theme in this story and invite children to write about family gatherings or birthday events they have experienced. Another option is to help children understand the writer's or illustrator's craft and try using some of the techniques they saw in the book. For example, after reading *Night Noises*, the teacher can call attention to how many of the "sound" words (*click, clack, crinch, crunch*) are written outside the text in a larger font and give students an opportunity to try doing that with a story they write.

Once students use writing to replicate the pattern of a book that has been read to them, they will be able to do the same thing with other books. For example, *Rosie's Walk* (Hutchins, 1971) is a simple picture book about a hen who goes for a walk and is totally unaware that her every move is being watched by a hungry fox. Through the sparse text, readers follow Rosie as she goes *over, under, through,* and *around* the different objects she encounters on her walk. After reading this book a teacher can invite students to create their own books about someone else's walk and then share them with the whole class. We have seen many examples of kids naming their books after themselves or a friend and showing some type of monster following them around their homes, classroom, and neighborhood. Since Rosie ends up safely back in the henhouse, these books always have happy endings. In this case, the literature provides a structure that supports students in taking on an authoring role. They also get an opportunity to practice reading as they are writing. Drawing a picture of someone going *over* a wall or *under* a gate requires an understanding of what those prepositions mean and will serve learners better than completing a worksheet on prepositions.

It Didn't Frighten Me! (Goss & Harste, 1981) is another predictable book that children can enjoy as a read-aloud and then use as a model for making their own books about things that do and don't frighten them. The phrase "One pitch black, very dark night, right after Mother turned off the light, I looked out my window only to see . . ." is repeated on each page with a different potentially scary object. Once they have made books following this pattern, they can be encouraged to generate their own starting sentence and use it in the same way to create a book about a different topic. For example, they might decide to start with "One sunny day when I went out to play . . ." and create a book about things they like to do outdoors.

Ten Little Bears (Hague, 1999) is a counting rhyme. "10 Little Bears/Time to rise and shine/One stayed in bed/Then there were nine" (p.1). After listening to all of the trouble that each of the bears gets into, children delight in coming up with their own problem, and the result can easily become a class book. *Where's Spot?* (Hill, 1980) provides the same supportive structure young children can use to build reading and writing strength. This book invites readers to lift flaps as they search for a missing puppy.

Writing down what students say. The language experience approach (LEA) was first introduced by Roach Van Allen (1976). Educators who advocate this approach "are concerned with helping beginners learn to bring their own knowledge and experiences to bear in constructing meaning from the printed word" (Weaver, 1994, p. 57). In other words, teachers begin with the language and experiences of learners and use their own words as reading material. Typically, a student (or group) dictates a text that is read over a number of days or weeks. Some teachers make LEA texts into books that become part of the classroom library. The thinking is that learners will find it easier to read their own words than reading words written by other people because they will be more natural.

LEA can be used with literature in a number of ways. Students might make their own pattern books as described above or they might write about an experience they connect with a book. The important point is that reading is seen as an active process of constructing meaning. Readers do not simply absorb a text and know what it's all about; they have to participate purposefully in the meaning-making process (Kucer, 2008; Goodman, 1996).

The Language Experience Approach is useful with anyone just learning to read, as well as with someone who has been turned off to reading. Older students can be invited to share special memories and experiences, talk about their hobbies, or sound off about what really bugs them. Their words can be transcribed and used as reading materials. The advantage is that the reader already knows what the text is going to say in terms of both language and content as he or she has just dictated it. Building off their own sense of language and their own knowledge of the world makes the reading process both predictable and manageable. LEA is also the basis for transcribing adolescents' favorite songs and using them as reading materials.

One of the advantages is that these materials are often very engaging and of high interest to this age group.

Key Issues in Implementation

While we highly recommend teaching reading with children's literature, we know that many teachers face obstacles when they wish to implement a literature-rich reading program. In this section we will address three of the most common obstacles: leveled books, decodable texts, and the faulty assumption that children who learn to read in literature-rich programs do not learn about phonics.

Why are leveled books an obstacle? One issue that many teachers bring up when they are thinking about using literature to teach reading is that their district requires them to use leveled books and many of the selections they want to use are not leveled. Typically, leveled books are texts that have been analyzed and labeled according to a set of predetermined criteria. Once the books are identified as being at specific levels, they are sold in sets to schools. Often the books are the same ones that can be found in the library, but they now have an identifying level symbol that seems to make them more instructional in nature. Of course there are still plenty of books that have not been leveled and these books are not used in classrooms that require teachers to use only leveled books.

The leveled text phenomenon has evolved from Marie Clay's original idea of using book levels as a way to give "young readers the support of familiar, predictable, repetitive, and rhythmic language patterns as well as tight text-picture match" (Brabham & Villaume, 2002, p. 439). We agree that predictable books are a marvelous way to help emergent readers begin because of the many supports these books offer. Teachers would do well to look through the leveled book lists that many libraries make available on the Internet. In light of the background interests that a student has, often an appropriate title presents itself. But this can also be a problem. Most book leveling is done by formulas that completely ignore the background knowledge of readers. We know from years of comprehension studies that children can read more difficult books than they might normally read if the book is about a topic they know a lot about or are interested in.

What about book choice? Although leveled book advocates argue that students in leveled book programs do have choice, the choice is only among books in a container labeled with a particular level or colored dot. There are unintended consequences from this leveling. Students who can only read from container C, for example, know they are much poorer readers than students who can choose from container E. We seriously question this sorting and labeling of readers. The practice is particularly deleterious for older reluctant readers. Since leveling schemes don't pay attention to what readers bring to a text, knowledge that could assist older readers in understanding harder books is not considered.

Katie DiCesare (2008) wants her first graders to experience success in reading words and stories. "But most of all," she says, "I want them to love reading" (p. 40). To promote this love of reading, she invites her students to help in developing themes for book baskets that include both leveled and unleveled books. The baskets they compile feature topics like picture reading, rhyming, fairy tales, nonfiction, poetry, and individual authors like Kevin Henkes, Mem Fox, and Eric Carle. Focusing on themes instead of levels is one way to make use of leveled books without getting into the situation where children define themselves as readers according to their current reading level.

Decodable texts are one way that books are leveled. Based on readability formulas that were used in the past, decodable texts are perceived to be easy books because they have short sentences and few long words. The problem is that writing to fit readability formulas always leads to distorted, inauthentic texts. While putting tight constraints on vocabulary can make texts technically more decodable, this practice can also produce contrived language that is hard to understand. Ken Goodman (1996) makes this point convincingly when he points out examples of supposedly simple sentences like "Father! See Spot run" that are linguistically complex and difficult for children to comprehend. He notes that children often read this as "Father sees Spot run" because the syntax sounds more natural to them (p. 76).

We see the pervasiveness of leveled books and decodable texts within these sets as a situation that needs further critical inquiry. On the one hand, we agree with Kathryn Mitchell Pierce's (1999) conclusion: "I don't have anything against grouping books into broad levels based on readability. Such groupings make it easier for teachers, parents, and students to select reading materials" (p. 373). But we also agree with her conclusion that leveling can inhibit children's ability to see themselves as multi-dimensional readers.

Think about what kind of reader you would become if the only books you were allowed to read were in a container with a green dot. This is not how to raise readers. As Szymusiak and Sibberson (2001) wisely note:

> If we know that children are unique and the reading process is complex, why would we limit our ability to match children with books by relying on a leveled list created by a person or company that doesn't know our children? (p. 15)

These authors tell a teacher story about getting carried away with leveling and decodable texts: A teacher, they report, came to their librarian friend and asked for "a book on hamsters for my third grade class project that has to be level M" (p. 16). They saw this as the height of "leveling mania," and we agree.

What about phonics in literature-based programs? One criticism of literature-based programs is based on the faulty assumption that children who learn to read with literature end up not being able to use phonics skills to help them read. A study done by Gambrell and Palmer (1992) challenges this assumption. These researchers compared first and second graders' knowledge about reading and writing in literature-based classrooms and conventional classrooms. Children in conventional classrooms used a basal reading series for instruction and children's literature during voluntary reading time while children in literature-based classrooms used literature for instruction and for voluntary reading.

The authors concluded that children who experienced literature-based instruction used phonics more often, had a better understanding of the pleasure of reading, and had a better understanding of the purposes of writing. They were more likely to say that they would try to sound out words they didn't know than children in the conventional classrooms who more frequently said they would ask for help if they didn't know words. In other words, the children who were taught through literature showed more skill in using phonics to help them read than children who were using basal reading programs. This made them more independent readers as well since they were more likely to use what they knew to help themselves instead of asking for help.

Working With Linguistically and Culturally Diverse Students

It is important to point out that students who have not been raised in mainstream middle class families are not devoid of experience. They know a lot and one of the best strategies for working successfully with them is to tap into their experiential base. The same is true about children who speak a language other than English. These kids should not be thought of as being unable to express themselves. We simply need to use what language they have to support them in learning

English. This means that when everyone else in the class is writing in a journal, students who speak a language other than English are writing in a journal too. The idea is that everyone writes in whatever language they feel comfortable and they use pictures to illustrate their work. All students are given the opportunity to share what they have written or drawn.

Ours is a multicultural work. Immigration in its multiple forms is the mode of the world, not the exception. Successful teachers build from the linguistic and cultural resources that children bring with them to the classroom. For example, Myriam Revel-Wood had a Polish child who spoke not one word of English join her class one fall. She included him in everything the class was doing including keeping a journal, the one activity, besides math, that he did more of than anyone else. While everyone else wrote their journal entries in English, this boy wrote his in Polish. Although he was always included in literature discussions, he rarely spoke. After Christmas, he suddenly began to contribute and by the end of year a visitor could hardly tell him from the other children in the classroom. Stories like this one are important. They show that most of what any of us knows about language we have learned from being in the presence of other language users as they went about their daily lives. We are also reminded that a student's native language is the foundation for learning new languages.

The key to success in working with new language learners is to invite them in and ensure that they are not isolated. When teachers see these children as providing new potential directions for the curriculum, instead of being difficult to work with, everyone benefits. It is also important for teachers to get into the habit of searching the Internet since more and more children's books dealing with other cultures (and other languages) are becoming available and can be shared with the entire class. As we have said before, all children need to see themselves in literacy before they themselves will become literate. For this to happen, they have to assume the identity of literate people and see how literacy relates to them and the lives they live.

One example of a reading program dedicated to the importance of children seeing themselves in their reading materials is the "Integrated Reading Curriculum" (IRC), which focuses on African American culture. Tambra Jackson and Gloria Boutte (2009) describe how this curriculum uses "liberation literature" (a term they credit to Virginia Hamilton) to "reflect the children's images," introduce them to others of their race who have made a difference, and encourage them "to involve themselves in community service, no matter what the circumstances" (p. 115). The authors note that literacy is taught through "an activity-oriented curriculum intended to excite, motivate, stimulate, arouse, expose, inspire, delight, enchant, and rejuvenate" (p. 111). They contrast this approach with school programs that are narrowly focused on the mechanics of reading and test scores. In schools using the IRC philosophy,

> the goal is to help readers fall in love with books: the stories, the characters, the pictures, the ideas, and the values. The IRC seeks to give non-readers an overwhelming desire to read—which is a basic step toward doing it. (p. 112, italics in original)

In other words, both the methods of teaching and the materials make a big difference. "When books serve as mirrors for African American students and reflect their worldviews in positive ways, the possibilities for literacy are increased" (p. 114). We would extend this line of thinking to other cultural groups as well. It's important to look at school and classroom collections to see if there are gaps in terms of books that feature characters representing different ethnicities and/or cultures. While we agree with Jackson and Boutte that African American children are often "given the message that they are invisible, unimportant, and inferior" (p. 112), we see that problem extending to other non-mainstream groups as well.

Technology Extensions and Electronic Resources

Fan fiction is a genre of writing in which readers of popular literature create new stories to "extend storylines, create new narrative threads, develop romantic relationships between characters, and focus on the lives of underdeveloped characters" (Black, 2009, p. 398). For example, http://fanfiction.mugglenet.com/ features original Harry Potter stories written by fans.

The NewLits.org site also has examples of digital storytelling. Glynda Hull and JuliAnna Avila describe this genre as follows: "Two to five minute movies, the stories usually begin with a written script that is eventually accompanied by images, photographs, artwork, or snippets of video; a musical soundtrack; and the author's voice reading or performing the script" (retrieved July 22, 2010 from https://newlits.wikispaces.com/Narrative+and+digital+storytelling). We see all of these technology developments as positive in that they move children's and adolescent literature into formats that will no doubt be attractive to young people who have grown up in the digital era. For them, participating in online literacy activities might provide the impetus to keep them engaged in reading and critical language study.

Assessment

There are many commercial reading tests for beginning readers but they often provide decontextualized information like how well and how quickly students can sound out nonsense words. This type of assessment shows growth in terms of only one cueing system, graphophonemics. It does not provide information on the student's use of syntax or whether he or she is focusing on making meaning (semantics). In addition, this type of assessment is not built on a "real" reading experience since nonsense words are not what readers normally encounter. Instead of relying on commercial reading tests, we recommend that teachers look for changes in their students' actions and attitudes. For example, we think one sure sign of growth is that we see children doing more than simply trying to sound out words. Another sign is that they are making high quality miscues. Textbox 3.1 provides ideas for assessing a beginning reading program.

Textbox 3.1. Assessment

We know we are doing a good job teaching kids to read when they are:

Choosing to read when they have free time.
Talking with their friends about favorite genres, books, and authors.
Recommending books to their friends.
Using all of the cueing systems to figure out hard words.
Making high quality miscues.
Not giving up on new books that seem hard.

We know the classroom environment is supportive of children learning to read and write when:

It is an environment that is rich in spoken and written language.
Students are able to make choices and are held responsible for their own learning.
Students are encouraged to take risks and their approximations are valued.
Students are invited to use reading and writing in personally relevant ways.
Students are invited to experiment with using language to achieve different purposes.

Invitation: Developing A Miscue Ear

The goal of this invitation (see Textbox 3.2) is to help participants develop the ability to analyze miscues and make quick decisions about whether to correct or ignore them. This is a useful strategy for both teachers and students to learn. Chris taught it to her fifth and sixth graders and noticed that the number of annoying corrections during oral reading decreased substantially.

Textbox 3.2. Invitation: Developing A Miscue Ear

Miscues happen when readers change a text while reading aloud. While some see miscues as mistakes that need to be corrected, we see them as providing valuable information on how readers are trying to make sense of a text. Miscues can show readers' strengths as well as their weaknesses. Developing a "miscue ear" means that teachers (and students!) can quickly analyze miscues and decide if they interrupt the meaning of the text or not. If not, they are considered to be "high quality" miscues and there is no need to correct them. This invitation provides an opportunity to examine a reader's miscues and think about what might be learned from them.

Materials & Procedures

- A sample "marked up" text is provided to show one student's miscues.
- You can also make your own examples from taped student readings. Include copies of the text for participants to mark up as they listen to the tape.

1. As a group, review the markings and what they indicate.
2. Discuss each miscue in terms of what information it provides about the reader.
3. If you were this student's teacher, how would you respond to each miscue? Would you correct it? Why or why not?
4. What other information do you need to evaluate this student's reading? How might you obtain it?

Other Notes

1. This invitation can also be used with upper elementary and middle school students. Once students learn to analyze each other's miscues, they will stop correcting unimportant errors and will concentrate on meaning instead. This will make the classroom more peaceful and they will also become stronger readers as they work together to decide whether they have heard a high quality miscue or not.
2. Sample marked up "text":

Monesha
Before Monica went to bed she looked out (of) her window

very
and saw the moon. The moon looked (so) ∧ near. "I wish I

Monesha   she
could play with the moon," thought Monica, and ∧ reached

```
up                                        started
∧ for it. But no matter how (much) she stretched, she

         reach                          Monesha
could not touch the moon. "Papa," said Monica to

had
her father, "please get the moon for me." Papa got a very
long ladder. He carried the (very) long ladder towards a
very high mountain.
──────────
Key: ∧ = Insertion of word not in text.
( ) = Omission of a word in text.
```

Professional Development

This section has two parts. The first part, "Collaborative Kidwatching" (see Textbox 3.3), provides an invitation that can be done by small groups of practicing or prospective teachers. The second part provides a selection of professional articles that relates to different aspects of this chapter. Depending on your study group's interest in older or younger readers and current "hot topics," the articles listed in Table 3.3 can serve as resources for guiding conversations and raising new questions.

Textbox 3.3. Collaborative Kidwatching (Goodman, 1978)

Together with the teachers at your grade level, identify a child whom you all feel is struggling with reading and writing.

Over the course of the next week everyone makes as many observations as they can of this child, noting when he seems engaged, when he seems disengaged, what things he seems to like to do, with whom he likes to play, to whom he goes when he is hurt and so on. Observations on the playground, in the cafeteria, as well as the classroom are valuable. Also take note of what he struggles with in terms of schoolwork. Collect examples if possible.

At your next meeting take turns sharing what you have learned for the purpose of exploring a single question, "What would we have to do to be successful with this child?" Jot down various recommendations. There is no need to defend choices at this point in time. The object is to generate as many ideas as possible.

During the next week try out one of the ideas and report back what happened. Talk about what success was achieved and what might be tried next.

As an aside, we (Jerry and Chris) want to say that when we worked with teachers to open the Center for Inquiry in Indianapolis, this was our staff's weekly professional development activity. Each week we identified one student, made as many observations as we could on that student, and then met to talk about what we might collectively do to insure that child's success. This professional activity not only helped us grow but also supported our school's goal of not letting any child fall through the cracks.

TABLE 3.3.   Suggestions for Further Reading

Poonam, A., Martens, P., Wilson, G., Altwerger, B., Jin, L., Laster, B., & Lang, D. (2005) Reclaiming literacy instruction: Evidence in support of literature-based programs. *Language Arts*, *83*(1), 63–72.

Do children learn about phonics when teachers use literature as the foundation of their reading program? Researchers found that children learning to read through commercial phonics-based programs were not significantly better than students in literature-based programs in terms of phonics use, accuracy, or comprehension. In addition, students in literature-based programs were found to use more strategies, take more risks, and take action when what they read didn't make sense.

Cunningham, A. & Shagoury, R. (2005) The sweet work of reading: Kindergartners explore reading comprehension using a surprisingly complex array of strategies. *Educational Leadership*, *63*(2), 53–57.

This article will be especially interesting to teachers who work with kindergarten and first grade students. The authors provide numerous examples of young children learning to dig deep as they are also learning to read. They show how comprehension strategies can be taught right from the beginning.

Brozo, W. & Tomlinson, C. (1986) Literature: The key to lively content courses. *The Reading Teacher*, *40*(3), 288–293.

This classic article describes how trade books can be used to help older students understand the textbooks used in their content courses. While textbooks are often dry and not very inviting, literature brings new topics to life.

four
Choosing
Books
Diversity Counts

Lee Heffernan was teaching third grade across the hall from a special education classroom some years ago. There was a boy, Evan, who was autistic and regularly ran into her room and played with the computers until his teacher retrieved him. His teacher asked if Evan could visit Lee's room for a short period each day. Lee agreed, but was worried about how much of a distraction Evan would be. Over time, Evan started to fit in more and stayed longer. Lee decided to read aloud *Ian's Walk* (Lears, 1998), a book about a boy with autism and his sister Julie. The kids made connections with Evan and many of them related to Ian, the character with autism, rather than the sister Julie as Lee had expected. Instead of focusing on Julie's irritation with her brother being so different, the students focused on Ian's feelings of frustration at not being allowed to do things his way. One girl made the connection, "Evan loves to smell the chalkboard just like Ian liked to smell the bricks." A series of conversations and literacy events about disabilities followed and the students decided that almost everyone had something that was different about them (Heffernan & Lewison, 2000).

Serendipitously, Lee found an editorial in the local paper about a bill in the state legislature that would provide additional funding for services for people with developmental disabilities. The editorial described how the state had an extremely poor record of serving this group and had been placed on a "Hall of Shame" list along with 12 other states. Because of their connection with Evan, the kids felt very strongly about this issue and decided to write letters to their state senator. For example:

Dear Senator,
I support House Bill 1114. I want to get out of the Hall of Shame. We have a kid in our class. He is handicapped. I hope he gets the support he needs. Please help us.
R.J

In these letters of pleading to vote yes on the bill to help kids like Evan and to get their state out of the Hall of Shame (Heffernan & Lewison, 2000), students were taking action to get things done in their world.

This story is significant. We see Lee building curriculum from the everyday occurrences in her classroom and using *Ian's Walk,* a book that the students enjoyed, to open up new conversations about living with people with disabilities, an enterprise in which they were involved daily. She used a book to disrupt the commonplace notion that talking about Evan and people with autism was not an acceptable part of classroom life. In an organic way, the class started digging deeper by paying attention to the plight of a group that is often marginalized (Harste, Breau, Leland, Lewison, Ociepka & Vasquez, 2000). Lee took the additional step of tying students' discussions to larger sociopolitical issues—the bill before the state senate. In the tradition of Lankshear and McLaren (1993), students used literacy to engage in the politics of daily life. Instead of being bystanders, they used literacy as a powerful tool to communicate their feelings about a consequential issue and potentially influence change in the community. This classroom story demonstrates the power that books can have on our personal lives, how they can change social practices in the classroom, and how they can also be the impetus for taking action and getting real work done in the world.

We see a strong connection between the books we choose to read and critical literacy. This connection underpins our goals of growing literate beings who are competent and confident readers and writers, who think critically, and who have a commitment to making the world an equitable place for all.

There are three main genres of children's literature we use regularly in classrooms—books about *social issues, multicultural* experiences, and *international* stories and global events—that have the potential to open up new spaces that break down boundaries between ourselves and "the other" (Said, 1978). By "the other," Said refers to false negative assumptions or romanticized images of groups of people we haven't experienced face-to-face. The best of social issues, multicultural, and international children's literature shatters images of "the other" by presenting characters who are both like ourselves and those who are very different from us. In these books, characters are portrayed in realistic, dynamic, non-stereotypical, and multi-dimensional ways. Although the three categories of books often overlap, we decided to separate them to delve into the values and commitments that each brings to our teaching. What follows are three principles that underlie our beliefs.

Principle #1: Books About Social and Political Issues Open up New Curricular Spaces

There is one type of children's and young adult literature that we have written about extensively and have witnessed making both large and small differences in classroom life and the lives of students—*social issues* books (Harste et al., 2000). This realistic fiction genre includes books that have the potential to build students' awareness of how systems of meaning and power affect people and the lives they lead. They invite conversations about fairness and justice; they encourage children to ask why some groups of people are positioned as "others." These stories do not make difference invisible, but rather explore how differences in culture, language, history, class, gender, sexual orientation, and race *make* a difference. We saw this demonstrated in the way Lee called attention to the issue of autism in her classroom by reading *Ian's Walk.* Social issues books can enrich our understanding of history and life by giving voice to those who have traditionally been silenced or marginalized. They make visible the political and social systems that attempt to maintain economic inequities and show how people can begin to take action on important social issues (Lewison, Leland, & Harste, 2000).

Although *Ian's Walk* is a book that most teachers would use in class, there are social issues books that some teachers find too disturbing or uncomfortable to use. For example, when teaching a college course on diverse children's and young adult literature, Karla Möller had a few members of her class suggest including "variations in sexual preference" as a topic of study. This caused quite a stir with some students and Frances used the words "deviant" and "sinner" to describe homosexuals. She felt discriminated against when her religious perspectives were challenged by class members and the instructor. On the other hand, Susan, a lesbian, felt victimized by Frances's words and by some of Möller's attempts to keep all class members engaged in dialogue (Lewison, Leland, Flint, & Möller, 2002, p. 222).

As part of Möller's course, the class read Jacqueline Woodson's *The House You Pass on the Way* (1997), a book about how 12-year-old Staggerlee and her family are set apart from the community because her "father had married a white woman" (p. 5). In addition to other difficulties, Staggerlee realizes that her attraction to a girl will probably bring her more trouble. In discussing this and other books that address sexual preference, Möller notes:

> During small group sharing, many class members commented on the bullying and overt harassment with references to homosexuality that have become common in schools, but added that they felt unprepared or unwilling to address this issue. While class members did not find agreement or easy answers, many noted they were changed by the readings, the discussions, and their writing . . . As days passed, many students began making connections between the unjust treatment of homosexuals and the experiences of other oppressed groups in the past and present . . . Class members experiencing conflict in their feelings about homosexuality did not suddenly switch their views. The discussions touched on chords that were for many integral to their entire belief systems—and all major shifts take time. However, it was clear through class members' words and actions that reading *The House You Pass On the Way* and participating in class discussions helped many face personal and societal biases head-on in productive ways. (Lewison et al., 2002, pp. 222–224)

As Möller points out, the books themselves are important and can serve as springboards for digging deeper into issues, feelings, and perspectives. Like Möller, we are especially interested in the critical conversations that follow the reading of these books—conversations that focus on diversity and difference, injustices in society, and, at times, people working together to make a difference in the world. Many have asked us why we use books that foster risky conversations, those that often deal with issues usually kept outside of the classroom door. Why use "authentic and brave" literature (Ballentine & Hill, 2000) when there are so many safe books in print to use with students? Put simply—there is a remarkable vitality, an aliveness, a level of intellectual engagement that occurs when kids have the opportunity to read about and discuss important controversial topics that intersect with their lives. These "dangerous" real-world conversations, as Sonia Nieto (1999) describes them, stand in stark contrast to the lifeless, routinized discourses that flow from commercial reading programs that have come to permeate many elementary and middle school classrooms. When critical conversations become part of the regular curriculum, school has the potential of becoming an exciting place where stimulating intellectual work is the rule rather than the exception.

As another example, Amy Wackerly, a second/third grade teacher, read *Voices in the Park* (Browne, 1998) to her class. This book is a story about social class and status, recounting the interactions of two families when they were in the park at the same time. One family consists of a bossy wealthy mother and her rather shy son. The other is a despondent out-of-work father and his outgoing young daughter. Before reading the book a second time, Amy told the kids that they would be "retelling the story from a character's point of view." After the second reading, she put them into groups that contained representatives of all four characters and invited them to assume the role of their assigned personality as they talked through the story without rereading the actual text. Through the ensuing conversations, it became clear that students understood how four people who experienced the same events could come away with very different perceptions. To do this, they had to challenge the common sense notion that there is only one way to see "the facts" of any event (Lewison, Leland, & Harste, 2008).

Amy brought this understanding from *Voices in the Park* to bear on a class problem. She had received several complaints from children about the amount of name-calling that was going on at school. After students connected name-calling to bullying, she invited them to think about why bullies might be doing what they do in the first place. She talked about how she doesn't think of herself as a bully, yet sometimes she finds herself acting in a mean or bossy way at home. She challenged the students to put themselves into someone else's shoes and think about what might be going on in that person's life to make him or her act like a bully. The students came up with very sophisticated responses and Amy used these to create a number of scenarios and activities where students took on the roles of bullies and those being bullied. They were engrossed in the dramatizations, actively involved in figuring out why they engage in bullying themselves, and tried out different ways to respond when under attack. (Lewison et al., 2008).

The work that Amy did with young children helped them understand the social practices that make us read people in certain ways. They examined how to uncover the meanings the author may have wanted us to believe, how to connect what we read in books to our own lives, and how we can connect books to larger social issues. This allowed students to consider multiple perspectives in ways that positively affected their lives and the school community. We see *Voices in the Park* serving as a touchstone text, a significant book that teachers go back to numerous times during the year for multiple purposes (Calkins, 1994; Laman, 2006; Wood Ray, 1999). Whenever issues of bullying resurfaced during the year, *Voices in the Park* could be returned to as a lens from which to examine new problematic issues from a place of expertise.

Other researchers have found similar levels of engagement as Lee and Amy did when students read and discuss controversial books. Ballentine and Hill (2000) describe how their second, third, and fourth grade students' "less-than-enthusiastic literary engagement" led them to look for "literature that would heighten . . . students' self-awareness" (p. 11). They turned to multicultural literature, believing that "truths like racism, depression, and abuse as well as acceptance, elation, and caring could become topics for our children's meaningful discussions" (p.11). Using books that "strain against the boundaries of district adoptions or that deviate from the kinds of texts that teachers usually select" (p. 13) may seem like a needless risk, but after describing their year-long study using multicultural children's literature and their students' engagement and insights, Ballentine and Hill noted that "our children's voices—in discussion, in explanations of their art, and in their dramatic enactments—continually reminded us that the risks we were taking in our teaching made sense" (p. 19). We agree with them.

Principle #2: Authentic Multicultural Literature Matters

Another category of books that opens up spaces for breaking down boundaries and misconceptions of "the other" is multicultural literature. It is important that these books are used in all kinds of classrooms with all kinds of kids. The purposes of using multicultural literature include:

- making society a better place by exploring the human condition and related socio-political issues (Sims Bishop, 1992);
- liberating us from preconceived stereotypes (Howard, 1991);
- providing a broader view of the world (Landt, 2008);
- crossing borders to understand similarities and differences among ourselves and others (Landt, 2008); and
- helping students of all backgrounds see themselves in reading (Landt, 2008, Sims Bishop, 1992).

These purposes seem quite similar to those for social issues books, and they are. One major difference we see comes from the multiculturalists' determination to find "authentic" literature. Below, we present some of the major characteristics of culturally authentic multicultural literature and the controversies around these features.

Who writes culturally authentic literature? Common wisdom dictates that insiders can better portray the everyday lives of characters, understand the attitudes and cultural specifics of a group, and write books that particular groups can claim as their own (Sims Bishop, 1992). Despite this criterion, multiculturalists are quick to point out that some non-insider authors spend lots of time in the communities they portray and can do a sensitive job in presenting realistic, non-stereotyped characters and situations (Short & Fox, 2004; Sims Bishop, 1992; Yokota, 1993). In addition, membership in a particular group doesn't mean an author is immune from inadvertently perpetuating stereotypes (Short & Fox, 2004). But whether the author is an insider or not, cultural accuracy is key. It's clear that what "culturally authentic" means is contested, but there are some places where insider authors probably have the edge on non-insiders. For example, generally they write books that don't lump characters into "cultural conglomerates" (i.e. Koreans as simply Asian, Kenyans as Africans, etc.) and that don't exclude cultures such as religious groups or European Americans (Yokota, 1993). To make matters more complicated, examining cultural accuracy is tricky. Cultures are dynamic and changing so "there can never be a simplistic scale for evaluating authenticity;" there is always variance (Short & Fox, 2004, p. 378).

For whom is culturally authentic literature written? Multicultural literature has the potential to offer insights into the experience of all human beings. This means that literature can help us grow as socially conscious beings who are aware of political and social issues that are often directly related to race, class, language, ethnicity, gender, sexual orientation, age, ability, and more. At the same time, this literature can allow us to see how complex social issues have permeable boundaries and impact us all. An exemplary culturally authentic book can build bridges of understanding between the reader and people in other groups, hopefully influencing how "they will live in this culturally pluralistic world" (Yokota, 1993). This "cross-cultural understanding occurs when people begin to accept that there are different ways of thinking and different values in other cultures" (Louie, 2006, p. 447).

Culturally authentic literature allows children to see themselves in books. In the words of Rudine Sims Bishop (1992), "if literature is a mirror that reflects human life, then all children who read or are read to need to see themselves reflected as part of humanity" in a positive way (p. 114). This means finding books in which people from non-mainstream groups are portrayed as leaders, not just followers, and aren't the only characters who have problems or are expected to forgive someone. Sims Bishop asks us to put ourselves in the place of the reader and ask if we would be offended or embarrassed by a book we decided to read to our students. As important as this point is, there is another aspect that goes beyond seeing ourselves in books. Unless children in their daily lives can see themselves in literacy, reading will always remain something that's not for them (Harste, Woodward, & Burke, 1984). As teachers, our first job is to help children see themselves as literate beings and then assess how accurately they and their cultures are represented in the materials and literacy practices we teach.

Details matter. Junko Yokota (1993, pp. 159–160) points out the importance of rich details in multicultural literature, believing that accurate details are often best handled by being embedded in the text, thus becoming more natural and less didactic. These details include authentic dialogue and relationships; historical accuracy; the strategic and sensitive use of language, colloquial speech, and dialects; undistorted images; and non-stereotypical illustrations (Landt, 2006; Short & Fox, 2004; Sims Bishop, 1992; Yokota, 1993). We have found some teachers who question the inclusion of embedded details in multicultural literature. For example, in a children's literature class Chris taught, a white teacher questioned whether colloquial dialogue in *Stars in the Darkness* (Joosse, 2001) was a positive element of the book, thinking it was stereotypical. Then another white teacher brought up the part in the back of the book about how the author wanted to represent "the street rhythms" of the real Richard, the main character in the book. At that point an African American teacher said that it was fine to use that speech style but another black teacher didn't agree and said it perpetuated stereotypes. So, the debate goes on. We like this conversation because dialect is relevant to the credibility of text and larger social issues. The type of debate that occurred in this case can start needed conversations—not only among teachers, but also with our students. We also believe debates about (in)appropriate cultural or language details are a good way to initiate discussions on reading the word and the world (Freire, 1970) in more equitable ways.

As an example of why authentic characteristics are so critical, we recount a story told by Rhonda Harris Taylor (2000), a Choctaw woman. Rhonda was in the children's section of a chain bookstore in Oklahoma during the Christmas season and spotted a list of recommended books to buy for kids. To her disbelief, at the top of the list was *The Indian in the Cupboard* (Banks, 1985). This book has repeatedly received extremely negative reviews by the Native American community for its insulting stereotypes of the Indian character, Little Bear. These include distorted images "of the Indian as *savage*, a paternalistic role for the White protagonist, and an auxiliary role for the Indian character as the faithful sidekick" (Taylor, 2000, p. 373, italics in original). Little Bear (an Iroquois) is portrayed as dangerous, blood thirsty, speaking English in monosyllables, primitive, superstitious, needing a White person (a boy in this case) to guide him—in short, the stereotypical Indian we've seen for years in Hollywood movies and on TV (p. 372–375).

If we go back to the criteria for selecting multicultural literature, we can ask a series of questions of *The Indian in the Cupboard.*

- Is the book written by an insider or someone who has extensive experience with the Iroquois culture?
- Would Native Americans claim Little Bear as one of their own?
- Does the book build cross-cultural understanding between Native Americans and other groups?
- How would a Native American child who reads this book feel?
- How authentic are the language and relationships in the book?

From this simple assessment, it is clear that *The Indian in the Cupboard* comes up short. But, what is most infuriating to Taylor is that the book gets rave reviews in mainstream media, library, and teaching publications in both Britain and the U.S. Teachers and librarians trust

TABLE 4.1. Useful Resources for Assessing Cultural Authenticity

Book Awards	Web and Book Resources
Coretta Scott King Award (African American)	**Asian American:** http://www.asianamericanbooks.com/
American Indian Youth Literature Award (Native American)	http://www.cynthialeitichsmith.com/lit_resources/diversity/asian_am/asian_am.html
Pura Belpré Award (Latino/a)	**Native American:** http://www.oyate.org/
Tomás Rivera Award (Mexican American)	Slapin & Seale (1992) *Through Indian eyes: The native experience in books for children,*
Sydney Taylor Award (Jewish)	Philadelphia, PA: New Society Publishers*
Américas Book Award (Latin American, Caribbean, or U.S. Latino/a)	**African American:** http://www.childrenslit.com/childrenslit/th_af.html
Carter G. Woodson Book Award (topics related to ethnic minorities and race relations sensitively and accurately)	**Multicultural:** http://www.isomedia.com/homes/jmele/joe.html (includes separate sections for a number of ethnic groups)
Jane Addams Book Award (effectively promotes peace, social justice, world community and the equality of the sexes and all races)	Harris, V.J. (1997) *Using multiethnic literature in the K-8 classroom.* Christopher-Gordon Publishers **International:** http://wowlit.org/ (Worlds of Words from the University of Arizona)
Notable Social Studies Trade Books (emphasize human relations, represent a diversity of groups and are sensitive to a broad range of cultural experiences)	http://www.csulb.edu/org/childrens-lit/proj/nbgs/intro-nbgs.html (IRA: Notable books for a global society—you will need to use a search engine for the latest lists)

* We love this book, but it's difficult to get. Look for it at your public library.

these professional reviews, but Taylor stresses that we must "understand that favorable reviews in mainstream sources are not a guarantee of either authenticity or the absence of cultural stereotyping" (p. 382). She, like Landt (2006), stresses the importance of finding reliable sources for evaluating books that depict cultural groups other than our own. Landt goes to two places when she is unsure about the cultural authenticity of a book—cultural book award winners and websites devoted to individual cultures (p. 686). Table 4.1 lists book awards and websites compiled from Landt's (2006, pp. 686–687) research and our own.

Principle #3: Using International Literature Matters

A third category of literature that opens up new conversational spaces is international children's and young adult literature. These books are not always easy to find in classrooms. Much of traditional school study of "other countries" is accomplished through history and social studies textbooks. But leaving out the engaging stories of people from across the globe shortchanges our students. Why should young people only get abbreviated, single perspective understandings of the world beyond the country where they live? Tomlinson (1995) eloquently describes how children's literature can bring an enhanced sense of reality and hope to the history curriculum.

Unlike textbook accounts and television coverage of war, which most often focus on acts of aggression, well-written trade books focus on the results of aggression—the uprooted and ruined lives, the suffering from pain and sadness, and the waste of lives, energy, and resources. If the violence in these stories can convince young people they must find peaceful ways to settle their differences, it is justified. (p. 45)

Using a wide range of international books provides a number of important benefits. These include:

- reducing ethnocentrism by being able to "look at other cultural groups without a perspective of either superiority or inferiority" (Lo, 2001, p. 84);
- enriching units of study by including insider knowledge on international issues that might be otherwise missing (Brewster, 2008; Lo, 2001, Short, 2009a);
- eliminating the patronizing or exotic tone that is often present in works by outsiders (Stan, 1999); and
- reflecting the cultural and language diversity of the students in our classrooms (Lo, 2001).

When using international children's literature, Short (2009a) cautions that often these studies "take the form of theme units that focus on superficial aspects of a culture through a limited study of the 5fs—food, fashion, folklore, festivals, and famous people" (p. 5). Using international literature calls for treating the content in these books in complex ways, often using multiple texts on the same issue so students can gain in-depth rather than shallow understandings of intricate global concerns.

We have found three issues related to international children's books that are worthy of further discussion.

Using literature about the developing world and cross-cultural studies increases understanding of difficult global issues. Diakiw (1990) makes a strong case for using international literature focused on the "less developed regions of the world. These regions, normally the least studied across the curriculum, are the source of the majority of immigrants and refugees to North America and Europe" (p. 296). Diakiw argues that issues of poverty, famine, and war are probably better addressed in classrooms with caring teachers rather than in front of the television set. We agree with Diakiw and want to emphasize that it takes more than a caring teacher and a good piece of literature to address issues of the developing world in classrooms. Because of the economic and social complexities of developing countries, we urge teachers to bring in a wide range of strategies and materials to augment international children's literature focused on developing regions, so that stories can be understood in larger political and global contexts.

Short (2009a) created a useful curriculum framework that stresses the importance of studying global issues through *cross-cultural studies* which "provide an opportunity for children to examine the complexity and diversity within a particular cultural group" (p. 5). As an example, Short describes a study on Korea after students had already focused on the complexity of culture within their own lives. Books that focus on Korean culture, both in the U.S. and in Korea include:

- *Cooper's Lesson* (Shin, 2004). Mixed heritage Cooper is confused about his identity. He doesn't speak Korean and is frustrated in Mr. Lee's Korean grocery where only Korean is spoken. Despite language barriers, the two come to understand each other and the issues in their lives.
- *The Name Jar* (Choi, 2003). After being teased about her Korean name on the bus on the first day of school, Yoon-Hye is thinking about changing her name and gets help from children in her class. In the end, after a talk about her Korean heritage from her mother, Yoon-Hye decides to keep her own name.

■ *When My Name Was Keoko* (Park, 2002). Two siblings, Sun-hee and Tae-yul struggle to keep their identity during the Japanese occupation of Korea before World War II. The story was inspired by the author's family stories.

As was mentioned earlier, Short cautions that cross-cultural studies often end up being superficial, tourist curricula, so finding a variety of literature that "reflects complexity in terms of the economic, social, political, aesthetic, moral, historical, and geographical contexts of a cultural group" is critical (2009a, p. 5, based on Begler, 1996). Another part of Short's framework, *inquiries on global issues*, highlights "difficult social, political, and environmental topics such as violence, human rights and social justice, environmental degradation, over-population, poverty, language loss, race and ethnicity, and economic imperialism" (p. 7, based on Collins, Czarra, & Smith, 1998). We find Short's focus on complexity in cross-cultural studies and in-depth inquiries into global issues important components of studying developing regions of the world.

Authenticity issues in international children's and young adult literature. Deborah Lo (2001) has identified three types of books that fit into the categories of international, global, or transcultural literature (p. 84). One of the main characteristics of international literature that she identifies is that these books were originally written outside of the United States in a language other than English and then translated. Translations raise a number of questions. How accurate is the translation? Which books get published? Are they only books that publishers think will be popular (Joels, 1999)? What ends up being published in the United States or other English speaking countries does "not represent a microcosm of the greater worlds of international children's literature" (Stan, 1999, p. 168). In addition, getting published does not guarantee quality or accuracy, nor does it mean that the books that get published have important themes.

A second category of international books features texts originally written in English, but in a country other than the United States. A good example of this is *Fleeing the War* by Malawian educator Steve Sharra (1996). This children's book was based on adaptations of stories Steve heard from refugees who fled the 16-year civil war in Mozambique and settled in Malawi. The book was written in English and, as with many books in this category, won a prize (in this case the British Council writing prize in Malawi).

A third category of international children's literature consists of books that were written about another culture by a long-term participant in that culture. As an example, *Afghan Dreams: Young Voices of Afghanistan* (O'Brien & Sullivan, 2008) was created by award-winning photojournalist Tony O'Brien and filmmaker Mike Sullivan. The book gives voice to Afghan youth's stories from all walks of life—street workers, students, pickpockets, carpet makers—all who wish for peace in their country. Each of the stories is accompanied by a striking photograph of the young Afghan person who relates his or her experience. Although created by outsiders, *Afghan Dreams* is focused on local knowledge and is not patronizing.

We have found that author's notes at the beginning or end of international books written by informed outsiders often give rich details about the region and the particular issues presented in the book. These notes are extremely helpful for teachers in expanding their knowledge of particular world situations and also helpful in suggesting additional resources for classroom use. Many of the international books we use are in this category. But, even with extensive author's notes, we interrogate international children's literature as we would any other type of book and ask questions like:

Whose story is being told in this book? Whose story is left out?
Who benefits from the story being told in this way? Who is marginalized?

No matter how authentic or politically correct books appear, we still have the obligation to teach our students to question, interrogate, and "trouble" any texts we read. We agree with Short (2009a) who, building on the work of Paulo Freire (1970), stresses "all of the components of a curriculum that is international should be permeated with 'critically reading the word and the world'" (p. 8). This means digging in, understanding how differences make a difference, and uncovering how power relationships are often implicit, being seen as what's natural and normal. Our job is to help kids read deeply and critically whether the text is a book, a TV show, a situation on the playground, or a documentary about a developing country.

Getting our hands on international children's and young adult literature can be difficult. As advocates of using international children's literature, we agree with Susan Stan's (1999) observation that literature designed to expose students to global societies, cultures, and issues to foster international understanding is often seen by teachers and librarians as "not ours" (p. 169). Generally countries like the United States, with a long-standing children's literature tradition, are affluent and have structures such as libraries, bookstores, and publishers to support the availability of children's literature. Smaller, less affluent countries, even those with strong literate and artistic traditions, often find it economically unfeasible to publish books in English (p. 169) or if the books are published in the United States, there are often problems with printing agreements between countries. In developing countries or countries with low literacy rates the rare publishing of children's books is often due to "the efforts of volunteers, individuals, local nonprofit organizations, and outside funding from nongovernmental organizations" (p. 171). Steve Sharra's book about refugees in Malawi is an example of this (1996). In other situations, war and/or political ideologies can cripple the publishing of children's books, even in places that have a strong tradition of publishing children's books. As Stan points out, "countries that have emerged from colonial rule . . . have often faced the prospect of beginning a children's book publishing program totally from scratch" (1999, p. 172). Also, when publishing starts in developing countries, textbooks are often the first order of business, not children's literature. As a result of all of these complex issues, American students read very few of the world's children's books. We are often faced with using children's literature written by cultural outsiders. Some of these books are excellent, but it's important to note that many books presented as "international literature" really aren't.

Some international books that are easier to find include graphic novels that focus on international issues. Graphic novels are usually narratives depicted with artwork in comic book format, although there are some graphic novels that also use photographs. Textbox 4.1 includes some international graphic novels we especially like.

Textbox 4.1. International Graphic Novels

- *Persepolis: The Story of a Childhood* (Satrapi, 2003). This graphic novel is an autobiography of a young girl's life during the Islamic Revolution in Iran. It is a riveting tale of war, death, and the struggles of coming of age in a conflict-torn country (young adult book).
- *Maus: A Survivor's Tale: My Father Bleeds History* (Spiegelman, 1986). This graphic novel is based on Spiegelman's interviews with his father, a Holocaust survivor. The Holocaust is portrayed in comic form with the Jews as mice, the Germans as cats, the Poles as pigs, the French as frogs, and the Americans as dogs (young adult book).

- *The Arrival* (Tan, 2006). In this wordless graphic novel we see the traumatic journey of one immigrant to a new land; Tan's incredible drawings make it like no place we have seen. The book depicts many of the issues immigrants must face (new language, new food, new kinds of work), but in a fantastical way that lets the protagonist stand for any person (young adult book).
- *Alia's Mission: Saving the Books of Iraq* (Stamaty, 2004). This graphic novel tells the amazing story of Iraqi librarian Alia Muhammad Baker as she rescues thousands of books from her library in Basra before it comes under attack during the 2003 American invasion. The library was destroyed in the war (elementary book).

As an example of the complexities involved in using international children's literature, we share the experience of Lee Heffernan and Mitzi when they used children's literature for a semester-long focused study on Afghanistan in Lee's third grade classroom. At the time, Mitzi had been working in Afghanistan for three years on a development project designed to rebuild teacher education programs at sixteen Afghan universities and Lee was coming one summer to help conduct workshops. Since Mitzi and Lee were both interested in Afghanistan and many students in Lee's class had relatives in the military, they decided to make it the topic of a focused study.

For years Lee and Mitzi had enacted critical curricula that connected the political and the personal, the public and the private, but never the global and the local (Shor, 1999). This study was a perfect opportunity. As context, students at Lee's school were not making sufficient *Annual Yearly Progress* according to the state high-stakes reading test and most teachers were using programmed instruction materials. Lee took the risk of putting aside the scripted books to have kids read and write about Afghanistan. The resources Lee and Mitzi used for this focused study included a text set about Afghanistan (see Textbox 4.2), two newspaper articles, YouTube videos, and PowerPoint presentations of Mitzi's trips to Afghanistan and refugee camps in Pakistan.

Textbox 4.2. Afghanistan Text Set

- *Afghan Dreams: Young Voices of Afghanistan* (O'Brien & Sullivan, 2008)
- *Afghanistan: The People (Lands, People, and Culture)* (Banting, 2003)
- *Cool Maps for Curious Kids #2: Afghanistan, an Unauthorized Tour of* The Land of A Thousand Splendid Suns *and* The Kite Runner (Zimmerman, 2007).
- *Count Your Way Through Afghanistan* (Benson & Haskins, 2006)
- *Four Feet, Two Sandals* (Williams & Mohammed, 2007)
- *I Come from Afghanistan* (Weber, 2006)
- *Listen to the Wind* (Mortenson & Roth, 2009)
- *Nasreen's Secret School: A True Story from Afghanistan* (Winter, 2009)
- *The Roses in My Carpet* (Khan, 1998)
- *Three Cups of Tea: One Man's Journey to Change the World … One Child at a Time* (Young Reader's Edition) (Mortenson & Relin, 2009)

TABLE 4.2.   Graphic Organizer on Responding to Text

Text Title: _____

Question:	**S**urprise:
Semantics: Meaning	
Important:	**W**riting **T**opic:

Source: Graphic Organizer developed by Lee Heffernan (2000).

As each resource was shared with students, they jotted down a question, something important about the book/resource, a surprise, and a writing topic in their sketchbooks (see Table 4.2).

After the students responded, their questions and issues were discussed in small and large groups. Students then drew a picture and wrote a short story in their sketchbooks. The unit culminated with the students interviewing the Afghans who were studying at Indiana University and using the material in their sketchbooks to write social narrative stories that were translated into Dari and later used by English learners in Afghanistan. Lee and Mitzi ended the focused study by having the students fill out a survey about the project and they conducted small group interviews. The focused study was a success—students learned about Afghanistan, their social narrative books were used as reading materials in Afghanistan, and most students loved the project.

Stepping back and examining the resources available for this focused study illuminates many issues about international children's literature. In addition to books, newspaper articles and YouTube videos added a depth that was needed for students to grasp some of the complexities in this developing country. Although most books about Afghanistan were written by outsiders, two books about refugees were written by authors who had lots of experience with refugees and refugee camps. *The Roses in My Carpet* (Khan, 1998) was written by a Pakistani woman and *Four Feet, Two Sandals* (Williams & Mohammed, 2007) by a Somalian woman.

In thinking back on Stan's (1999) article about the issues of finding quality international children's literature, we agree that it was difficult to find books written by Afghans. On the other hand there were many wonderful books to be had. Not as successful as the majority of literature were a few didactic books that attempt to "teach" about Afghanistan. These are plentiful and easy to find. *I Come from Afghanistan* (Weber, 2006), one of these books, was rated the least liked resource by the students in Lee's class. In this book nine-year-old Bahishta tells the story of her life in the U.S. as an Afghan American. It is a "food, culture, and holiday" type of book, a book that Short (2009a) would probably refer to as tourist curriculum. At first Lee and Mitzi said they would never use it again, but changed their minds when they realized that the students' critiques of the book were insightful enough to create stimulating conversations about why some books are better than others. Even third graders could see the difference between books that dealt with real cultural issues and those that presented superficial depictions of people.

With communications technology bringing globalization and a shrinking world to our doorsteps, we shortchange students if international studies are not part of our regular curriculum. We have found using international children's literature is a good place to start.

Key Issues in Implementation

From the work we do with teachers we see two main issues that can limit the use of social issues, multicultural, and international books in classrooms.

Curricular mandates. With moves to adopt mandated reading programs in elementary and middle schools, many teachers feel that they have little or no flexibility or time in the day for using quality children's literature. In some cases, these mandated programs have resulted in a reduction of time, or in a few extreme cases, the elimination of content area subjects such as social studies and science. Manzo (2005), in an *Education Week* article titled "Social Studies Losing Out to Reading, Math," discusses the unintended consequences of the No Child Left Behind legislation. She laments that:

> Johnny may be learning more about reading and mathematics, but he may have little time to study the discoveries of Columbus, the tenets of the U.S. Constitution, or the social and political causes of the Civil War. (p. 40)

Manzo discusses the research of Theodore K. Rabb, a professor of history at Princeton University and a founder and board member of the National Council for History Education. Manzo quotes Rabb when she points out,

> The unintended consequence of No Child Left Behind has been to put history into an even more marginal position . . . It is clear that, with some notable exceptions nationwide, the amount of class time given to history, especially in the first eight grades, has been shrinking. (p. 40)

In some schools, the narrowing of curriculum has limited or even curtailed the use of social issues, multicultural, and international books, which greatly enhance students' understanding of subject area studies (social studies, history, and science).

We also believe the narrowing of content curriculum can have dire consequences for students learning about democracy and citizenship. If the history/social studies curriculum is limited and not open to discussions of controversial issues that are prevalent in social issues, multicultural, and international books, what kinds of demonstrations of democracy are we passing on to students? Kelly (1955) argues for giving students and teachers the freedom to make choices about curriculum. As a strong advocate of student selection of curricular topics, he assumes that young people will bring current issues into the classroom—many of which are unsettled and contested. Kelly points out the futility of teaching about democracy when the freedom of students and teachers to think and make choices about what materials to use is restricted (Lewison et al., 2002).

Avoiding controversy. Although there are many courageous teachers who use social issues, multicultural, and international books regularly in classrooms across the country, there are also many who are concerned about using books that realistically depict racism, class conflict, and violence—afraid these books may be too disturbing for children (Leland, Harste, Ociepka, Lewison, & Vasquez, 1999). "Some of these books are controversial and some people wish to protect children from controversial issues and the books about them" (Bargiel, Beck, Koblitz, O'Connor, Pierce, & Wolf, 1997, p. 482).

As an example, take the book that Amy Wackerly used with her second and third graders, *Voices in the Park* (Browne, 1998). This book is unique in a number of ways, but we find it especially important because it focuses on issues of class and socioeconomic status, concepts not often found in children's books. Some time ago, after Chris had shared this book with a group of teachers, several said that they thought it would be a good vehicle for promoting classroom discussions, but others disagreed. They said that the book was "too sad for young children." One teacher said that as a parent, she would object to having her child exposed to the book. "My daughter doesn't have ideas like this and I don't want someone putting them into her head. We don't talk about stuff like that at home." Another teacher agreed, claiming that "We don't have problems like this at our school. Everyone in my class plays with everyone else, older or younger, boys or girls." When the accuracy of this statement was questioned, the teacher insisted that "there might be isolated problems, but these are the exceptions" (Leland et al., 1999, p. 71). Gallo (1994) argues "if we do not provide our students with a variety of literature—however controversial—and teach them to read it and discuss it critically, we cannot hope that they will ever develop into sensitive, thoughtful, and reasonable adults" (p. 118).

When talking to teachers who are worried about using social issues, multicultural, and international books, we point out that they are certainly not the only potentially controversial books used in classrooms. Some children's literature scholars argue that few children's books are really safe to use in the sense of being devoid of conflict. Lehr (1995) asks us to look closely at what seems to be innocent literature for young people:

> Issues of conflict cannot be avoided in writing realistic books for children. Even the safest of books for young people like *Dr. De Soto* by William Steig [1982], *Alexander and the Wind-Up Mouse* by Leo Lionni [1969], or *Chrysanthemum* by Kevin Henkes [1991] have underlying themes of prejudice and violence. Whether a mouse is about to be eaten by a fox, beaten by a broom, or mocked by peers, one cannot escape conflict in books for children. I chose these three titles to illustrate that conflict and pain reside in books that we consider safe, mundane, or even harmless. (pp. 1–2)

We applaud teachers who, despite mandates, use controversial books instead of prescribed programs that are often mind-numbing. These forward-thinking teachers are moving away from a curriculum of consensus and conformity toward one that values diversity and difference. As they use social issues, multicultural, and international books, they create curriculum that honors diversity, invites silenced voices to be heard, allows multiple perspectives to be explored, and helps students connect the local and the global. We are hopeful that by reading diverse literature and engaging in critical conversation, students will become cosmopolitan citizens, who embrace diversity and employ a view of the world "which conceives [of] cultural differences as neither absolute nor necessarily antagonistic, but deeply interconnected and relationally defined" (Rizvi, 2006, p. 32). By taking on cosmopolitan identities, students internalize the ideas of globalization and become citizens of the world (Beck, 2002; Heater, 2000; Miscevic, 1999; Lee, 2010).

Working With Linguistically and Culturally Diverse Students

Some people think that having students in our classes who don't speak fluent English is problematic, but it also can be viewed as a wonderful advantage. Since all students are capable and bring a wide range of experiential, cultural, and linguistic resources to the classroom, our job as teachers is to figure out ways to use these resources regularly and give them a place of prominence in "what counts" in our classrooms. As an example, in Risë Reinier's multiage (4–6 grade) classroom, Sara was a new student. She arrived in this country from Algeria speaking Berber, Arabic, and French. She didn't speak English. In this class, however, Sara was viewed as a capable, knowledgeable student who was admired for her knowledge of three languages. She was not perceived as deficient because she didn't speak English. Sara was able to participate by reading books in languages she understood and by writing in Arabic—a language that Risë neither read nor understood. Risë had a remarkable level of trust that Sara was doing "appropriate school work" in her writer's notebook. This level of trust is unusual and stands in stark contrast to more traditional models of ESL (English as a second language) instruction where it is important to know exactly what each student is producing—usually having the students work exclusively in English. During writing time in a more traditional ESL classroom, we might have seen Sara copying the alphabet or short texts in English from the board or from books. It is important to note that Sara did participate in regular ESL instruction, but there was no pressure for her to abandon the complicated stories she wrote in Arabic in order to move quickly into English writing (Lewison, Leland, & Harste, 2008; Van Sluys, 2008).

The way Risë encouraged Sara to write in Arabic for writer's workshop relates to a concept developed by Pat Thomson (2002) called the *virtual school bag*. According to this theory, children enter school with a virtual school bag full of all of the things they've learned at home, their language(s), abilities, and past experiences. Some students' school bags are more valued in classrooms and are metaphorically "opened" daily—while other, less privileged children are rarely allowed to open their bags and use the cultural resources they've acquired at home. "Closed bags" position many students as disadvantaged. Sara was fortunate in being able to open her virtual school bag daily in Risë's classroom (Lewison, Leland, & Harste, 2008).

Pat Thomson came up with the idea of virtual school bags by drawing on Pierre Bourdieu's (1986) notion of *cultural capital*. In a school setting, cultural capital is the knowledge, resources, ways of thinking, and dispositions that are valued in classrooms and can be used to accomplish school tasks. These are the social practices that count in school. Normally, we might think of Sara as lacking in cultural capital because she couldn't speak or read in English, but in Risë's classroom, where differences were perceived as valuable assets rather than obstacles to be overcome, Sara was encouraged to use her ability to read, speak, and write in a language other than English as cultural capital. From this example, we see that the teacher is in a powerful position—one of being able to *expand* or *restrict* the types of cultural capital and social practices that are valued in the classroom.

Teachers can choose to use social issues, multicultural, and international children's literature as one way to make classrooms places that invite students from all types of backgrounds into the "literacy club" (Smith, 1988) rather than restricting membership to only those who come from homes where certain languages and literacy practices are used (Lewison et al., 2008).

To expand the cultural capital of our second language learners, we recommend using dual language books. This is a marvelous genre of children's literature that provides the stories written in English as well as a second language. In Spanish, there is an abundance of these resources and there are often sets of books, one written in English and one in Spanish. Table 4.3 provides a sample of dual language books written in Spanish and English.

TABLE 4.3. Sample of Dual Language Books in English and Spanish

Books	Theme
¡Si, Se Puede!/Yes, We Can!: Janitor Strike in L.A. (Cohn, 2002).	This is the story of a Mexican immigrant whose mother cleans offices at night and helps to organize a janitors' strike in Los Angeles. There are author's notes that help with discussions about politics and labor issues.
Friends from the Other Side/Amigos del otro lado (Anzaldua, 1995)	This story depicts tensions between undocumented Mexicans and Chicanos already living in Texas. The rich story includes references to a visit from the Border Patrol (la migra), the hardships of daily life on the border, and also the dignity of immigrants and citizens of Mexican descent.
Book Fiesta!: Celebrate Children's Day/Book Day; Celebremos El dia de los ninos/El dia de los libros (Mora, 2009)	Children's Day/Book Day is now celebrated annually in Mexico, the same date as Mexico's Day of the Child. In an author's note, Mora has suggestions for celebrating children's literacy in one's own community.
La mujer que brillaba aún más que el sol/The Woman Who Outshone the Sun (Martinez, 1999).	This story recounts the legend of Lucia Zenteno who arrives at a Oaxacan mountain village in central Mexico and is feared by villagers because she is different from them. She is banned from the village and their precious river leaves with her.
The Harvest Birds/Los pajaros de la cosecha (Lopez de Mariscal, 2001).	In this story, Juan has big dreams of becoming a farmer like his father and grandfather. But when his father dies and the land is divided, there is only enough for his two older brothers. Juan receives help from the harvest birds on how to become a farmer by keeping weeds around the edges of the land and respecting nature.
Antonio's Card/La tarjeta de Antonio (Gonzalez, 2005).	Antonio is fascinated with words because they express powerful feelings. This is the story of how Antonio tries to find the right words for a Mother's Day card to express his love for his mother and her partner. His classmates make fun of his mother's partner and Antonio has to make a decision about speaking up for himself and the people he loves.
The Invisible Hunters/Los cazadores invisibles (Rohmer, Chow, & Viduare, 1997).	This is a retelling of a Nicaraguan folk tale of three brothers who find a magic vine when they are hunting that can make them invisible. To obtain the magic, they must promise never to sell the meat they hunt and never to hunt with guns, only with sticks. When European traders arrive, the brothers forget their promise. There is an environmental theme running through this book.
My Papa Diego and Me/Mi papá Diego y yo: Memories of My Father and His Art/ Recuerdos de mi padre y su arte (Marín, 2009)	This book is written by Diego Rivera's daughter and recounts her childhood growing up in Mexico through her memories around occurrences related to Rivera's paintings of children. This is an insider look at a larger-than-life father and the lessons he passed along to his children.

When we have students whose primary language is other than Spanish, we are often faced with few materials in their primary language. Table 4.4 gives a sampling of dual language books that teachers might find helpful for classroom use with students whose primary language is other than English or Spanish.

TABLE 4.4.   Sample of Dual Language Books in a Variety of Languages

Language	Book	Theme
Korean	*Cooper's Lesson* (Shin, 2004)	Mixed heritage Cooper (Korean & American) is confused about his identity. He doesn't speak Korean and is frustrated in Mr. Lee's Korean grocery where only Korean is spoken. Through conversation, the two come to understand each other's issues with language barriers.
Tagalog	*Lakas and the Makibaka Hotel/ Si Lakas at ang Makibaka Hotel* (Robles, 2006)	Lakas helps his Filipino community stand in solidarity when their apartment building is going to be sold. The story focuses on *makibaka*, the spirit of struggle.
Hebrew	*A New Boy* (Tal, 2007)	Boris is a new Russian immigrant to Israel who doesn't know Hebrew and experiences all kinds of problems including bullying. This is a story about the difficulties of friendship when there are language barriers.
Japanese	*A Place where Sunflowers Grow* (Lee-Tai, 2006)	This story takes place in a Japanese internment camp during World War II. Mari finds moments of solace and self-expression in the art school, a little-known part of the internment camps.
Vietnamese	*Going Home, Coming Home/Ve nha, tham que huong* (Tran, 2003)	Amy is confused when she takes a trip to Vietnam, her parents' home. This story addresses the issue, "Where is home?"
Mandarin	*China's Bravest Girl* (Chin, 1993)	Hua Mu Lan convinces her father to let her go to war to protect her country. She later marries her best friend and fellow officer, but only after he agrees to treat her with respect and equality.
French	*Petit Singe cherche son refuge/Little Monkey's One Safe Place* (Edwards, 2005)	Little Monkey is frightened by a storm and runs home to his mother. She reassures him that even in the vast jungle there is always one safe place for him.

Technology Extensions and Electronic Resources

There are two particular electronic resources we especially like for working with social issues, multicultural, and international children's literature (in addition to the resources listed in Table 4.1). They include author interviews and online read alouds.

Author interviews. Although more difficult to find with international books, we have found a number of online author interviews that are very helpful to use in classrooms. These include:

- **Christopher Myers:** http://www.readingrockets.org/books/interviews/myersc. In this interview Myers talks about how everyone has stories to tell, how his poor Brooklyn neighborhood influenced his writing, and how reading touches every part of his life.
- **Janet Wong:** http://www.readingrockets.org/books/interviews/wong. In this interview Wong discusses the influence of growing up in Korea Town in Los Angeles, how she changed careers to become a writer, and her reflections on some of her books.

- **Pam Muñoz Ryan:** http://www.readingrockets.org/books/interviews/ryan. Ryan discusses her childhood in Bakersfield, California, her books (that often feature strong female protagonists), and winning the 2002 Pura Belpré Medal for *Esperanza Rising*.

Online read-alouds. There are a number of social issues and multicultural books that are excellent resources. The best come from storyline online, produced by the Screen Actors Guild Foundation. Here are three of our favorites.

- *White Socks Only* (Evelyn Coleman, 1996): http://www.storylineonline.net/. Read by actress Amber Tamblyn, this is the touching story of grandma when she was a girl in Jim Crow Mississippi. She sneaks into town to see if what she heard was true—that you can fry an egg on the pavement if it is hot enough. The story unfolds as she comes across a drinking fountain with a sign reading "whites only." She knows exactly what to do. She takes off her black patent leather shoes and gets on the water fountain step with her clean white socks to get a drink. Then she is noticed by the white townspeople. Amber Tamblyn presents a great example of how anyone can read a book about an ethnic group other than their own.

- *To Be a Drum* (Evelyn Coleman, 1998): http://www.storylineonline.net/. Read by actor James Earl Jones, who also discusses his own struggles with reading aloud and stuttering, this book is a marvelous tale of inner freedom. Daddy Wes tells the story of the earth's first people living in harmony with the earth; the middle passage and slavery; resistance through song, talk, quilting, and beat; the heroics of the civil rights movement; and the incredible contributions African Americans have made to the United States and the world. The illustrations are magnificent by themselves, but are beautifully animated in this video.

- *No Mirrors in My Nana's House* (Ysaye M. Barwell, 1998): http://www.storylineonline.net/. Read by Tia and Tamara Mowry from "Sister, Sister," this multicultural book is about a girl growing up with her grandmother in a house with no mirrors, no stereotypes. We found it a bit problematic in that it diminishes the problems of poverty, but this makes for great conversations. The author is a member of *Sweet Honey and the Rock,* and the a-cappella group singing the second reading of the book is pure joy.

Assessment

How can you assess the use of social issues, multicultural, and international children's literature in your classroom? We believe that examining students' written and artistic responses to these books is a good way to assess their understanding of complex social and global issues. In addition, Textbox 4.3 provides a list of observational questions you can ask yourself to assess the impact of these books on students and how you have integrated them into your curriculum.

Textbox 4.3. Assessing the Impact of Social Issues, Multicultural, and International Children's Literature

You can tell when social issues, multicultural, and international children's books are having an impact by answering these questions:

- Do students find stereotypes and inauthentic characters while reading? Do these issues become the focus of class discussions?

- When students are asked about their best-loved book, do some choose social issues, multicultural, or international books as their favorites?
- Are social, political, cultural, and global topics a regular part of your curriculum?
- Do social, political, cultural, and global topics become the center of classroom conversations even when you didn't start them?
- Are kids making comments that show they feel connected to other places in the world and/or global issues?

Invitation: Book Brochures

Book brochures (see Textbox 4.4) are a wonderful way for an entire class to learn about many different social issues, multicultural, or international books in a short amount of time. This is accomplished by students making brochures about books they have read that highlight exemplary literature of a particular genre (i.e. international books).

Textbox 4.4. Invitation: Book Brochures

Book brochures are flyers advertising books that are created and read by students. A book brochure usually is focused on one particular type of book. In this case: social issues, multicultural, or international.

Materials & Procedures

- Art paper in various colors or 8 ½ x 11 sheets of copy paper
- Art supplies including crayons, colored markers, scissors and glue

1. Most students find folding an 8 ½ by 11 inch of paper into three sections gives them an easy way to segment what they include in the brochure. Here is an example of the types of elements a book brochure on a multicultural book might include.

   Front of Brochure:

   Section 1: Title, author, illustrator, publisher, copyright date. Illustration showing why you liked the book.

   Section 2: Short synopsis.

   Section 3: Why this book is exemplary: *(What makes it a good multicultural book?)*

   Back of Brochure:

   Section 4: Why you think other kids in the class should read this book.

   Section 5: A drawing, poster, or bumper sticker to help sell your book.

   Section 6: Questions you have about the book.

2. After all of the students have completed a book brochure, share. Invite students to take notes of those books they wish to read.

Extensions

Book Circles is a more formal sharing of book brochures. Students are arranged in groups of four around tables. Students come to Book Circle with their book, their brochure, and a literature log to jot down the names of titles they may want to read.

Round 1: Each child at a book circle table gets to tell about their book and show their brochure.

Round 2: One child stays at each table and the rest of the children move so they are with completely different people than in Round 1. As with the previous round, each child at a book circle table gets to tell about their book and show their brochure.

Round 3: Roaming. Everyone gets up and goes to look at book brochures and books that they missed in Rounds 1 and 2. This is a relaxed time, part reading brochures and part skimming books.

Reflection: At the end of Book Circle time, have children discuss what went well and what they'd like to do differently next time.

Professional Development

Engagement 1—Gender issues and children's literature. In her chapter called "Gender Issues in Books for Children and Young Adults," Shirley Ernst (1995) provides an informative history of studies on gender and children's literature. She discusses how studies from the 1970s and 1980s showed:

> Stereotyped behaviors such as girls working in the kitchen and boys riding bikes . . . Boys were generally shown as independent, problem solvers, active, and in charge of situations while girls were often portrayed as dependent, problem causers, passive and followers. (p. 67)

Surprisingly, when she later asked teachers to bring in ten books chosen randomly from their classroom libraries, the gender equity in the books still leaned toward males as main characters and stereotypes were still strong. This engagement invites teachers to explore gender issues with more current books (see Table 4.5).

Engagement 2—Questioning authenticity. One anti-war book that many teachers use with elementary students is *Faithful Elephants: A True Story of Animals, People, & War* (Tsuchiya, 1951/1997). We have used the book many times ourselves. This book was originally written in Japanese for a Japanese audience. It is a very touching and heart-wrenching story about the poisoning of the animals at the Ueno Zoo in Tokyo so they wouldn't escape if bombs hit the zoo. Especially poignant is the tale of the elephant keeper and his three elephants. We have never questioned the authenticity of this book until recently reading an older article by Kawabata and Vandergrift (1998). This article challenged our prior beliefs about the book. The pairing of the book, *Faithful Elephants*, with the article has led to incredibly complex discussions among teachers (see Textbox 4.5).

TABLE 4.5.   Are They Really Better or Not?

Work in pairs and go to your school, university, or community library. Pick five *picture books* randomly off the shelves from different parts of the library. If you pick an older book (before 1995), put it back and choose another. Fill a chart with five rows, one for each book. Here's what goes in each row.

Survey of Picture Books

Title:

Author (identify whether male or female):

Copyright Date:

Who was the main character(s) in the book (identify as male or female/ethnicity)?

How is the main character(s) portrayed (independent, dependent, problem-solver, problem-causer, active, passive, cute, strong, etc.)?

How would you evaluate the main character(s) for gender role stereotypes?

Chart the group's findings and discuss the current state of children's literature regarding gender equity and stereotypes.

Textbox 4.5. Questioning Authenticity

Have someone in your group read the book *Faithful Elephants: A True Story of Animals, People, & War* (Tsuchiya, 1997) aloud and discuss your response to the story and ways you might use the book in your classroom. Then read "History into Myth: The Anatomy of a Picture Book" (Kawabata & Vandergrift, 1998) in *Bookbird*, volume *36*(2). Discuss the article in relation to your previous discussion of *Faithful Elephants*. Also discuss if you would use the book in the same ways your group had previously shared or would do something different with it. There are no right or wrong answers on this one, just a lot of food for thought.

The set of readings in Table 4.6 are focused on social issues, multicultural, and international children's and young adult books. We have used these readings in teacher study groups and found them helpful in fostering discussions that relate theory to classroom practice.

TABLE 4.6.   Suggestions for Further Reading

Social Issue Books	Multicultural Books	International Books
Leland, C., Harste, J. C., Ociepka, A., Lewison, M., & Vasquez, V. (1999). Exploring critical literacy: You can hear a pin drop. *Language Arts, 77*(1) 70–77.	Louie, B. Y. (2006). Guiding principles for teaching multicultural literature. *The Reading Teacher, 59*(1), 438–448.	Short, K. G. (2009a). Critically reading the word and the world building understanding through literature. *Bluebird: A Journal of International Children's Literature, 47*(2), 1–10.
This article discusses both problematic issues and productive learning in classrooms when teachers read children's books that have the power to engage students in "critical" conversations about issues of power and social justice, and how systems of meaning in society position educators. It offers descriptions of 12 such books for children, lists chapter books, books for older readers, and books about taking social action for social justice.	In this article, Louie offers seven principles that teachers should pay attention to when using multicultural literature in classrooms. These include issues of authenticity, understanding character's worlds and perspectives, relating self to the text, the value of having variants of the same story, and why it is important to encourage students to talk, write, and respond throughout reading the multicultural texts. Louie reports on a study in a fourth-grade classroom in which her principles were applied in teaching four variants of the Mulan story and watching Walt Disney's "Mulan" video.	This article describes a collaborative project that involved elementary teachers integrating international literature into their classrooms without using a "tourist approach." Short provides a very useful framework for creating a curriculum that's international. It includes focusing on personal cultural identities, cross-cultural studies, integration of intercultural perspectives, and inquiries into global issues.

five

Supporting Literature Discussions

Ann Mennonno teaches in a multiage second/third grade classroom in a public school located in downtown Indianapolis. Because children had questions, Ann decided to do a literature study around the topic of immigration. She specifically looked for books that contained family histories and reasons why various groups of people immigrated. Despite all of the recent finger pointing and name calling regarding controversial topics like *hiring practices, immigrants, illegal immigrants*, and *Mexicans*, she wanted the students to understand that this was not a new issue. They too, more than likely, were the descendants of immigrants.

Before initiating this literature study, Ann wanted to find out what the students in her classroom already knew about the topic. To do this, she used a strategy called ***Graffiti Board*** (Short, Harste, & Burke, 1996). A graffiti board provides an informal and low-risk way for students to share what they know or think they know about a topic. In this case, Ann used it as a curricular device to find out what previous experiences the children in her classroom had with immigration. She taped a large sheet of blank paper to the chalkboard, wrote "IMMIGRATION" in the center, and left different colored markers on the chalk ledge. Students knew that they could go up at any time that day and add their thoughts to the graffiti board. The next morning, Ann counted 13 question marks on the paper and realized that a significant number of her students had no idea what the word meant. She also noted that other children had a variety of correct and incorrect ideas. Some of these are listed below with their original spellings.

- I thek it is when someone's mad.
- I think it means when people immigrate.
- I think it is when someone goes to a new contry.
- I think immigration is when 2 parts of the earth combine to make a mountain.
- I think it is underwater hibernation.

While teachers can never be sure about the kinds or depth of prior knowledge their students will bring to school with them, they can be sure that there will be a wide variety of understandings and misunderstandings.

In preparation for this literature study Ann had pulled together a set of books on immigration (see Textbox 5.1). She looked for books that offered different perspectives on immigration and told about the problems that immigrants frequently encounter. She hoped that some of the books would connect to experiences her students had heard about or encountered. This initial collection included stories about immigrants from many different countries. These people had come to America for a variety of reasons and under a variety of conditions. Ann told her students that this set of books on immigration would continue to grow. She said she would be on the lookout for additional books and asked the students to think about what else they might want to add. Textbox 5.1 shows the set of books Ann had ready at the beginning of the study.

Textbox 5.1. Ann's Initial Collection of Immigration Books

My diary from here to there (Perez, 2002)
Coming to America (Wolf, 2003)
Molly's pilgrim (Cohen, 1983)
One green apple (Bunting, 2006)
When this world was new (Figueredo, 1999)
My name is Yoon (Recorvits, 2004)
Hannah is my name (Yang, 2004)
The color of home (Hoffman, 2002)

The first book shared as a read aloud from this set was *My Diary from Here to There/Mi diario de aqui hasta alla* (Perez, 2002). Ann showed the front and back book covers to the children and asked them to make predictions about the story: *Who* is in it? *Where* is it taking place? *What* is happening, and *why*? Ann took the time for predictions because she knew it would encourage students to observe closely and to make connections. True to her expectations, the children's predictions generated lots of conversation:

- One boy pointed out that the picture on the front cover showed a car with luggage on the roof. He predicted that someone was moving to a new home and the suitcases on top of the car probably had clothes inside.
- A classmate noted that the picture looked like it was nighttime. "It might be about someone on a long trip," she observed. "Sometimes my family drives all night when we are taking a long trip."
- Another girl added that she knew what a desert looked like because she went to one on her summer vacation and that's what the picture looked like to her.
- Other children were interested in the map on the back cover and named the states it showed. They predicted that someone was moving between Mexico and one of the bordering states like Arizona, New Mexico, Texas, or California.
- One boy wanted to talk about the fact that the title of the book was printed in both English and Spanish. He predicted that this might be "one of those books where you can pick which language you want to use."

- Someone else pointed out that this book had a seal for getting an award and wondered what "Pura Belpré Honor Book" meant. Ann took a moment to talk about how they might find out using the Internet.

Because the discussion showed no sign of slowing down, Ann finally intervened and said they had to stop so there would be time for reading the book. As she read aloud, Ann stopped occasionally to talk about the book and ask whether any of the children's predictions were being validated or challenged.

To culminate the first day of literature study Ann invited the children to write a sentence of their choice, draw a picture to illustrate it, and then share it with the class. As might be expected, the children's responses showed great variation. Some wrote about people they knew who had moved to a new place: "Amada moving away from her friend reminded me of when my friend Sabrina moved away because she was really nice. She moved to New York. So far away." Another child wrote, "It reminded me of when my dad went to jail when I turned one year old. It made me sad and I cried for a whole week." His picture (Figure 5.1) shows someone crying and reaching out while a car drives away. In this case, the process of making a connection allowed him to tell a family story that was important to him. Lily wrote about a story she heard on a radio program: "A family from Mexico got kicked off of the bus because they weren't legal residents." Her drawing (Figure 5.2) shows a bus with two unhappy people standing next to it.

Literature studies can go in different directions and serve lots of purposes. How long a literature study lasts depends on what questions you and your children have and what you want to get accomplished.

FIGURE 5.1. Connection to *My Diary from Here to There/Mi Diario de Aqui Hasta Alla* (Sam).

A family got kicked off the bus because they wert legal residents.

about Illigal immigrants from mexico.

I heard a radio program

FIGURE 5.2. Connection to *My Diary from Here to There/Mi Diario de Aqui Hasta Alla* (Lily).

Principle 1: Literature Discussion Groups Support Reading as a Social Event

Readers thrive in an environment that not only allows but also encourages them to interact with others. Although we might have romantic visions of a solitary reader happily curled up with a book, we know that this solitary reader also looks forward to sharing his or her thoughts about the book with someone else who has read it. That's why different types of literature discussion groups are so popular in classrooms and the larger world—readers want to see if others feel as they do or have different reactions to a text. One quick way to see how others have reacted to a book is by examining book reviews. Teachers photocopy reviews of books being read and make them part of the discussion. While this might be difficult reading for younger children, older students often enjoy seeing how "professionals" judge the books they are reading. Two excellent sources for reviews of children's and adolescent literature are *Horn Book* and *School Library Journal*; both are accessible on the web.

Peterson and Eeds (1990) refer to sharing thoughts about books as "grand conversations." They explain that in literature rich classrooms, there are no pre-determined questions or answers. "Real books have no manuals to tell teachers all the things they must do and when to do them. The story contained in each book stands on its own" (p. 5). When participating in grand conversations, teachers and readers talk together to generate interpretations of what the author has written and figure out how they want to respond to it. They recommend letting students know that it is "*their* ideas that . . . make the dialogue work" (p. 62).

Many of the teachers we work with see ***Partner Reading*** as a good first step in giving students opportunities to talk about what they are reading. Kathryn Mitchell Pierce (1996), for example, describes how she has students read with a partner at the beginning of the year. Since she eventually wants her students to participate in larger literature discussion groups, she sees partner reading as "a manageable starting place" (Pierce, 1996, p. 156). While students are doing partner reading, they can also engage in a strategy called ***Say Something*** (Short et al., 1996). Readers engage in Say Something while reading silently or while taking turns reading aloud. In both cases, they decide ahead of time how often they will stop reading (for example after every paragraph or at the end of each page) and ask a question, make a personal connection, or predict what might be coming next. ***Literature Circles*** enrich the partner reading experience by adding more voices and more perspectives. Once students have been successful with partner reading, they are ready to start working in small groups. The idea of literature circles is built on the assumption that "through conversation and dialogue, readers have the opportunity to explore their own half-formed ideas, to expand their understandings through hearing others' interpretations, and to become critical and inquiring thinkers" (Short et al., 1996, p. 479). Talking about the same story with others in a small group gives readers time to refine their interpretations and expand their understandings.

There are many ways to organize literature circles. We like to ask both our college students and kids in schools to get into groups of three or four and identify what we call critical moments from the story or non-fiction article that they would like to talk about. We explain that a critical moment is when something happens in the story or appears in the text that catches their attention and seems to be especially important. They take turns sharing their ideas and other group members offer opinions for why they think they made those particular choices. A similar process can be followed to invite students to identify stereotypes in the texts they are reading. We have found that although students frequently can provide a definition for the concept of stereotyping, they often have a harder time finding stereotypes in the books they experience (Leland, Harste, & Clouse, in press). ***Taking Inventory, Quotable Quotes, Key Ideas*** and ***Patterns & Surprises*** are other strategies we have used to begin book conversations about books or articles (see Chapter 10 for descriptions of these curricular invitations).

We also know teachers who like to begin by assigning ***Roles in Literature Circles***. Each student is given a different task. One student might provide a summary of the story being discussed; one might generate questions; one student might make connections between the events in the story and real-life experiences; one student might be the wordsmith, identifying important words and phrases in the story; and another student might take responsibility for mapping the story through sketches to help classmates keep track of characters and events. Harvey Daniels (1994), an early advocate of giving specific roles to group members, provided role sheet handouts in his first book about literature circles. He suggested that teachers assign roles to students and give them the sheets to fill them out and bring to the discussion. In his 2002 book on literature circles, however, Daniels modifies his original position and warns that reliance on roles can lead to discussions that seem mechanical rather than conversational.

As might be expected, there are multiple perspectives among educators about how literature discussion groups are defined and enacted. For example, Barbara Lehman (2007) argues that these groups should be "student selected based on students' interest in specific works selected from a choice of texts offered by the teacher or suggested by students" (p. 39). We also know teachers, however, who assign specific readings and still invite their students to engage in small groups that they refer to as literature discussion groups or literature circles. Ann Mennonno describes Readers' Workshop in her classroom as a time when she teaches mini-lessons on various reading strategies that she thinks her students are ready to learn. Kathy Short and

Kathryn Mitchell Pierce label the time when they teach mini-lessons as guided reading time to distinguish it from literature circles time (1998). We recommend that teachers not worry so much about the exact terms they are using, but focus more on the idea that students need time and opportunities to "just talk about books" as well as to learn strategies for becoming better readers.

Principle #2: Text Sets Support Powerful Conversations

A ***Text Set*** is a collection of books and other resources that provides many different perspectives on a topic. Text sets can serve as a resource for exploring topics of interest to you and the students in your classroom. Since text sets are multimodal, they can include more than just books. Pictures, textbooks, commercial videos, songs, maps, diaries, and audio or videotapes of classroom visitors who have first-hand knowledge of the topic and are willing to share their personal experiences are valuable additions.

Text sets help learners connect what they already know to what is new. They push the boundaries of a group's collective thinking by providing multiple perspectives on any topic. After reading or hearing many stories about immigration, Ann's children will have a better understanding that all immigrants don't have the same situations, reasons for moving, or goals. They also will probably have many new questions as well. While it may sound counterintuitive, a major benefit to using text sets is that they make objects of study more complex instead of simplifying them. We hope to find some books in every text set that don't have happy "storybook" endings since that will better reflect real life. Not all immigrants are successful in achieving their goals. We want children to see that real life is complex and messy, with few easy answers. That understanding might provide insight when their own lives become complex and messy. (See Resources on our website for text sets on war, homelessness, bullying, racial issues, gender and a variety of other topics: www.routledge.com/cw/leland.)

We also want to make it clear that text sets and the books and other materials in them are never "neutral" or "innocent." Like all texts, they were created by people who could never be totally objective, even if they thought they were. So we recommend that students get into the habit of asking critical questions about everything they read. The ***Becoming a Text Analyst*** strategy encourages students to ask themselves questions about power and privilege (Luke & Freebody, 1997).

- Whose story is being told in this book, video, article or other text?
- Whose story is left out?
- Who benefits from the story being told in this way? Who is marginalized?
- How might the story be different if it was told from someone else's perspective?

Questions like these might be asked about individual books or about the text set as a whole. Students can work together to synthesize their findings and draw some conclusions about patterns that can be seen across the entire text set. Are most of the books and other materials offering a positive or negative view of the topic? Why might that be the case?

Investigating a Disney princess text set. Karen Wohlwend (2009) used Disney princess dolls as a text set and studied kindergarten children who frequently chose to play with these dolls during their free choice time. She explained this choice by noting that a number of researchers (e.g. Walkerdine, 1984; Steinberg & Kinchloe, 1997; Christensen, 2000) have previously suggested that Disney fairy tales position girls as helpless victims who are destined to wait around for a prince to rescue them. They questioned whether these books and associated toys might serve to "reduce the heroines to happy homemakers-in-waiting" (Wohlwend, 2009, p. 59).

To test the hypothesis that children who played with Disney princess dolls might simply accept the passive female roles that are portrayed in many Disney stories, Wohlwend provided numerous opportunities for a group of children to play with the dolls. She invited them to make up stories about the dolls as they interacted with each other and with new doll characters they added. Her conclusions might be surprising to some. Wohlwend observed that while the children often started out with the familiar plots of Disney books and films, they also extended and revised these plots in ways that allowed the princess dolls "to take up more empowered identity positions in child-ruled imaginary spaces" (p. 58). After spending extended time with a text set that included books, toys and movies (seen outside of school), the kindergartners in this study did not simply go along with the stereotypes embodied in the Disney princess dolls. Instead they created new identities that fit better with their own ideas of what it means to be a girl or a boy.

Investigating a Fairy Tale Text Set. Amy Wackerly invited her second and third graders to become text analysts as they investigated a fairy tale text set. To prepare for this literature study, Amy divided her class into small groups and gave each group a traditional fairy tale to read and discuss. Stories in this text set included *Cinderella, Sleeping Beauty, Snow White and the Seven Dwarfs,* and *Peter Pan.* Amy also gave each group some markers and a piece of chart paper so they could take notes while they were reading. She invited them to jot down their thoughts on these questions:

- Who was strong or weak in the story you read?
- Who had power?
- Were there any differences between how women (or girls) and men (or boys) were portrayed?

At first the children seemed to be more interested in writing down what they already knew about these stories than in actually reading any of the books. They noted that Cinderella, Sleeping Beauty, and Snow White were all beautiful and the princes who rescued them were brave. They further observed that older women in these stories often had power but they were mean. (Cinderella's fairy godmother was the notable exception to this rule!) After the children settled into reading and had progressed through most of their books, Amy asked them to write down some notes about what the characters actually did and whether they had power or not. This activity led to some interesting conversations within the different groups.

After a lengthy discussion, the *Peter Pan* group decided that the female characters in their book "didn't do anything important." Third grader Emily observed, "Mostly the girls were just there. Wendy took care of her brothers but she didn't have any power like Peter Pan or Captain Hook." The group reading *Sleeping Beauty* had a similar conversation and decided that their title character also had no power. They wrote on their poster: "Sleeping Beauty really did not do anything but sleep." When Amy brought all the groups together to share their findings, one conclusion the children came to was that none of the beautiful female characters had any power at all. Another was that boys did more interesting things than girls. They got to fight, save people, and choose the person they wanted to marry.

In a subsequent writing activity, Amy asked her students to identify the different characters' positions and talk about how the book they read positioned girl and boy characters. Did they see themselves in the same way? Second grader Maddie was in the group that read *Cinderella*; she was unhappy with how both the female and the male characters were positioned. She wrote (in her original spelling):

I think the girls should be strong and tuff. I want the girls to show those guys just what we do. I want a girl who is tuff, independent and not always the danzil in destrist. I want a tomboy girl. And I want a boy who doesn't like a girl for her looks. I want a boy who loves a girl for who she is.

Third grader Vivien was in the group that read *Sleeping Beauty*. She was also unhappy with how girls were positioned and noted that in this story, boys had a lot of power. She went on to say, "This is totally not fair!"... I don't see myself as a weak person. I think I am powerful. Women are small but mighty."

This fairy tale text set was a starting point for Amy's second and third graders to think about power and agency. By positioning them as critical thinkers and by giving them books and time to read, think and talk, Amy's students started questioning some common cultural myths about the roles of women and men.

There are several other strategies that teachers might use to support children in digging deeply and in taking action. The **What If?** strategy is one way to challenge stereotypes and encourage thinking that extends traditional stories. For example, with the fairy tales, we might ask "What if the princess suddenly turned into a superhero and broke right through the prison walls?" Or "What if we made the story so that the prince got captured and the princess rescued him?" We might also ask children to rewrite the fairy tales in ways that challenge the original stories. Writing **Emancipatory Fairy Tales** (Lewison et al., 2008) involves changing the setting, plot, or characters of an existing story to make it more equitable. A third strategy is to gather text sets for the same story and invite students to compare and contrast the different versions. There are, for example, many versions of the Cinderella story and while many of them are "more of the same thing," some provide different interpretations that are well worth exploring. For example, see *Cinder Edna* (Jackson, 1994).

Principle #3: There Are Multiple Goals and Multiple Strategies for Literature Study

In this era of a narrowing curriculum it is important that you and your students understand why it's so important to engage in literature study. You might be called on to explain why you take the time to have your students read and discuss literature instead of plugging them into commercial programs that come with the promise of higher test scores. We work with schools that use children's and adolescent literature as the foundation of their reading programs and they consistently score well on standardized tests. Regardless of test scores, however, we have found that it makes a big difference when teachers and students are able to provide an articulate explanation for what they are doing. In the following section, we provide a partial list of reasons for doing literature study that can also be tied into most standards for developing higher level thinking skills. We wish to acknowledge the Internet and the many anonymous teachers and colleagues who contributed to this list. With each reason or goal we also suggest instructional strategies that might be used to support your work in this area. While the strategies can be mixed and matched across the entire list, we hope that our selections will provide some snapshots of what literature study might look like in different contexts. Table 5.1 provides a summary list of reasons for doing literature study and a sample instructional engagement for each. Taken together, the reasons for teaching with literature and the strategies for doing it cover the big picture of curriculum—what we think of as the most important issues and topics. If you ever find yourself in the position of having to explain why you *want* to use literature, the list of reasons in this chapter can be used as initial talking points for the discussion.

Many of the teachers we work with use the first part of the year to introduce instructional strategies from the list to the whole group and pair them with individual read aloud books as Ann did with *My Diary from Here to There/Mi Diario de Aquí Hasta Allá*. Once students are comfortable using the strategies, they can adapt them as needed to support their children's reading and understanding of the various texts they encounter.

TABLE 5.1.   Reasons for Literature Study with Sample Engagements

#1: Literature study allows us to benefit from the insights of others.	Quotable Quotes Save the Last Word for Me Patterns & Surprises
#2: Literature study opens our minds to the ambiguities of meaning.	Subtext Strategy I-Statement Charts
#3: Literature study helps us understand our place in history.	Family Stories, Neighborhood Stories Oral History Projects
#4: Literature study encourages us to question "accepted" knowledge.	Mini-Inquiry Book Chart-a-Conversation Six-Box Literacy Response Strategy
#5: Literature study deepens our understanding of how language works.	Discourse Analysis for Kids Becoming a Text Analyst
#6: Literature study encourages us to explore ethical complexities.	Written Conversation Process Drama: Writing in Role Process Drama: Conscience Circle
#7: Literature study helps us understand and use the elements of text.	Story Mapping
#8: Literature study teaches us to support our points of view and expand our interpretations.	Literature Response Little Books Character Maps
#9: Literature study helps us develop empathy for those who are unlike us.	Cultural X-Rays I-Statement Charts
#10: Literature study allows us to have both an aesthetic and a critical experience.	Readers' Theater Process Drama

#1: *Literature study allows us to benefit from the insights of others*. Literature represents our collective human knowledge base, including beliefs, self-perceptions, philosophies, assumptions and interactions with the world at large. Some of life's most important lessons are subtly expressed in literature. We learn these lessons only if we pause to think about what we read.

Suggested strategies. One strategy we find useful for getting readers to pause and think more deeply about what they are reading is called *Quotable Quotes*. Students are asked to record a passage they found memorable or significant on the front of an index card and what they want to say about the quote on the back. When students later meet with others in their text set group, they engage in an activity called *Save the Last Word for Me* (Short et al., 1996) and take turns sharing their quotes without saying why they chose them. Other group members respond to each quote and say why they think it got selected. Then the person who wrote down the quote gets the last word about why she or he thinks it is important. If time permits, we also like to have the group look for *Patterns & Surprises* across the whole set of quotes. This activity involves putting all the cards out on the table and moving them around to form categories. Quotes that don't fit into any of the identified categories can be characterized as surprises or anomalies.

#2: *Literature study opens our minds to the ambiguities of meaning*. While people argue that they "say what they mean and mean what they say," in reality, language is both maddeningly and delightfully ambiguous. Ambiguity, double entendres, and nuance give our language depth and endless possibility. Literature study gives us access and develops appreciation for deep thinking and multiple perspectives. Since all readers bring different background experiences to what they are reading, different interpretations are always being generated.

Suggested strategies. Jean Anne Clyde (2003) developed what she calls the ***Subtext Strategy***. Children use one post-it note to document what the main character in a story is saying and another post-it note to suggest what that character might be thinking, but not saying. Sharing these post-it notes supports everyone in understanding what might be going on that has not been said directly. For example, in the chapter book *Old People, Frogs, and Albert* (Wilson, 1997), the main character (Albert) is afraid of the elderly residents he sees on the porch of the Pine Manor Nursing Home as he walks home from school everyday. He thinks they look and act strange. But then Mr. Spear, his reading tutor and good friend, has a stroke and ends up at Pine Manor. Albert's teacher thinks he will want to visit Mr. Spear so she arranges to take him there after school. As Albert hesitates to go in, a classmate senses his discomfort and offers to visit Mr. Spear for him. Albert quickly says, "I'm okay," but then his feet seem to stick to the sidewalk. While using this book and strategy with a group of third graders, Chris wrote, "I'm okay" on one post-it note and "I'm really not okay because I'm scared to go in there!" on another to show what Albert was thinking.

Another strategy that helps students understand that different people see things differently is an *I-Statement Chart* (Leland & Harste with Huber, 2005). Students fold a piece of blank paper into three columns. In each column they identify a different character. Students write a statement for each character showing what that person might have been thinking during a particular part of the story. Figure 5.3 shows an example prepared by a fourth grader for the book, *Stars in the Darkness* (Joosse, 2001). This is a book about a family dealing with the older son's participation in gang activities. His younger brother and mother are both upset by what they see him doing and want him to stop.

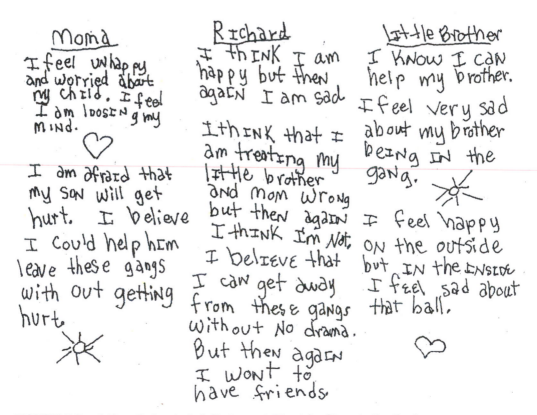

FIGURE 5.3.   A Fourth Grader's I-Statement Chart for *Stars in the Darkness*.

#3: ***Literature study helps us understand our place in history.*** History is about people who were products of their time and their own intricately woven value systems. Literature study enhances our appreciation of history's complexity, which in turn expands our appreciation of present political complexities and better equips us to predict and prepare for the future. History gives us statistics; literature lets us experience the human tragedy.

Suggested strategies. The children in Ann's class who talked about moving to new places opened the door for making a collection of family stories on immigration. Students might interview their parents and grandparents to collect stories about their own families' immigrant origins as part of a larger oral history project. These pieces can be written up or collected via audio- or videotape. Regardless of the final form, family and neighborhood stories will add to the initial text set on immigration by connecting with the students on a more personal level.

#4: ***Literature study encourages us to question "accepted" knowledge.*** Human progress often results from the rejection of assumed "facts." The difficulty lies in spotting our own unexamined assumptions. The more ideas we expose ourselves to, the more likely we are to notice that some of them contradict what we think we know. This motivates us to reconsider and revise our views.

Suggested strategies. Given the confusion and questions Ann's students had about immigration, a good next step is to invite each child to make a ***Mini-Inquiry Book*** out of a single sheet of paper (Lewison et al., 2008) and label it "Questions About Immigration." Children use this little book to jot down a question they have about immigration at the top of each page. Questions they had at the beginning of the study and new questions that come up as they read more of the books in the classroom text set to find answers to their questions are all appropriate. More often than not, further reading generates further questioning and fuels a continuing cycle of inquiry.

We also like to use literature response strategies that encourage readers to linger in texts and engage in a process of rethinking their initial interpretations. Pat Smith developed ***Chart-a-Conversation*** for this very purpose (see Table 5.2). After reading, students use the chart to write down one thing they liked about the text, one thing they didn't like about it, a pattern they noticed, and something they found problematic about the text. They write something in each column then draw a line under it and make additional entries. For example, someone reading *Holly's Secret* (Garden, 2000) thought that it was problematic to talk about lesbian parents at all in a children's book. Since this strategy invites participants to discuss what they see as problematic, there is an underlying assumption that it's okay to disagree. Our experience tells us that diversity and difference are more important in classrooms than sameness and consensus.

TABLE 5.2.   Chart-a-Conversation

LIKE	DISLIKE	PATTERNS	PROBLEMS

*#5: **Literature study deepens our understanding of how language works.*** Sticks and stones may break our bones, but words can hurt us too. Literature study hones language skills and teaches new and valuable techniques for communication. Poets use word play, rhythm, and sounds to recreate an emotional feeling as they deliver messages that often go well beyond the words and phrases themselves. So do speechwriters, politicians, and advertisers. "Where's the beef?" "Ask not what your country can do for you; ask what you can do for your country." "Crisp and clean and no caffeine!" All of these ideas sound good and are therefore easy to buy into. But something that initially sounds great might not stand up to deeper scrutiny. That's why we need to maintain a critical perspective and keep digging deeper.

Suggested strategies. According to Hilary Janks (2005), it is important to build critical language awareness. "When we are confronted by a text that we agree with, it is easy to imagine its positive effects, and hard to see its negative effects" (p. 34). ***Discourse Analysis for Kids*** and ***Becoming a Text Analyst*** are strategies that focus on figuring out how language and power weave together within the choices authors make. Pushing students and ourselves to respond to uncomfortable questions like "What assumptions are hidden in this text?" and "What is this text trying to get me to believe?" can move us in the direction advocated by Janks.

*#6: **Literature study encourages us to explore ethical complexities.*** Because literature provides multiple perspectives, readers are constantly challenged to rethink their initial ethical conceptions and sometimes their condemnation of others' actions. Few issues are simply black and white, and those that are, we want to color gray.

Suggested strategies. ***Written Conversation*** (Short et al., 1996) provides a context for students to discuss a topic by writing back and forth to each other without saying anything out loud. We have seen many instances where a seemingly simple question led to a discussion in which it quickly became clear that there was no simple answer. ***Process Drama*** contains several strategies that teachers can use to support children in examining ethical issues. In talking about the ethics of a boy taking his teddy bear back from the homeless man who found him in the book *The Teddy Bear* (McPhail, 2002), one group of second graders were invited to ***Write in Role***. Their task was to decide whether the child should leave the teddy bear with the homeless man or take it back. After writing, they formed themselves into a ***Conscience Circle*** to share their decisions and explain their thinking.

*#7: **Literature study helps us understand and use the elements of text.*** All stories have structure and common elements. Once students learn to identify these elements in literature, they can use them to develop a better understanding of how authors construct stories and to organize their own original stories when they write.

Suggested strategies. Story Mapping can be a useful strategy for helping students figure out how stories are put together. To help students prepare for writing their own stories, Chris used this strategy to teach her fourth and fifth graders about basic elements like character, setting, and plot. Since plot was often the most difficult element for kids to understand, she used a mapping structure that broke it down into a problem, some attempts to solve the problem, and resolution. Figure 5.4 shows a story map made by a sixth grader for the adolescent novel, *The One Hundredth Thing about Caroline* (Lowry, 1983). In this story, the main character is horrified to hear her mother's new friend say, "The kids have to be eliminated." At the end of the book, she discovers that he was not talking about eliminating her, but about the characters in a book he was writing. This student used story mapping to understand what she was reading and as a strategy for planning her own original story.

*#8: **Literature study teaches us to support our points of view and expand our interpretations.*** Providing evidence for our interpretation of a story or poem is an important part of literature study. When we build a solid case in support of our opinion, we also build self-confidence in our ability to use language to get things done in the world.

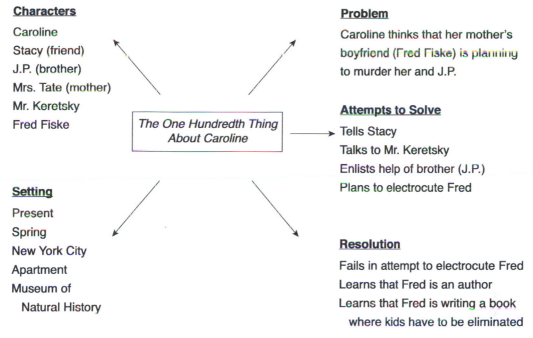

Characters

Caroline

Stacy (friend)

J.P. (brother)

Mrs. Tate (mother)

Mr. Keretsky

Fred Fiske

The One Hundredth Thing About Caroline

Problem

Caroline thinks that her mother's boyfriend (Fred Fiske) is planning to murder her and J.P.

Attempts to Solve

Tells Stacy

Talks to Mr. Keretsky

Enlists help of brother (J.P.)

Plans to electrocute Fred

Setting

Present

Spring

New York City

Apartment

Museum of
  Natural History

Resolution

Fails in attempt to electrocute Fred

Learns that Fred is an author

Learns that Fred is writing a book
  where kids have to be eliminated

FIGURE 5.4.   Story Map for the Adolescent Novel, *The One Hundredth Thing About Caroline.*

Suggested strategies. We have found *Literature Response Little Books* to be very helpful in keeping track of the characters in what we call multi-view books (Lewison et al., 2008). These books are written so that the different characters take turns speaking for themselves. They use first-person narrative to describe what they are thinking and what they see other characters doing. Since there is no narrator, it's up to the reader to remember what each character says and how this connects to the overall plot and what the other characters do and say. *Bat 6* (Wolff, 1998) is a great example of a multi-view book since it features the voices of 21 different characters as they try to make sense of a violent racist act perpetuated by a sixth grade girl. A Literature Response Little Book constructed by a fifth grade student for this book included a listing of the characters and a few points about each one. For example, his entry for the character Tootie at the beginning of the book included the following notes: "Bear Creek Ridge team, catcher, wants to get Aki (a Japanese-American girl) on her team." His entry for Tootie near the end of the book said "Saw Aki get attacked but wasn't sure how much to tell. Didn't want Shazam to go to reform school."

Constructing a character map is another strategy that provides a structure for supporting interpretations and keeping track of evidence. In this case, readers are encouraged to gather information from the book that relates to the characters being studied. For example, the adolescent chapter book *Seedfolks* (Fleischman, 1997) is about how a community garden impacted 13 different people. We could introduce this idea by mapping out the characteristics for one of the thirteen people as a large group and then ask smaller groups to work on the rest of them. Figure 5.5 shows a sample map for the character Kim in *Seedfolks.*

#9: *Literature study helps us develop empathy for those who are unlike us.* Too often our circles of concern are very narrow. Literature study helps us expand that realm of concern beyond the things we personally experience.

Suggested strategies. *Cultural X-Rays* is a strategy developed by Kathy Short (2009a). As a specialist in international children's literature Kathy wanted to create a strategy that supported children in thinking deeply about cultures and how the various peoples of the world were alike

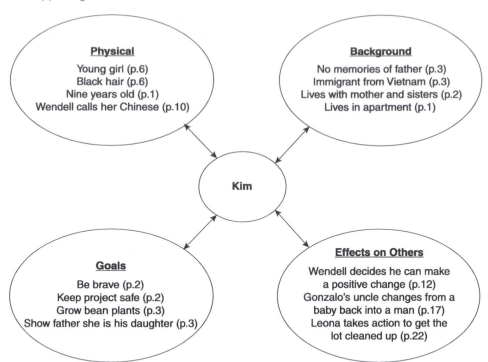

FIGURE 5.5.   Character Map for *Seedfolks.*

and different. *Cultural X-Rays* asks students to draw a sketch of the main character in the book they are reading. Next they are told to put a fairly large heart in the center of that character. In the area of the heart students are invited to write down what it is he or she truly values. Outside the heart they are to note all the things that are different from themselves such as the clothes that are worn, the kind of housing that is available, the things the character spends his or her time doing. *I-Statement Charts* are another good way to support children in thinking about how the perspectives of characters might differ from each other as well as from their own.

    #10: *Literature study allows us to have both an aesthetic and a critical experience.* While we believe that the emotional lived-through experience of literature can transport us to new dimensions, we also agree with Cynthia Lewis (2000) that an aesthetic experience can involve critical thinking. In other words, the pleasure that comes from making personal connections to texts is not necessarily diminished when we are also able to deconstruct power relationships and understand how we are being positioned as readers of particular texts.

    Suggested strategies. Strategies like readers' theater and *Process Drama* can provide both an aesthetic and critical experience for students as they engage in the activity of bringing characters to life. Readers' theater works particularly well with books that have a lot of dialogue. Copies of the text can be highlighted in different colored pens. While the teacher often acts as narrator, students can be assigned different parts to bring the conversation to life. Multi-view books are great for readers' theater since each character's part is already separated out. Process drama supports students in thinking "off the page," in terms of how characters are feeling and what they are thinking. Both teacher and students are invited to step into different roles and continue the story in new ways. Donna Adomat (2009) worked with drama to support two very different kinds of readers, both of whom had difficulties with reading comprehension. Her research demonstrates how working with drama supported these children's in-depth thinking through a story. Carmen Medina (2004) worked with Latino children. By building off of the students' knowledge of pop culture she was able to use drama to support these students' ability to read their everyday world more critically.

Brian Edmiston (1993) describes an instance in which a teacher read a traditional version of *Jack and the Beanstalk* aloud and then invited his first graders to act out going up the beanstalk with him. Taking the role of Jack's neighbors, some of the children pretended to find gold coins and put them into their pockets. At that point, their teacher took the role of the giant and asked them why they were taking his money. The children didn't know what to say. Some denied taking the coins while others admitted they had them. When the giant asked them to give the coins back to him, some ran away with the gold and others stayed to talk to the giant. "The students were making up a drama together, but they were also concerned with one theme of the story: taking other people's things" (Edmiston, 1994, p. 250).

The goal of this activity was to challenge the children to think about this story differently. Traditionally, the giant in this story has been positioned as a "bad guy" and no one wonders if stealing gold from him is problematic. Bringing the giant into the drama in a way that raises questions about the actions of Jack and his neighbors puts a different spin on the situation. Is it okay to steal from people we don't like? Or is stealing always wrong? Edmiston suggests adding characters like friends of the giant or police officers, even though they might not appear in any version of the story since these characters could add other perspectives. Instead of worrying about getting the story right, Edmiston suggests that it's more important to create opportunities for students to see the story through different lenses.

There are many traditional and not-so-traditional literature response strategies that teachers can use to help students develop a deeper understanding of whatever texts they are reading. We have touched briefly on a few of them here but want to emphasize that our list is not exhaustive. We encourage you to experiment with different strategies and see for yourself which ones work best in different contexts and with different books. While you will no doubt decide that some strategies are more useful to you than others, we believe that they can all be helpful tools to have in your teaching repertoire. Even more important than the strategies, however, are the reasons we have provided for doing literature study in the first place. It's easy to get caught up in activities without stopping to think about how helpful they are in developing your students' ability to think critically. We have tried to make the case in this chapter that literature study can do two very important things at the same time: It can help students see school as a place where learning about real life takes place and it can help teachers address standards in a way that keep students interested.

Key Issues in Implementation

We see literature study as the core of any classroom reading program. Authentic literature study involves students reading lots of texts, discussing their reading with others, and using writing and the arts to develop their ideas about how texts might be positioning them and others. Students have some choice about what they read and get multiple opportunities to participate in partner reading and literature discussion groups. We also know that in this era of accountability that appears to have gone crazy, everyone is nervous about meeting standards and being able to show that students are making progress. Fortunately, literacy standards are generally broad enough to encompass authentic literature programs as well as the artificial skills-based programs that try to teach to the test. In this section we respond to potential questions teachers might have about how to use literature when they are required to use a basal reading program, how to keep track of where kids are and how to ensure that the time spent working in literature groups is beneficial.

How can I teach with literature when my district requires me to use a basal reading program? The opening vignette for this chapter describes a teacher planning a literature study on immigration. We know that many teachers are required to use a basal reading program and are not as free as this teacher was to design curriculum. However, we also believe that there are many ways to "use a basal" and not all of them are incompatible with what was happening in the vignette. First, it is good to remember that many commercial reading programs include stories that were originally published as trade books. For example, a second grade basal text published by Harcourt (2007) contains a story about a boy who lives in Chinatown. This story was originally published as a picture book called *Chinatown* (Low, 1997). The picture book *A Day's Work* (Bunting, 1997) introduces readers to a Mexican boy who is trying to help his immigrant grandfather find work. This story is part of a third grade text published by Pearson/Scott Foresman (2008). When basal publishers buy trade books to use in their reading programs, they sometimes alter the text to control the vocabulary and ensure that students are introduced only to new words that align with previous phonics instruction. We also know of cases where the basal version of the story omits some or most of the illustrations from the original picture book. While these changes can certainly make a difference for learners, it doesn't change the fact that there is some good children's literature in basal readers.

The problem is that commercial programs often fail to provide an in-depth experience that invites students to see a topic from multiple perspectives and develop deep understanding. Ann's children didn't read just one story about immigration and then move on to a story about owls. They interacted with a text set that provided multiple opportunities to learn about immigration. Both of the stories mentioned above would be great to include in a study on immigration. While the formal reading program might only provide one or two stories, you can extend the topic by finding others with different perspectives. In addition, all of the teaching strategies Ann used in the vignette can also be used with the stories in a basal. Chris learned the hard way that asking the so-called "comprehension questions" at the end of the story did not support her first graders' comprehension even though the teacher's manual implied otherwise. We know there are better ways to build comprehension and have provided many examples in this chapter for you to try.

How can we keep track of so many kids reading so many books? Many of the teachers we work with prefer to have four or five books (or text sets) on different topics all going on at the same time. Students sign up for the book or topic they wish to explore and meet to plan how much reading they will do in between meetings to talk about what they have read. Teachers meet regularly with all of the groups over a grading period and make sure every student in the room has had an opportunity to participate in a group with them. Teachers also ask groups to plan and post a schedule of what they are going to be doing during their group meetings. These postings help students stay focused and let the teacher know when it might be a good time to visit or observe a particular group. For example, a group of seventh graders reading *Ironman* (Crutcher, 2004) decided to spend their literature study time reading chapter one of the book and engaging in a written conversation about the chapter. When their teacher stopped by to see how they were doing, he jumped into the written conversation and noted that there were a number of comments and questions about the main character's fascination with TV star Larry King and almost as many focusing on why this kid was having so much trouble with his English teacher. He also observed that one student was adding very little to the conversation and made a note to talk privately with that student later about what was going on and what support she needed to participate more actively.

How do we ensure that the groups are working? Watson and Davis (1988) suggest that the teacher's role is crucial in getting literature circles or discussion groups to run smoothly. "Literature study groups do not have much of a chance if the teacher fails to accept his or her primary role as a contributing member of the group" (p. 65). In their study, Suzanne Davis, a fifth grade teacher, "never asked students to do anything that she was not willing to do herself" (p. 63). As an authentic group member, she read the same books and responded in her own literature log. By "authentic member," we mean that she wasn't simply watching and evaluating them, but was doing what students in the group did. When Davis shared her log entries with students, her examples were not provided as the model to which all students should aspire, but as a demonstration of how one might respond to literature. Villaume and Worden (1993) take this a step further and suggest that groups will be more successful if teachers provide support though a three-pronged strategy of demonstration, facilitation, and instruction. They note that these components are to be integrated concurrently throughout the process, not introduced or focused on sequentially:

Demonstration involves teachers demonstrating how to do something, like making an initial response to a text or being a productive member of a literature discussion group. When teachers position themselves as group members, they can make a conscious effort to act more like participants than judges. Instead of pronouncing students' responses as right or wrong, they can provide an example of how to elaborate, probe, and offer alternative ways of thinking. In short, they talk *with* students instead of *at* them.

Facilitation involves encouraging students to expand on their observations and to talk directly to each other instead of to the teachers. When teachers notice that some students are monopolizing the conversation, they can facilitate by inviting others to talk about their ideas as well. Facilitation also includes helping students recognize and construct open-ended questions, seek clarification when needed, and connect their responses to the responses of others.

Instruction includes mini-lessons on a variety of topics spanning the range from simple topics like how to participate in a literature discussion to more sophisticated topics like developing the concept of a personal response. "A personal response was introduced as a *seed*. Good seeds grew in discussions; bad seeds withered and died because there was nothing to say about them" (Villaume & Worden, 1993, p. 466).

What data can we collect to show progress? Individual reading logs are one good way we know to show students' progress over time. The format of these logs may vary according to your instructional and evaluation needs but, at the very least, they will include information like the book title, author, genre, date of beginning and finishing the book, and the student's opinion of the book (see Table 5.3). Logs also provide a way to see which books students might have started but didn't finish. Some teachers have kids complete a set of pre-determined responses for each book they read. These might be presented as response stems like "Three things I like about this book are . . ." or "I would (or would not) recommend this book to my friends because . . ." Some teachers require students to include a summary of the book, although we much prefer seeing students' responses to the story rather than a rehashing of what happened. While uniformity might make the whole process easier, we have found that varying the structure at different times of the year tends to make the record-keeping less tedious.

Although we do not advocate a competition to see who can read the most books or singling children out in any way, we also realize that there are times when sheer numbers can help parents, administrators, and the larger public understand what a literature rich reading program entails. So it is a good idea to have students keep track of what they are reading and to celebrate the progress of the whole class with others outside the class. This can be done via a class newsletter, by posting reviews of books read in the classroom, or by having each student keep a detailed written record. Progress summaries might be shared with parents at the end of each grading period or at pre-selected intervals during the year. Milestones like a hundred books being read and discussed by class members might also be publicized and celebrated.

TABLE 5.3. Sample Book Log

Book	Started	Finished	Author	Genre	My Opinion	Who might like it

Working With Linguistically and Culturally Diverse Students

Literature study is inherently good for linguistically and culturally diverse students for three main reasons. First, as described earlier in this chapter, literature study is social. Students work in groups and get to hear what others are thinking. English language learners (ELLs) benefit from being included in conversations and being invited to contribute what they can. Other group members can also be supportive by talking through difficult concepts or phrasing in the text. Second, teachers who value literature study can create text sets that highlight different cultures and even different languages. This means that the dominant culture is not always privileged. Stories and information about other cultures and other language groups are just as important. (See Chapter 4 for a list of dual-language books and information about multicultural and international books.)

Finally, texts sets are multimodal in nature. This means that they contain more than reading material. Linguistically and culturally diverse students might learn more from videos, maps, or art than from simply reading a book because they provide more options for making meaning.

Technology Extensions and Electronic Resources

We encourage you to check out teachertube.com which contains videos that might be useful to both practicing and pre-service teachers. It's a free site, but you must register and sign in each time you wish to access it. The video we recommend to accompany this chapter is called *Literature Circles*: http://www.teachertube.com/members/viewVideo.php?video_id=145. Created by a group of teachers from the Carol Morgan School in the Dominican Republic, this video provides a demonstration of how to do literature circles with participants playing specifically assigned roles. The following roles are used in this demonstration: discussion director, summarizer, connector, vocabulary enricher, and character captain. Each teacher describes his or her role before they put all the roles together to talk about the picture book *The True Story of the Three Little Pigs* by Jon Scieszka (1996). After viewing the video, we like to have viewers use a strategy we call ***Three Pluses & a Wish*** to talk about what they have seen. This strategy invites participants to jot down two or three points about what they thought was especially strong in the video (or whatever is being evaluated) as well as one area that they wished had been done differently. For example, individual students in one college class came up with the following pluses and wishes after watching the video:

Plus—I like how the teachers took turns explaining each role.

Plus—After watching the teachers, I think I can do it too.

Plus—One teacher made a great point about how many of us are as "big and bad" as the wolf since we eat meat too.

Wish—I wish they had used a book that had more to it.

Wish— I wish they didn't worry so much about being on task. Aren't people supposed to talk in a literature circle?

Wish—I wanted to see them talk about a book without using roles so I could compare the two ways.

We also encourage our students and colleagues to make their own videos of how they do literature discussion groups or literature circles so that multiple perspectives are highlighted and people have choices to consider. The most dangerous aspect of videos like this is that they might come to be seen as "the right way" or "the wrong way" to do it and that belief can discourage further conversation.

Assessment

How will you know if literature study is going well in your classroom? First, it helps if you have some concrete goals for what you are hoping to accomplish. Which practices do you see as most important in building a strong foundation for future literature study? Which strategies are you going to teach and when will you give students opportunities to use them in meaningful ways? Once you get started, we recommend that you sit in with various groups, observe closely, and take notes so that you can give feedback to students with specific examples later. What are you seeing and hearing during the time you provide for literature study? Are students' actions and attitudes changing? Textbox 5.2 provides suggestions for assessing literature study in your classroom.

Textbox 5.2. Assessment

We know literature study is succeeding when we see students doing these things:

- Sharing books and seeking out other kids to read with.
- Directing their comments to each other during group time instead of talking only to the teacher.
- Giving serious consideration to different points of view and occasionally changing their perspectives as a result of hearing other opinions.
- Taking the responsibility to manage their own discussions without the teacher present.
- Following the schedules they create and post for managing their time during literature study.
- Using the various strategies on their own as a normal way of responding to their reading.

TABLE 5.4. Six-Box Graphic Organizer

Something important I want to remember. . .	A question I have. . .	An image I relate to this book—SKETCH IT!
Something unexpected. . .	A connection I made with this book. . .	Something I could write about. . .

Invitation: Six-Box Literature Response Strategy

The *Six-Box Literature Response Strategy* uses a graphic organizer (see Textbox 5.3 and Table 5.4). All of the topics on the graphic organizer encourage in-depth thinking about the text and support students in looking at the story through different lenses.

We like to use an "edgy" book with this strategy so that there is plenty to think about after reading it. One of our favorites is *Freedom Summer* (Wiles, 2001), a picture book about two young boys who learn that racial discrimination will not end with the Civil Rights Act of 1964. Although the law decreed that the town swimming pool and other public places were to be open to everyone, regardless of skin color, some people looked for ways to defy the new legislation. In this story, the two friends (one black and one white) race to the swimming pool with eager anticipation since it will be their first chance to swim there together. As they approach their destination, however, they are stopped in their tracks by the sight of town dump trucks filling the pool in with tar. Rather than integrate, some town officials have decided to destroy the pool for everyone. Our college students have told us that hearing this book as a read aloud is like getting kicked in the stomach. They are so shocked that they don't know what to say. A few always ask to see the book so they can check the ending and make sure they understood it. When we pass out the six-box graphic organizer, however, their indecision seems to fade and they immediately get to work. The topic is so intense that they suddenly have many ideas to express.

Textbox 5.3. Invitation: Six-Box Literature Response Strategy

As literacy educators we want to support broad reading as well as in-depth reading. Sometimes when students are reading broadly they encounter books that deal with topics that leave them speechless. A series of prompts can get them started as well as support them in thinking deeply about what they have read.

Materials & Procedures

- Multiple copies of the graphic organizer (see Table 5.4)
- Writing materials
- A selected piece of children's literature

1. After reading, distribute copies of the graphic organizer to everyone. These prompts invite students to take a variety of perspectives. Encourage students to put something in each of the boxes on their sheet.
2. Once students have completed the graphic organizer, invite them to become researchers. Ask students to cut their responses apart so that the responses to each prompt can be examined as a set. For example, one set of responses would be "Something important I want to remember about the book …" while another group's set of responses would contain everything students in the class responded to "A question I have …"
3. Form students into six groups to analyze each response set. Ask students to read through all of the responses in their set and to be alert to patterns or categories they see forming. Encourage groups to identify "anomalies" or responses that do not fit their categories.
4. Once categories have been formed, invite students to construct some type of graph that summarizes their findings.
5. Have groups present the categories they found, themes they see emerging, anomalies, and conclusions.

Other Notes

This strategy works well with all ages. Younger children can be encouraged to use their own invented spelling and to do more drawing if that is helpful. Older students can be introduced to more complex methods of analysis and encouraged to present their findings in more sophisticated ways like through bar graphs or pie charts.

The second part of this strategy takes place after students have filled something into each of their six boxes. We encourage students to think about how some of the responses reflect similar themes and suggest that they move the boxes around to form physical groups. We also encourage them to identify "anomalies." We define anomalies as responses that they didn't understand or that didn't seem to go with any others.

Once categories have been formed, each group is invited to present their findings. When an anomaly is presented, we invite the author to talk about what he or she was thinking at the time, though we also say it's okay to remain anonymous. As we have engaged students in this strategy over the years, we have noticed that some wonderfully divergent thinking frequently comes out of the anomalies.

Professional Development

Literature study can be an enlightening and enjoyable experience for practicing and prospective teachers, especially when they have an opportunity to try out new strategies with colleagues and then share their thoughts on how these ideas might be used with different books.

Table 5.5 provides summaries of three professional articles that focus on doing literature study with kids at different age levels. Each article offers "nuts and bolts" advice for implementing new approaches and shares examples for how students responded to these ideas. We recommend that you read these articles in groups and follow the reading by doing one or more of the strategies described in the article your group read. This is also a good time to revisit the three guiding principles of the chapter:

- *Principle 1: Literature Discussion Groups Support Reading as a Social Event.*
- *Principle 2: Text Sets Support Powerful Conversations.*
- *Principle 3: There Are Multiple Goals and Multiple Strategies for Literature Study.*

How do the professional articles address these principles? How can they support you in setting up a critical literature-based classroom?

TABLE 5.5.   Suggestions for Further Reading

Clyde, J.A. (2003) Stepping inside the story world: The subtext strategy—A tool for connecting and comprehending. *The Reading Teacher, 57*(2), 150–160.	Leland, C., & Harste, J. with Davis, A., Haas, C., McDaniel, K., Parsons, M., & Strawmyer, M. (2003) "It made me hurt inside": Exploring tough social issues through critical literacy. *The Journal of Reading Education, 28*(2), 7–15.	Smith, K. (1995) Bringing children and literature together in the elementary classroom. *Primary Voices K-6, 3*(2), 22–30.
Jean Anne Clyde explains her work with the subtext strategy. Teachers may find it useful to read the article together and follow it with a picture book or short story so they can try doing the strategy and getting feedback from each.	This piece describes how five teacher education interns moved from wondering if critical literacy was appropriate for their students to engaging in inquiry projects that focused on the actual use of these books in classrooms. A number of different literacy response strategies that can be used with both older and younger children are discussed and samples of student work are shown.	Karen Smith's classic article provides a wonderful glimpse into a successful fifth/sixth grade literature study program. The author describes how her instructional approach changes during the year to match students' development and needs. She also discusses how she deals with problems and distractions.

six

Inquiry Into the World Through Focused Studies

During her first year as a teacher, Heather Rock[1] was a member of a teacher study group that had been exploring critical literacy. As a result of her work with this group, she planned to begin the year with a focused study on U.S. History (the fifth grade social studies curriculum), only with a twist. A focused study is an inquiry into a topic that can take place over days, weeks, months, or even the entire school year. Heather felt strongly that students needed to hear and recognize the voices typically left out of most accounts of history, especially those in textbooks. So her study focused on: *How and why are historical events told differently in various texts?*

Heather began the year by having students read Michael Dorris's *Morning Girl* (1992)—a chapter book about two Taino children and their daily lives on a Bahamian island just prior to the arrival of Columbus in 1492. Her students met in *Literature Circles* to discuss it, which was an enjoyable enterprise for the class. In literature circles, kids meet in small groups to discuss particular pre-agreed upon segments of text, which in this case were chapters of the book. During these meetings, one significant concept that many students commented about was being able to see the same situation through different eyes, as the book is told in alternating chapters from the point of view of a brother and sister.

Heather had timed the reading sections so her class would finish the book the day before Columbus Day. On the final page of the book there was an image of Morning Girl hurrying back to the village to find the right people to help the newly arrived visitors as they disembarked from the ships. As students independently finished the book, gasps of disbelief disrupted the silence. The epilogue is taken directly from Christopher Columbus's journals and describes his view of the native people: "They are very well formed . . . They do not carry arms nor are they acquainted with them . . . They should be good and intelligent servants" (Dorris, 1992, p. 74). Students rushed

---

1 This vignette was modified from an unpublished account written by Heather Rock.

to find their friends to see if they had read the epilogue yet. They were appalled that Columbus was thinking of making people like the characters they had come to admire into servants.

The next day Heather's students began digging deeper by comparing various accounts of Columbus's life and journey including the book *Encounter* by Jane Yolen (1996). This story is also told from the point of view of a young Taino boy. Throughout the book he tries to warn his people against welcoming the strangers who seem more interested in gold than in friendship. During the read aloud, Heather reported that students expressed a sense of uneasiness. Where was the adventurous hero they had learned about in previous years? Heather asked the class to examine the large color diagram of the "Columbian Exchange" in their fifth grade textbook. Students noted that servants (or slaves) were not one of the "products" being carried back to Europe and were unsure of why this was left out.

Because of the students' curiosity, Heather decided to find out more about Columbus by reading Howard Zinn's *A People's History of the United States: 1492 to Present* (2003). She read about the extreme measures taken by Columbus and his men when they became desperate for gold. For example, Zinn notes:

> they ordered all persons fourteen years or older to collect a certain quantity of gold every three months. When they brought it, they were given copper tokens to hang around their necks. Indians found without a copper token had their hands cut off and bled to death. (p. 4)

Heather was amazed at how little she actually knew. She told her students that she didn't learn much about Columbus in her own schooling and then explained what she had learned from the Zinn book. This began a conversation about whether or not more explicit information about Columbus belonged in textbooks. Students brainstormed possible reasons it would be left out, "It could make parents mad that their children are learning this stuff," explained one student. Another suggested that Heather could be sued for telling them the truth about Columbus. Heather could barely disguise her shock and asked the student why he thought this. "Well," he replied, "they've sued for a lot less."

This discussion made Heather a bit nervous. She felt that both she and her students were leaving their normal comfort zones on how to "do" school and history. They were no longer passively receiving knowledge from the texts they read. Students realized that their textbook was only one version of history. Heather reported that her students began to discuss resisting the traditional celebration of Columbus Day and instead consider how the Tainos would feel about Columbus Day if their people had not been wiped out by European violence and disease. One student explained his thinking:

> I think that Columbus isn't really a hero and he didn't really discover a new world because there were already people there that knew it wasn't Asia, Europe or India. I think Columbus Day is a holiday because it is important that he brought a lot of new people here.

Heather said that her students felt empowered by their newfound knowledge of Columbus and took action (the third part of our mantra) by publishing an article in their classroom newspaper and distributing it throughout the school. This article contained content that would have previously made Heather worry, but the more she worked out of her comfort zone, the more she realized how powerful this space was for student learning. The focused study could have ended here, but because of student interest (and her own) Heather extended the study to new, but connected areas. As the year progressed, she helped her kids seek out the stories of those who have typically been silenced.

- Students studied the history of slavery in the U.S. by comparing descriptions of the Middle Passage in several books about colonial times.
- They counted the number of times women were mentioned in a textbook chapter on founding the colonies and questioned why they didn't get more attention.
- This led to a related inquiry into what women were doing during colonial times.

Heather used a variety of sources for studying U.S. History including Joy Hakim's *History of US* series (2007), several picture books such as *From Slave Ship to Freedom Road* (Lester, 1998), as well as biographies and primary sources whenever possible. Heather used the textbook most often as a companion to the other texts she was bringing into the classroom. By comparing the textbook to other sources, Heather's students frequently discovered that there were facts missing or that the tone was very different.

These focused studies went on for half the year as Heather and her students moved beyond Columbus and what really happened when he landed in the New World to how Columbus and women were portrayed in textbooks and how other historical events played out in textbook narratives. Heather's class added onto this base by starting another focused study that explored young people who made important contributions to history, but were left out of textbooks. Heather brought in sources such as *Connecting Children Past and Present* (Fresch, 2004) and *We Were There Too* (Hoose, 2001). From these sources and a number of historical fiction children's books, students in Heather's class chose to research and find out more about a particular "kid in history." These inquiries went on for weeks and included time for whole class reflection. Students often brought in news articles, song lyrics, books, or an artifact related to a young person one of their peers was studying. Though they were conducting individual inquiries about specific children, there was always a feeling of connectedness and shared learning among class members.

As the year was coming to an end, Heather and her class discussed what kind of culminating experience might be most fitting for this focused study and decided to create a "Kids in History Museum." Each student created an exhibit for his/her kid. Nearly all of the exhibits had pictures and text on poster boards that included photos or sketches of the focal young people, a history of their work and achievements, and timelines of what else was going on in the world at the time. Some of the exhibits had the creator dressed in costume, some included quizzes for the visitors to take after spending time at the exhibit, and some provided videos, news articles, books, and music of the time.

Heather had her students form committees to divide the responsibilities: creating posters and banners to be displayed in the museum, making flyers to be hung around the school and taken home, writing letters to the local newspaper, and figuring out where in the school to set up the museum. Over 500 people visited throughout the day. Mitzi attended and was amazed at the extensive exhibits the students had created and how knowledgeable they were about their "kid" and the related time periods.

Heather said that during reflections, her students agreed that the museum was a success, even if it wasn't perfect. She noted that her students had developed creative ways to take action and teach others the information they found so important. They also incorporated music, costumes, videos, and props as they took on the roles of knowledgeable experts, eager to share their information with others. Heather said it was clear that the students knew more than the key facts they had displayed in their exhibit. She related some exciting moments, such as newspaper reporters interviewing students and photographers documenting the event. But probably most important was the sense of shared work and accomplishment that students experienced as a result of being inquirers into parts of history that most adults didn't know about.

Principle #1: Focused Studies Open New Possibilities for Inquiry

From Heather's vignette we can see how one significant children's book, in this case *Morning Girl* (Dorris, 1992), led to a year-long series of focused studies into how historical events are portrayed in textbooks versus other texts. The culmination was an in-depth inquiry into kids who made a difference in history, but were left out of most textbooks. Focused studies are usually whole class inquiries into a broad theme or topic that highlight the interests of students, a curricular unit of study (as we saw with Heather's fifth grade history curriculum), or a social justice concern that arises during the year.

Silvers, Shorey, and Crafton (2010) describe focused studies as students working together as part of a community of practice (Wenger, 1998) where young people "learn about their world [and] . . . take on shared endeavors to accomplish goals . . . By collaboratively pursuing socially meaningful work, the community of practice provides an opportunity to learn together while developing an identity of participation" (p. 382). This participation usually starts with an essential question (Berghoff, Egawa, Harste, & Hoonan, 2000) that is "broad enough to uncover the full depth of the topic, yet narrow enough for students to connect with personal interests and find authentic avenues for exploration" (Bird, Libby, Rowley, & Turner, 2002, p. 25). For Heather's Kids in History focused study, her class decided to explore the question: *How have kids made a difference in history?*

The ways focused studies play out in different classrooms can vary tremendously. In contrast to what happened in Heather's classroom, Jerry prefers to start the year by having small groups engage in 24-hour focused studies. He asks students to inquire into something they've always wanted to learn about. In a 24-hour period they read something about their topic, interview someone, and have a hands-on experience. Everyone reports back on both what they've learned and the successes and problems of the inquiry. Talking about things that didn't go well is very helpful in planning the next inquiry. Whatever the length, we have listed some common components that teachers include in focused studies (although it is certainly not necessary to incorporate all of these components).

Focusing questions. These questions come from the students. In Heather's case, after a few read alouds and class discussions about kids in history, the students really wanted to find out more about these hidden heroes in history. As a class, they came up with the big question, *How have kids made a difference in history?* In helping students formulate their wonderings and puzzlements into questions, we have found it is often useful for teachers to help students craft questions that have more than one response, encourage multiple perspectives, open up new areas of exploration, or explore critical issues. One strategy we especially like is having students keep ***Mini-Inquiry Books***, where they write down individual questions as they arise during a focused study. In this way kids can keep track of and not forget their personal questions, conjectures, and issues in need of further exploration.

In order to have guidelines and direction for individual inquiries, Heather created some guiding questions for students to consider during their research into kids in history. Here are some examples:

- What are some of the most important things to remember about your kid in history?
- What were the different ways that kids interacted with adults and how were the adults portrayed in your sources?
- What were the different kinds of actions your kid took? Which of these were working with a system or against a system?
- Whose voices were heard and whose were absent in the sources you found?

These guiding questions served instructional purposes and were more specific than the overall focusing question created by the students based on what they passionately wanted to study.

Planning to plan. This is a process where teachers start considering activities that students might experience during the focused study. Aside from the ideas and systems of knowledge (understandings from different disciplines) we may want students to experience during the study, we are also guided by what learners already know and want to find out (Berghoff et al., 2000). For example, Heather began planning the "kids in history" focused study by using a concept map to brainstorm the potential directions this inquiry could take. She wanted to leave it open for student ideas, but also have a sense of purpose. This planning began by gathering an initial set of books, songs, and videos.

Initiating experiences. One way of "jump-starting" a focused study if a topic doesn't arise naturally from what's happening in the classroom is through initiating experiences (Bird et al., 2002). These engagements help children connect their personal experiences, knowledge, and questions to the issues and controversies that will be explored in the focused study (Burke, 1998). The engagements can also provide common experiences from which the class can embark on the inquiry cycle. The possibilities here are endless—a read aloud, video, fieldtrip, journal entry to a provocative question, speaker, song. Whatever the activity, its role is to signal that the focused study is underway (Berghoff et al., 2000).

Devices for organizing and sharing. These devices are used regularly by students over the course of the focused study. They document accumulating information and knowledge learned during the focused study and allow students to look back on their growing understandings and expanding group expertise (Burke, 1998). One way to make this visible to the whole class is by using an audit trail (Harste & Vasquez, 1998) or learning wall. This is usually a wall of the classroom where students choose and display the important artifacts and experiences that track the trajectory and critical moments in the focused study (see the *Assessment* section in this chapter for more details on learning walls). Other devices include journals, maps, webs, or any way for students to keep track of what they are learning and record the new questions that arise as they delve deeper into the focused study. Assessment is naturally related to the devices for organizing and sharing since these artifacts present concrete ways for students and teachers to look back and assess learning and growth. Many teachers have students go back and review these artifacts and write reflections about the focused study and what they learned.

Learning center invitations. These open-ended learning activities help children explore the focusing questions in social and creative ways. The invitations encourage students to make meaning using a variety of sign systems (art, music, drama, dance, mathematics). They also provide students with opportunities to gain new perspectives on the topic that they might not otherwise consider (Bird et al., 2002). Carolyn Burke (1998, p. 2) describes the properties of invitations. During these experiences:

- Attention is focused on meaning making.
- Students interact in social and collaborative ways.
- Students are able to use disciplinary knowledge, sign systems, and ways of knowing.
- Students are exposed to current information and if possible, cutting edge perspectives.
- Students are actively engaged in one focused experience, not a series of exercises or activities.
- There is potential for students to ask new questions that lead to further inquiries.

As part of the Kids in History Museum, Heather's students created their own learning center invitations for visitors to engage in when they visited the museum. One of these asked visitors to take on the role of particular kids in history as they walked through the exhibit so they could interact with other kids in history. A disappointment that some of Heather's students expressed was that some of the visitors didn't take on the persona they were given and took much more passive roles than what students had envisioned. The students had tried, although unsuccessfully, to create an invitation that would get visitors out of the traditional role of simply being a tourist or spectator at the museum.

Conceptually related texts and media. These focused study engagements feature multiple and varied sources of information (books, magazines, newspapers, videos, graphic novels, TV clips, YouTube videos, etc.) that provide alternative perspectives and create opportunities for complex connections. The term we use for these sources is a *Text Set* (see Chapter 5). Text sets often form the core materials of focused study inquiries. Even though we have a wide range of materials, there are times when students may focus on reading a single text. Groups of students meet, read, and delve into the significant meanings of a text. As we saw in the literature circle reading of *Morning Girl* in Heather's class, this includes forming critical analyses of issues presented in one book and then extending these insights to other sources.

Exploring critical issues. These engagements often fit seamlessly into a focused study, but in case they don't, we create invitations that question everyday assumptions and have students apply different inquiry methods to study specific real-world questions. These inquiries take students beyond the school walls and encourage them to deal with social, political, or community issues. For example, Mitzi created a focused study called: *How can we share space at home and in school?* She invited students to go beyond the main focus of the inquiry and explore how conflicts between individuals and governments over private and shared space often make the news. She introduced news articles about people quarreling over neighbors' houses, trees that blocked views, barking dogs, and parties that were too loud. Mitzi also brought in articles about citizens protesting the city's plan to build a park, a dump, or a freeway. She and the students discussed how protesters like these are sometimes called NIMBYs (Not In My Back Yard!).

Interested students were invited to find other examples of "space" disputes in the newspapers. After collecting a variety of articles, they compared the various conflicts they found and put them into categories. They discovered that some conflicts were more frequently reported than others. They noted how the conflicts were resolved, if at all. They also were invited to propose their own solutions to the problems and/or evaluate the solutions adopted by the participants in the conflict. In this way, the personal and social issues that students were examining in the main focused study took a political turn.

Culminating experiences and celebrations. These activities help children pull together their current understandings of the inquiry, celebrate what they've learned, and reflect on their accomplishments. Culminating experiences:

> bring closure to the unit . . . and put them [students] in the role of teacher as they create presentations or exhibitions that communicate what they have learned. We think about who the audience will be for their public demonstrations of learning and often use this time to bring in parents and people from the community or other students in the school. (Berghoff et al., 2000, p. 92)

This creates the potential that student learning will have an impact on the larger community.

Small group work within focused studies. Although focused studies usually involve the whole class, often students break up into small groups to pursue specific sub-inquiries. Silvers et al. (2010) described what happened during a first grade whole class focused study on Hurricane Katrina when all the students became interested in the disaster because of the extensive media coverage. One small group in Mary Shorey's classroom was especially interested in the topic and desired to become experts on the social and political issues involved in the response to Katrina. They named themselves the Hurricane Group (despite this being the overall topic of the focused study). As the authors explain,

> These students were using multimodal tools [drama, music, art, gesture, etc.] to construct and share their learning as they explored a critical issue of great national importance. In the process, they were expanding their awareness of what it means to be a good citizen and what their responsibilities were as citizens to help others. (Silvers et al., 2010, p. 394)

Here is an example of writing from one member of the Hurricane Group who was trying to understand the inequities that happened during this disaster.

> Some people had money and could buy things and get out when the hurricane happened but the poor people were poor and couldn't buy things and couldn't survive and went to the Superzone (Superdome) to be safe, but they weren't. (Silvers et al., 2010, p. 394)

Silvers and her colleagues explain how this group of five students sought out their first grade teacher two years later, wanting to resurrect the Hurricane Group as another hurricane started up in the gulf. This focused study was a powerful presence in these students' lives and they saw their group not as something that ended with their graduation from first grade, but rather as a viable group of collaborators (community of practice) that could be reconvened if necessary.

Principle #2: Author Studies Connect Kids With Writers

Eighth grade teacher Carol Porter (1998) describes her work with co-teacher Evelyn Hanssen in planning and implementing an author study by talking about planning to plan, student choice, initiating experiences, student and teacher generated invitations, multimodal publications, and culminating experiences. This, of course, is similar to the procedures we outlined for focused studies, but here the spotlight is on a particular author. In Carol's class the author was Robert Cormier, writer of the famed *The Chocolate Wars* (1974) and *I Am the Cheese* (1977), among many other books. Carol started the unit by having the whole class listen to book talks by students who were previously involved in Cormier studies. Carol documents the work of one student, Tanya, whose group chose to read *The Bumble Bee Flies Away* (1983). She shows the choices and commitments that Tanya made during the author study including taking a field trip to meet Robert Cormier; reading a second Cormier book, *I Am the Cheese*, with her group; reading short stories with another girl and writing letters back and forth to each other about their interpretations of the stories; writing poetry; writing a comparison paper for *The Bumble Bee Flies Away* and *I Am the Cheese*; taking on the role of a critic when presenting book talks with a friend; and writing a self-evaluation (Porter, 1998. p. 110).

Two years later, Carol assembled a panel made up of former students for a teacher workshop she was conducting. Tanya was one of the panelists and said, "I remember I never had read any novels except Nancy Drew mysteries. Now I read all the time. All different kinds of books" (p. 104). Along with Tanya, the four other student-panelists told the teachers at the workshop (language kept in original):

- We got to choose what we wanted to read.
- Discussions were fun, too.
- I got help understanding the story better at discussions.

- Your group decides when you will meet to discuss and how far you will have to read.
- We also write and pick pieces we want to publish.

This group of adolescents did a great job of selling author studies to the teachers who attended Carol's workshop and had many questions for the students. As we've noted in both our own and colleagues' classrooms, author study inquiries are powerful curricular structures that have the potential to transform the identities of students and their investment in school.

The allure of authors. In the film, *Stone Reader* (Moskowitz, 2002, cited in Jenkins, 2006, p. 64), the writer/director Mark Moskowitz talks about the effect that author Joseph Heller had on him:

> They say one book can turn a kid on to be a reader for life. I was already a reader, but *Catch 22* excited me. It was the first book I read where the author's voice meant as much to me as the story or the characters. The first writer I wanted to know more about . . . the voice behind the pages was a friend I thought I could never find in life. (*Stone Reader*)

For Jenkins, the film highlighted human passion for stories and authors, and started her on a quest to find out why kids were enamored with certain authors as their favorites. She asked fifth graders to write to their favorite authors and analyzed their letters to find common patterns of response. The following are the four types of responses that were present in the students' letters— personal, biographical, literary, and reader interest (2006, pp. 65–66). We mention these four types of letter responses here because they all can become part of author studies and are ways for students to find excitement in reading, authors, and writing as we saw with Carol Porter's students. Author studies can help students find a passion for books, create bonds between readers and authors, and allow students to follow their passions.

Author study as multiple response. We find the work of Jenkins (2006) dovetails nicely with our perspectives on focused studies. She looked at the multiple ways teachers enact author studies and created an inclusive perspective she calls *author study as multiple response* (pp. 68–69). Below are three of Jenkins' six characteristics that we find unique to author studies and go beyond the characteristics we have already discussed in focused studies. Some of these characteristics came up in student letters.

First, there is often a focus on *literary analysis* during an author study because it "deepens and extends the reading experience." Here students linger in texts and dig deeper into the author's craft for two purposes. One is to better understand how the author pulls off writing a book "that takes us on a satisfying ride" (Fletcher, 2005, p. 1). The other is as a demonstration of ways we might write our own stories. A favorite author's book can serve as a mentor (Fletcher, 2005) or touchstone text (Wood Ray, 1999; Laman, 2006) and we can try out themes or devices that this author uses in our own writing. Students inquire into how authors construct their characters, common themes for writing, devices and techniques they use regularly, and particular uses of language that separate them from other authors. Frank Smith calls it *reading like a writer* (1983).

Ralph Fletcher shares a humorous letter he received from a class that points out just how closely they studied his work.

> Dear Mr. Fletcher,
> Our class liked your book FLYING SOLO. But why did you use the word <u>retorted</u> so many times? At first it didn't bother us, but pretty soon that "retorted" word was driving us crazy! You are a good writer, and we don't mean to be rude, but we think you should use the thesaurus more so you don't use a word too many times. (2005, p. 1)

Fletcher suggests that during author studies we encourage students to ask deep and probing questions about the way an author writes. He points out that it is important for students to understand that the choices authors make are deliberate and "books are not the result of arbitrary decisions but of the author's careful intentionality" (p.3).

Second, in author studies there is a focus on the *background of the author* that "heightens and intensifies the literary experience." Here students inquire into the author's life, interests, and body of work. As Ralph Fletcher puts it, "an effective author study helps students to know a writer from the inside out" (2005, p. 1). This can intensify pleasure and propel students to become enthusiastic readers and writers. Many authors now have their own web pages, videos, and interviews online, which are wonderful resources in these studies (Fox, 2006).

Third, there is a focus on *critical responses* to an author's work. Jenkins (2006) stresses the importance of challenging readers to ask Luke and Freebody's (1997) questions such as whose voices are being heard, whose values are being perpetuated, whose are being left out? Even though students love a particular author, it is still important that they question whether or not the author addresses issues of equality and justice in his or her body of work.

Author studies can be done with the whole class exploring the work of one author or groups of students conducting inquiries into different authors. There are as many ways to conduct author studies as there are authors. When the whole class is studying one author, read alouds are often a good way to introduce the study. During class discussions, students can start figuring out what makes this author different from others, what are common themes or issues that come up in his or her books, and what it is about this author's writing that they really like. When small groups of kids are studying different authors, teachers help them create affinity groups based on which kids like the same author. Textbox 6.1 shows the format that Chris uses for small group author studies.

Textbox 6.1. Small Group Author Study

- *Conduct* a web search for your author. Look for interesting aspects of your author's life and see if you can make connections to the characteristics of his or her writing.
- *Gather* several books by the author. Discuss what you notice about the books at first glance and what topics or themes (if any) are common for this author.
- *Read* and discuss at least three books by your author and decide characteristics you appreciate or don't really like. Consider how your group might share this author with other students in the class.
- *Revisit* the list of all the books written by this author and decide which new books your group will read and discuss.
- *Create* a poster or brochure to share with the rest of the class that includes the following:
    - o The author's background.
    - o His/her work (books written, accomplishments, awards, etc.).
    - o A list of the reasons your group likes or doesn't like this author's work.
    - o Critical questions you have about the author's body of work.
    - o Where other kids in the class can find more information about this author.

Directions for creating author brochures with college students can be found on the website that accompanies this book: www.routledge.com/cw/leland.

Author studies in early childhood classrooms. For most teachers, it's easy to picture how author studies would work with elementary and middle school students, but can they be used in the primary and early childhood classrooms? Kindergarten teacher Megan Hillegass (2005) answers that question with a resounding yes. She started her first author study by having students dig into the works of Robert Munch. She had so much success that she went on to have students inquire into the works of Alma Flor Ada, Lois Ehlert, and Ezra Jack Keats, to name a few. Hillegass points out that during her study of Robert Munch, she saw students creating a strong relationship with the author by selecting his books when they went to the library to choose their weekly book. She also found that young children are capable of learning about an author's style, the themes that are common in his or her books, and the types of illustrations that often accompany a particular author's writing. Finally, Hillegass is a proponent of author studies in early childhood classrooms because students are exposed to a wide range of great literature (2005, p. 5).

Principle #3: Genre Studies Encourage Digging Deeply

Lisa Siemens, who teaches six, seven, and eight year olds, spends the entire year having her students focus on the genre of poetry. She wants her students to fall in love with poetry, to understand its power, and appreciate the ways it can enrich their lives and get things done in the world. Lisa began one year by handing each child a box of crayons. She asked them not to open the boxes and to close their eyes while she read the following poem:

> *New Crayons*
> New Crayons
> wait
> breathlessly
> in boxes
> points poised
> to leap
> into rainbows
> and flowers
> and a thousand
> smiling suns.
> (Siemens, 1996, p. 236)

As the class discussed the poem, Lisa reported how one child, Charles, "saw crayons arguing in his mind," while Josh was disappointed that he didn't see anything (p. 236). Lisa assured Josh it was fine not to see anything. You can imagine the excitement when the boxes were opened and the students smelled the new crayons, drew pictures, and started writing. This simple activity started Lisa's students on an inquiry into poetry.

Lisa read the poems of a wide range of poets to her students and they began writing their own. As they listened to the poems Lisa read, students began to figure out what made poetry powerful—beautiful language, the inner feelings of the writer, the artistry of reading poetry aloud, the expression of strong emotions, the transformation of everyday objects and events into works of art, and the discovery that there is poetic language all around us, even in prose. Lisa's students used what they learned from published poets in their own writing. Near the end of the school year Lisa was curious and asked her students, "What is poetry?" Here are two of their definitions (p. 239).

A poem is like a big green
dragon waiting to blow
fire at the knight who
seeks the treasure. (Au)

What is Poetry?
Poetry is a bunch
of letters crushed together
that hide in your mind
and when you write
you don't even notice
that you wrote a poem. (Andrew)

As the year ended, Lisa noted how she was reminded almost daily that she was "living in the company of poets" (p. 240). By immersing her students in an extended genre study, Lisa saw her students going places with their writing where they would have never ventured before.

Although Lisa's vignette illustrates a lengthy inquiry into poetry, we know many teachers who spend only a week or two on a particular genre and then go on to another. There is no "right way" to address different genres of literature in your classroom. A wide range of genres will come into the curriculum naturally by students' independent reading choices. For some teachers, the book sharing that takes place after silent reading or discussions that follow read alouds are enough emphasis on genre. Others prefer that their students engage in a series of short genre studies. Or, as with Lisa Siemens, some teachers spend an entire year on a particular genre. We do know that discussing genres, whether informally or in genre studies, can enable our students to become savvy consumers of a wide range of literature. Hansen and Vasquez (2002) note:

> We teach our students about poetry, fantasy, and other genres as one way to appeal to their various interests and invite them into the world of readers. As we appreciate a genre in depth, we more clearly see the beauty of one book, the differences and similarities among many, and the multiple perspectives they offer. (p. 1)

In Textbox 6.2, we've included a list of a few of our favorite genres with a discussion of why we incorporate them in our curriculum.

Textbox 6.2. Selected Genres in Children's Literature

Fantasy and Science Fiction reading can expand students' thinking and help them imagine new worlds and new possibilities. These books also have the potential to foster explorations into why our world is the way it is, what new technologies may have to offer us, and what purposes our current institutions serve compared to those in other worlds. Although the lines can often blur, science fiction works usually have some basis in facts or new technologies, while fantasy works don't need to be tied to reality.

   Mystery reading, while extremely pleasurable for many students, can also help focus on characters, setting, and plot. By paying attention to these story elements, students have the opportunity to solve the puzzles presented in text. As an additional resource, the Internet has a number of sites that assist students in writing their own mysteries. For example, Scholastic has a site called *Writing with Teachers: Mystery Writing* (Nixon, 1995).

Graphic Novels and Picture Books can both be studied in terms of how graphic images impact the story being told. These multimodal works are often rich with multiple ways of interpretation due to the juxtaposition of images and texts. Students can examine how illustrations are used to set a mood or tone, or how they create messages.

Historical Fiction makes history come alive as authors place fictional characters in real times and places. In a critical curriculum, these books can also serve as starting points for critique as was done in Heather's class by asking students questions like whose story gets told and whose is left out of particular accounts of history.

Informational Texts serve to inform us about the world. These books can open up new worlds by presenting current knowledge on a wide range of subjects. Mitzi remembers a student who didn't want to read much of anything until he found a book on racecars in the library. As long as there was a supply of books about racing, Jim was always engrossed in a book during silent reading time.

Folktales, Fables, and Fairy Tales support discussions about the norms and values of society. Folktales often arise out of an oral tradition and usually have real people as characters. They often tell how things came to be the way they are, drawing on the human need for explanation. Fables are often animal stories that teach us how to behave in life. Fairy tales also point to how one ought to behave, but often with kings, queens, and dragons as characters.

Diaries* and *Memoirs help us understand the lives of others by giving us an insider view of how they think.

Realistic Fiction is a genre that focuses on real-life social and personal issues. We call these social issues books and they are described in detail in Chapter 4.

Genre studies allow students to dig deeper into texts. When we flood the classroom with a particular genre, students become detectives in figuring out how the genre works, which text is a great example of a genre, what authors do when they write these types of texts, and why some books in a genre appeal to us much more than others. Kids become experts and can take a hand at writing in a particular genre. Each genre has "distinctive features and structures that place varying demands on readers and writers" (Sharp & Martinez, 2010). Kathryn Mitchell Pierce (in Short & Pierce, 1998) keeps genre studies simple for her students. The basic routine is "browse, read, respond, analyze and make connections, write" (p. 4). Whatever the process the teacher uses to immerse students in a particular genre, the key is always making the study interesting for kids. This happens when students are able to ask their own questions and explore genres that focus on what's most important to them.

Key Issues in Implementation

Time is an issue that always comes up when we work with teachers on focused studies. How can you spend so much time on one topic? Teachers who implement longer focused studies point to how many curricular goals are accomplished in one focused study. For example, at Mary Shorey's school, the first grade curriculum "included a study of families, neighborhoods, citizenship rights and responsibilities, and needs and wants. It also included African American history" and reading and writing (Silvers et al., 2010, p. 388). Mary knew she wanted to teach the curriculum that was required, but make it more critical. Her focused study on Hurricane Katrina provided a framework for the mandated curriculum to be taught in a way that built on the interests and questions of the students.

On the other hand, focused studies can also be short. Remember that Jerry starts with 24-hour focused studies. He then moves on to 36-hour inquiries, week-long studies, and sometimes longer studies. Although the longer studies aren't necessary, we find most teachers who start out with shorter studies see the impact they have on students and slowly move to longer studies. We also believe that it is important for students to be able to opt out of a focused study if they are running into roadblocks on a topic or have found they aren't interested in what they thought they were. These students come to us with an alternate plan and find something else they'd rather study in depth.

The issue of time and planning is discussed often when we teach undergraduate and graduate classes in children's literature. Both Mitzi and Chris have teachers and prospective teachers interview groups of students and create focused studies with colleagues based on student interests and wonderings. Nearly all of the teachers and preservice teachers talk about being overwhelmed at the beginning of creating a focused study. What's surprising is that many students are not distressed by the length of the study, but rather by creating their own curriculum. There has been such a trend to "teach from the textbooks," that many are unsure and scared about how it would be possible to create such curriculum based on kids' interests. By working in groups, they soon find that thinking together is a resource that really pays off. For example, in Mitzi's class, Samantha Berkowitz (2010) wrote:

> My initial thoughts were that creating a focused study would be tedious work that would be time consuming, not work that would be enjoyable and valuable. Given the opportunity to choose any topic to research sounds like it should be an easy task, but in reality it was not so easy. Who would think that freedom of choice would be so difficult? It certainly was for me and it really forced my group members and me to brainstorm ideas. Things changed as I began to inquire about the project, asking specific questions and finding a topic of interest. I became excited to jump into this focused study as soon as possible.
>
> My group and I spent many hours on this project but it did not feel like a burden since the subject matter was one that really interests me. I learned several things along the way. I learned that the focusing questions are not questions directed to be answered in one simplistic way. In the beginning of the project I was creating questions that addressed only one concern and had one answer. I also learned that it is ok to make mistakes along the way. I also challenged myself to come up with ideas that were creative and interesting. After the completion of this focused study, I learned that this process of choice and not explicit direction is actually quite effective and a strong motivator for the student to work hard.

Working With Linguistically and Culturally Diverse Learners

In her work on author studies, Megan Hillegass (2005) makes a point of discussing how author studies provide a way to reach all students, especially reluctant, struggling, or marginalized readers. "When the focus is on the author and not the level of the book, all students can feel successful, involved, and interested in choosing books" (p.5). This is also true for focused and genre studies. It is always possible to have books on a variety of levels available for students and what's most important is that they find a book they can connect with to read and then contribute to class discussions and projects. The focus is not on levels, but the content of the books. This type of curriculum does not separate more proficient readers from less proficient ones, as often happens in schools. Instead everyone can read and contribute.

On the other hand, we find that students can often read at higher levels than we expect. Giving a student a book that is rich with illustrations and on a topic of her particular interest in the focused study can provide the clues needed for a young person to read beyond our and her expectations. Jerry notes how he has seen groups of boys that are drawn to informational texts working together relentlessly to figure out meanings. This can also happen with buddy reading. Our point is that even though focused studies provide the opportunities for bringing in books at a variety of levels, our job is to continue to help students push past the often artificial boundaries that define what they can read.

For students whose primary language is other than English, focused studies are a natural. Books can be available for students in a variety of languages. For example, author Alma Flor Ada has a number of books that are written in Spanish and English. Her books can serve as texts for author studies on immigration, being true to yourself, Latino folk tales, Latino holidays, and Latino daily life. She, like other authors with a wide variety of books, can become the focus of an author study.

Technology Extensions and Electronic Resources

Electronic resources are helpful for finding materials for focused studies. Author websites, genre study websites, topical websites, and YouTube videos are all wonderful resources for focused studies. Also, there are a number of websites that list bibliographies of books by topics (*Reading Rockets, Teachers @ Random, Apples 4 the Teacher*). Even online bookstores have proven to be extremely helpful in finding focused study books. In addition, there are many new digital publishing companies like Push Pop Press that bring books to life on computers, smart phones, and digital tablets.

With technology progressing at a rapid pace, video cameras coming down in price, and the advent of fairly easy movie production software such as iMovie, more and more teachers are having students create video presentations to share what they have learned in focused studies with their class, other classes in the school, parents, and the community. Some of these productions have ended up as public service announcements.

Assessment

There are a number of ways to assess focused, author, and genre studies. The devices students keep for organizing and sharing during the study are ready made for self, peer, or teacher assessment. The same goes for the products and/or presentations that are part of the study's culminating experience.

One of the best ways we know of assessing focused studies is through an audit trail or **Learning Wall** (Vasquez, 2004). The learning wall is a place where students and the teacher negotiate what artifacts to put on the wall that best reflect what the class has been learning, studying, and wondering about. Because of the public nature of the learning wall, students can reflect on, revisit, and analyze the learning that's happened in the classroom. This allows them to make informed decisions about where to go next in the study, a critical dimension of assessment. Early on in her book *Negotiating Critical Literacies with Young Children*, Vasquez points to an interview with Frank McCourt where he said, "nothing is significant until you make it significant" (as cited in Vasquez, 2004, p. xv). That's one of the notable aspects of a learning wall—the process of learning is made significant by putting it on the wall. Students, teachers, and parents can step back and examine the curriculum in ways that are usually lost because there is no public record of it. Figure 6.1 shows an example of a learning wall.

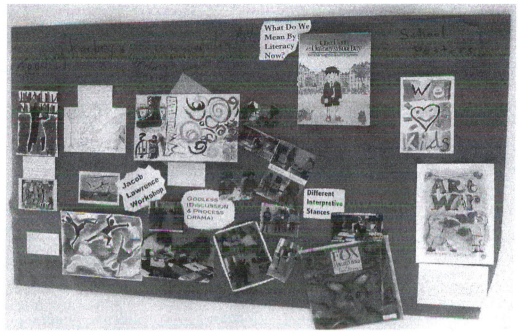

FIGURE 6.1.   Learning Wall (Anchorage, Alaska).

In addition, here are some questions that can be helpful in evaluating focused studies.

Textbox 6.3. Assessment

- During focused, author, and genre studies do students generate questions that lead to future studies?
- How engaged are students during the study?
- What new information and knowledge is generated during the study?
- How willing are students to present what they've learned to others outside of their classroom?
- How enthusiastic are students to start the next focused study?

Invitation: Illustrator Study

Illustrator studies are a great way for small groups of students to study an illustrator they find fascinating. They are great for any kid to engage in, but we have found them especially useful for reluctant and marginalized readers. Students are focusing on books, but pay special attention to the pictures (see Textbox 6.4).

Textbox 6.4. Invitation: Illustrator Study

Illustrator studies focus on the multimodal aspects of books, the shifting importance of illustrations and text, and the techniques used by particular illustrators. These studies work best if students have identified their favorite illustrators. A great resource to use in this invitation is the book *Artist to Artist: 23 Major Illustrators Talk to Children about their Art* (Carle, Mitumasa, & Blake, 2007). It's an anthology of children's literature illustrators that documents their individual stories. Each story contains information as to why they became a children's book illustrator, early sketches of their work, current self-portraits, and photographs of their art studios.

Materials & Procedures

- Sets of books by illustrators that students have identified as their favorites. These might include books illustrated by David Diaz, Kevin Henkes, Betsy Lewin, David Macaulay, Brian Pinkney, Jerry Pinkney, Chris Raschka, David Wiesner, Eric Carle, and others.
- A computer which students can use to find the websites of these illustrators or sites that are created about the artists.

1. In groups, students study the books of their illustrator and look for commonalities, differences, and surprises in the illustrations. They keep notes and describe what they notice about the style, tone, mood, and messages of the illustrations and how the illustrator uses line, color, shapes, etc.
2. On the Internet, students find biographical information about the illustrator and how they create their illustrations.
3. We adapted the following questions created by the Saskatoon Public Schools that can aid students in their illustrator study:
   o What things do you find in the visual text that are not present in the written text and visa versa?
   o What aspects are similar or overlap between the written and visual texts? Why do you think the author/illustrator made these choices?
   o What aspects differ greatly between written and visual texts?
   o How do the two meaning systems work together? (Saskatoon Public Schools (2004–09) http://olc.spsd.sk.ca/DE/pd/instr/strats/picturebooks/index.html).
4. Students may want to try out the style of the illustrator they are studying by creating their own artwork.
5. The group decides how they will present what they have found out about their illustrator to the rest of the class.

Professional Development

One of the most successful activities we've done in teacher study groups and in college classrooms is for teachers to work with their classes to create a focused, author, or genre study. The study group serves a number of purposes. It can be a place where teachers can find:

- suggestions for activities for the study;
- ideas for resources and books;
- feedback on student work they bring in to share;
- possible solutions for problems they present to the group; and
- help on assessing final student products.

Table 6.1 provides a list of professional articles for further reading.

TABLE 6.1. Suggestions for Further Reading

Focused Study	Genre Study	Author Study
Silvers, P., Shorey, M., & Crafton, L. (2010) Critical literacy in a primary multiliteracies classroom: The hurricane group. *Journal of Early Childhood Literacy, 10*(1), 379–409.	Damico, J.S. (2005) Evoking heads and hearts: Exploring issues of social justice through poetry. *Language Arts, 83*, 137–146.	Frost, S. & Sibberson, F. (2005) Author studies, *School Talk, 10*, 1–3.
This qualitative study describes how young children engage in multiple literacies while exploring personal inquiries about Hurricane Katrina in New Orleans, LA. The article illustrates the ability of children to ask critical questions, explore alternative perspectives, and engage in multimodal responses to construct and communicate meaning as they take social action.	This article describes the effectiveness of using poetry in a fifth grade classroom with students who initially saw poetry as "sappy." Through various poems and activities, these students came to see how poetry can be a catalyst for a provocative inquiry question such as, "What does it mean to be American?"	This issue of school talk has articles and ideas by Ralph Fletcher, Aimee Buckner, and Megan Hillegass. It covers author studies from a number of angles, including the perspectives of book authors and teachers. There are lots of practical ideas on how to conduct an author study.

seven

Multimodal Responses to Literature

Throughout history, the arts have provided humankind with ways to make and share meaning within and across communities. As cultures and technologies have changed and expanded, people continue to use visual arts, music, drama, dance, language, and other expressive modes to generate new ideas and pass them on to others. From a meaning-making perspective, a good language arts program should expand each and every student's communication potential.

Because the arts are so powerful in opening up new communicative channels, we draw on them as a way of encouraging both children and the teachers with whom we work to consider multiple perspectives. For example, at a summer institute in Toronto, we focused on how children's literature and the arts might be brought together to identify and respond to difficult social issues in today's world. We began by reading *Uptown* (Collier, 2000), a children's book that celebrates New York City, and followed up this reading by inviting participants to celebrate the greater Toronto area. Each participant created a page illustrating what he or she loves about this city. Sharing their views on highlights of their city helped participants to enjoy the experience. Since we also wanted them to dig deeply, we moved beyond the initial experience by asking them to identify areas of the city that were not represented and people who were left out.

Each day we deepened the discussion by introducing children's books that invited further conversations about people who were more or less invisible in participants' neighborhoods. For example, *A Street Called Home* (Robinson, 1997) calls attention to the "Shoe Shine Man" and the "Chicken Lady," people who might not be thought of as important or influential members of a community. Similarly, *Crow Boy* (Yashima, 1976) gave us an opportunity to talk about children who are marginalized in our schools. The book *King & King* (de Hann & Nijland, 2003) invited conversations about gay, lesbian, and transgendered youth who are often targets for

125

harassment and violence. *The Lady in the Box* (McGovern, 1997) opened up the topic of homelessness, another social issue that is rarely brought up in official school curricula. *Seven Brave Women* (Hearne, 1997) afforded us the opportunity to talk about gender inequities. *Going Home* (Bunting, 1996) brought up the issue of immigrants and the difficulties of having allegiance to two cultures. *Dave the Potter* (Hill, 2010) opened the door to a conversation about racism and about minority groups that are largely invisible in society, yet have talents that contribute significantly to the community. *Your Move* (Bunting, 1998) encouraged group members to think about gangs and why they are so appealing to many young people.

To help participants further develop the ideas that these important conversations brought to the surface, we asked them to create **Art Trading Cards** representing social issues that were important to them. Art trading cards are miniature works of art created on 2 ½ × 3 ½ inch card stock. The idea behind art trading cards is that these small pieces of art represent you—your "signature" as an artist and as a citizen. We invited participants to make their art trading cards using any kind of media, material, or artistic technique they wished. Figure 7.1 shows two examples of cards that participants created. Both cards deal with issues of identity. The first card speaks to the issue of diversity by using the colors of the rainbow to advocate for gay, lesbian and transgendered youth. The second card addresses the issue of multiple identities and how each of us is simultaneously gendered (*mommy*), labeled (*teacher, goddaughter*), and named (*Vivian, Flip, Podcaster*). This artist also included *alien* as that was how she perceived her treatment when she arrived in Canada as a new immigrant, despite that fact that she spoke perfect English. As one of several culminating activities in this institute, participants exchanged art cards with the artist's name and contact information on the back so that colleagues who had common interests could keep in contact as they continued to address social issues in their local school districts.

Given our changing world, it should not be surprising that our definition of the arts has to change along with our definition of literacy more generally. Today there are new ways to communicate beyond language, art, music, and dance. Literacy scholars frequently talk about *sign systems* as a way of showing that several complex meaning systems are simultaneously involved in a communicative event. Language, art, music, dance, drama, and movement are all systems of communication unto themselves in that they have an outward form as well as syntax

FIGURE 7.1.   Art Trading Cards:
Card 1—Gay, Lesbian & Transgendered Youth
Card 2—Multiple Identities.
Used with permission of the artist, Vivian Vasquez.

or ways of stringing these forms together. Within each system, meaning is conveyed by both the form used and the way that form is put into play. For example, size is an important element in the art trading card showing that gay, lesbian, and transgendered youth have more similarities than differences to each other and the larger population. The trading card focusing on multiple identities relies more on words than artistic elements to express the artist's intended meaning. Given these complexities, it is not surprising that today's literacy scholars use the shorthand notation *sign systems* to talk about the complexity of communication systems involved in media literacies, visual literacies, and even hybrid or evolving literacies (like hip hop) that highlight performance in the form of music, drama, language, poetry and dance.

The process of moving between and among language and art, language and music, and other ways of knowing is referred to as ***Transmediation*** (Suhor, 1984; Leland & Harste, 1994) and has been shown to generate new ideas and in-depth understandings (Albers and Harste, 2007; Siegel, 1984, 1995; Whitin, 1996). Siegel defines transmediation as "the process of translating meanings from one sign system (such as language) into another (such as pictorial representation)" (1995, p. 456). So, after reading a book like *More than Anything Else* (Bradby, 1995) that tells the story of Booker T. Washington learning to read, a teacher can invite students to represent what they think the story means using clay rather than through writing. Since students need to take what they understood from reading and transfer this understanding into a visual form, this is an instance of transmediation. Figure 7.2 shows the representations two students made of this book. In the first image, the student used a rather large chunk of clay and said, when asked, that this was her image of Booker T. Washington, an unmovable force in his pursuit of literacy. The student who created the second sculpture said that these were the skulls of all the members of Booker T. Washington's heritage crying out from their graves about the injustice of not being taught to read.

While language may still be the central sign system in language arts classrooms, the arts are integral to the processes of expanding communication and supporting oral and written language learning. We believe that in order to expand everyone's communication potential, the arts—in all their expressive forms—need to become a seamless part of the reading and language arts curriculum. This chapter highlights examples of how children's literature can be a vehicle for integrating the arts throughout the curriculum.

FIGURE 7.2.   Clay Representations of Booker T. Washington.
Used with permission of the artist, Peggy Albers.

Principle 1: The Arts Provide New Access to Literacy

One day when she was teaching second grade, Becky Lane read *Sylvester and the Magic Pebble* (Steig, 1969) aloud and then asked her students to use art to show what the story meant to them. Instead of talking and writing about the story as they usually did, Becky used **Sketch to Stretch**, a strategy that invited them to sketch what they personally thought the story meant. Chris was in Becky's classroom that day collecting field notes. She noticed that while most of the children appeared to be listening with interest while Becky was reading the story, one student (David) seemed to be paying more attention to a knot in his shoelace than to the story. When Becky finished reading and the other children eagerly began to draw, David stated that he did not know what the story meant to him and he did not know what to draw. Chris pulled up a chair and began to chat with the other kids in David's group.

In *Sylvester and the Magic Pebble,* a young donkey finds a magic pebble and accidentally makes a wish that turns him into a rock. Since he cannot wish himself back into a donkey without touching the pebble, he is stuck on a hillside and everyone gives up looking for him. Some children in David's group said they were drawing pictures of what they would wish for if they had a magic pebble. Others were drawing pictures of their families to express their feeling of how lonely they would be without them. They all agreed that it must have been terrible for Sylvester to be left alone like he was. David listened to the others but did not jump in and say that he felt the same way. Finally, he shook his head, sighed deeply, and said he would draw a picture of a time when he went camping.

Chris wondered how a camping trip would connect to the story but she decided to wait and see what David came up with. When she came back ten minutes later, she was surprised to find David hard at work on what was turning out to be a very detailed drawing of a tent, a tree, a squirrel, a storm cloud, and a boy cooking a hotdog over an open fire. The more he drew, the more enthusiastic and animated he became. When David started talking about his picture, the connections to the book were both obvious and surprising. While his classmates all seemed to regard the experience of being alone as something negative, David remembered how much he had enjoyed camping out by himself. He said he had a big family and they lived in a small apartment. "You know," he observed in a way that showed wisdom beyond his years, "sometimes it's nice to be alone" (Leland & Harste, 1995, p. 21). At the bottom of the picture he wrote, "It was fun. I had food!! I was alone!"

It's impossible to know whether David would have gotten as much out of this read aloud if he had not been given the opportunity to draw. We might hypothesize that engaging in art provided space for him to think more deeply about how the story connected to his life. While he was not immediately excited about drawing, engaging in it seemed to help him to remember the happiness he felt when he was camping on his own. It's also possible that just giving David an opportunity to figure out what he wanted to say made a positive difference. In either case, we think David's experience can serve as a reminder that multimodal responses are more than a nice "extra" in our literacy program. In some cases, they provide the means for students to create new identities and get their voices heard.

Gaining access through multiple art forms. A large body of research suggests that infusing the arts into all areas of the curriculum expands students' ability to communicate what they know and how they came to know it. Sanders and Albers (2010) suggest that when people have genuine questions and a desire to "try out different digital, visual, musical, spatial, dramatic (and so on) tools and techniques, they have the potential to say and do things that we have never before imagined" (p. 3).

Labbo's research (2006) makes a similar point. Providing opportunities to linger in text by using multiple art forms supports the taking on of multiple perspectives. Whitin (1996) asked students to sketch what they made of the texts they read over the course of a year. She found that even reluctant seventh grade readers grew by leaps and bounds. Importantly, students in both these research studies experienced for themselves that first draft thinking is not always their best thinking. Changing the lens allows us to think differently and come to different—and often more thoughtful—conclusions.

Martens, Martens, Croce, and Maderazo (2010) show how the integration of art instruction and reading instruction can support children in making meaning from picture books. They report a study in which the art teacher and reading teacher worked together with a group of third graders who were exploring picture books. The authors provide many examples of how children used art to help them construct meaning and conclude "students' comprehension was enhanced by studying art as a language" (p. 188). For example, after talking with students about how artists express the concepts of fear or danger through line and color, they observed that the children were trying out similar techniques as they used art to respond to other books. Their data show that the art lessons gave children in their study a new way of enjoying, digging deeper, and talking back to books.

Making meaning through different fonts. Some authors of picture books use different forms of typesetting to convey meaning. For example, the text in *Fox* (Wild, 2001) looks like something a young child might have produced. The letters are not uniform and the words are placed in various locations on the pages instead of in neat sections like in most books. This challenges the dominant discourse of how picture books are constructed and sets readers up for a different type of experience than they might have been expecting. In another example, *Click, Clack, Moo: Cows that Type* (Cronin, 2000) the text includes notes that look like they could have been typed on an old typewriter—and maybe by cows! *The Three Pigs* by David Weisner (2001) goes even further in challenging conventional forms. The story is told and illustrated in a way that makes it look like the characters are actually falling off the page and landing in different stories than the ones in which readers expect to find them. In this version of the familiar folktale, the pigs escape from the wolf by exiting the story and then reappearing later with a dragon they brought back with them from another story to protect them. One meaning readers might take away from all of these books is that nothing is permanent and traditional understandings are always subject to revision.

The use of different fonts can also be seen as a strategy for conveying meaning in texts (Hasslett, 2009). When fourth grade teacher Julie Copeland read *Voices in the Park* (Browne, 1998) to her class, the kids were fascinated with the way the fonts used for each of the four characters seemed to go with their personalities. They noted that the font used for Charles, the shy boy at the park with his bossy mother, was very light in comparison to the fonts used for the other characters. "It's like his voice is so soft that nobody can hear him," one of them observed. Others noted that the font used for Smudge, the friendly daughter of the out-of-work father, looked like something written by a kid who liked to have fun. Later in the literacy period that morning, Julie observed two children who were writing their own invitation on gender stereotypes. At first she was concerned that they were spending so much time finding an appropriate "boy font" and "girl font," but then she remembered the conversation about fonts in *Voices in the Park*. By the end of the work time, the children had designed what they called a stereotypical "girl font" with curling letters and intertwined hearts as well as a solid looking "boy font" with blocky letters and a clip art football helmet. Clearly the children were following Browne's example in thinking about how to make meaning multimodally as they challenged their classmates to think about gender in a new way.

Gaining access through music and dance. Other students might benefit from being encouraged to use music and dance to make sense of texts. There are a number of books that are written lyrically in an attempt to capture the flow and feel of music. Among our favorites are *Jazz on a Saturday Night* (Dillon & Dillon, 2007), *Rap a Tap Tap: Here's Bojangles – Think of That!* (Dillon & Dillon, 2002), *Hip Hop Speaks to Children* (Giovanni, 2008), *The Jazz Fly* (Gollub, 2000), *Bring on that Beat* (Isadora, 2002), *Who Bop?* (London, 2000), and *Bebop Express* (Panahi, 2005). Some books on jazz and the blues, for example, come packaged with CDs of the songs mentioned in the book. By talking about the feelings this music evokes and how the musician creates this mood, children gain a heightened understanding of not only the text but of history and their own cultural heritage. Texts that come with CDs include *Gershwin's Rhapsody in Blue* (Celenza, 2006), *The Jazz Fly* (Gollub, 2000), *Hot Jazz Special* (Hannah, 2005), *God Bless the Child* (Holiday & Herzog, 2003), *Ben's Trumpet* (Isadora, 1979), *Jazz* (Myers, 2006), and *No Man Can Hinder Me: The Journey from Slavery to Emancipation through Song* (Thomas, 2001).

To support the movement from language to music and vice versa, Jerry brought Orff Schuluerk musical instruments to the Center for Inquiry school in Indianapolis. After having a **Written Conversation** about a story that had been read aloud, students were invited to have a **Musical Conversation** about the same story. In written conversation students take a single sheet of paper and pass it back and forth as they talk about and make sense of a story just read. In musical conversation, students translate their meaning into a conversational set of musical sounds. We found that books with two distinct voices worked best. For example, *Little Blue and Little Yellow* (Lionni, 1995) share wonderful adventures. One day they can't find one another. When they finally meet, they are overjoyed and hug until they become green. Before beginning the musical conversation students can experiment with sound patterns to represent the two colors, the adventures they had together, and the climax of turning green. A third student might be enlisted to read the story as they accompany the reading with their musical composition. While any set of musical instruments can be used, we have achieved the most success using Orff Schuluerk and Zuzuki Orff xylophones that produce harmonized sounds.

Musical can also be used to support your writing program. *Once upon an Ordinary School Day* (McNaughton, 2005) tells the story of an ordinary boy who has an unordinary school day when an extraordinary teacher invites students to listen to music and then write about what they heard. While the book can be criticized in that it implicitly suggests that all instructional problems would be solved if teachers just added a little music to their instruction, it is, nonetheless, one step any teacher might take to put a new edge on learning.

Just as music has been found to help children understand new concepts, it also provides new lenses for older learners. After assigning reading about different approaches to professional development for teachers (Hawkins, 2008), Chris invited her college students to transmediate the text in any sign system they wished. While many students elected to draw or use clip art to show how they made meaning from the text, others opted for different forms like drama, poetry, and dance. *Brandon and Mike's X470 Interpretive Dance* (see http://www.youtube.com/watch?v=oVBNOPB7UjY) was created by two young men after doing the reading and searching for music that would support the points they wanted to make. In an interview after performing their dance, they explained that the key idea for them was the need for teachers to experience professional development that transforms their practice. In Hawkins' chapter, this kind of development is contrasted with the old training model that just tells them what to do. To show the traditional model, Mike (representing a teacher) makes the same movement over and over like he is beating on something. While that is going on, Brandon (representing a student) just sits there looking frustrated. He holds up a card with a D on it to show he is not doing well academically. When Brandon takes off his glasses, he enters into the role of another teacher and the dance now represents the transformative model. They move all around the classroom to show the importance of building community and collaborating to generate and share new ideas.

Then Brandon puts the glasses back on and goes back into the student role. But this time instead of talking at the student, the teacher is working with him and they are both enthusiastic. The project they are working on is a joint effort. At the end, the student holds up a card with an A on it to show that he is now achieving academic success.

After these students performed, audience members were invited to share what they thought the dance was attempting to communicate. The performers were encouraged to put on their "game faces" (not agree or disagree) while the other students thought aloud about what they had seen and what it might mean. The hypotheses ranged widely and the ensuing discussion was insightful. At the end of the class, a departing student was overheard telling a friend that she now understood the article "a hundred times better" than before she had seen everyone's transmediation. "It's like they all explained it to me in different ways. And some of them saw things I didn't notice when I read it."

Principle 2: Drama Supports Digging Deeply

As is evident in the instructional engagements already discussed, the arts can and do support a deeper understanding of text. In no instance is this more obvious than when children engage in drama. ***Process Drama*** invites students to use drama to make meaning of a text. Participants are asked to step into the text world and use their life experiences and their ways of knowing to make sense of what is happening as a text unfolds (Edmiston & Enciso, 2002; Enciso, 2011; O'Neill, 1995; Miller & Saxton, 2004). Students often enact alternate interpretations and in this fashion come to see the consequences of various actions.

Process drama uses a variety of techniques such as role playing, creating a still-life tableau, and conducting mock courtroom dramatizations in which key characters are put on trial as participants try to get to the bottom of an issue. What is important to remember is that dramatizations are not final interpretations, but rather in-process thought pieces meant to invite everyone to think more deeply and often more critically about a text (Ellsworth, 2005). Process drama can be used with readers at any level. We think it is especially helpful for those who seem to be having difficulty comprehending what they are reading, who seem to be detached from what they are reading, or who find it hard to imagine themselves in text. Teachers have found that acting out a scene initially helps students notice details that have been overlooked, and that these "noticings" often enhance comprehension.

Wayne Serebrin and Pauline Broderick (2009) used process drama to support their second grade students' understanding of *The Teddy Bear* (McPhail, 2002). This is the story of a young boy who loses his favorite teddy bear and then finds it much later in the hands of a homeless man. After arguing that it is his teddy bear, he ultimately decides that the homeless man needs it more than he does. By taking on this dilemma, the book provides an exploration of morality, ethics, and inequity in our society while capturing some of the tensions involved in everyday life.

In preparing for their use of process drama, Wayne and Pauline gave students time to view the illustrations closely and to comment on their observations. Students were encouraged to notice everything they could and to describe the images they saw and possible relationships among the images. To invite students to think deeply about the visual images in the text, open-ended questions were used: "Why do you think the boy and teddy bear are in the center of the illustration?" "Why do you think the artist chose these particular colors for the cover?" One of the things children noticed was that the book was set in a park. To support students in drawing on what they know about parks, Wayne and Pauline invited students to form small groups and create a ***Tableau***—a still picture using their faces, body positions, posture, gestures, space between themselves, etc.—to depict their experiences of what they do or have observed others do in a park.

Once all of the groups were ready, one group at a time presented their tableau to the rest of the class. As each group "froze" in position, the other students were invited to share what they saw in the tableau. Wayne and Pauline used the following questions: What are the characters doing? Can you tell who they are? How old are they? Are they related? How are they feeling? Their intent was to slow down the viewing experience and to invite students to observe nuances and details. As a culmination of the tableau experience students revisited the front cover illustration of *The Teddy Bear* to see what else they noticed after having time to think about their own and others' experiences in a park.

At this point, Pauline read the first part of the text. After talking about what additional things they learned about the story from reading these first few pages, the teachers introduced a strategy called **Student in Role** and invited participants to become a character in the story, portraying that person's actions and speaking his or her lines. Students were also told to be thinking about what they thought was on their character's mind, but left unsaid, at the time of the illustration. Wayne and Pauline then introduced **Tapping In**, the strategy of tapping on a student's shoulder to invite that student to share his or her thoughts and feelings. Students were invited to ask characters any question they wished. Some asked the mother and father characters how they felt when they found out their son lost his teddy bear. One student asked if they saw it as teaching their son a lesson about taking care of his belongings.

The next section that Pauline read told about the life the teddy bear had with the homeless man and how at times he felt afraid and lonesome, yet loved. The teachers stopped the story at this point and invited children to create a **Soundscape** that they described as a "sound picture." Students formed groups and generated the sounds (yells, rhythms, city noises) the teddy bear might be hearing. They also talked about smells as the homeless man and the teddy bear slept in a dumpster. During and after sharing, children talked about what effect this environment might have on the teddy bear and how it differed from his life with the boy.

While a more complete description of this group of second graders' experiences using process drama is on our website (www.routledge.com/cw/leland), we hope this description of how teachers used process drama while reading aloud is enough to give you a feel for process drama and why it is so powerful. When teachers are familiar with more of the forms process drama can take, there is no better tool for digging deeply into texts.

Principle 3: The Arts Support Readers in Taking a Critical Stance

In our book *Creating Critical Classrooms* (Lewison et al., 2008), we outline the social practices we see as important for citizens in the 21st century to have. The specific social practices we wish to develop are students' abilities to disrupt commonplace assumptions, interrogate multiple viewpoints, see things in their sociopolitical context and take action to promote social justice. For us, a critical stance entails being consciously aware and engaged, entertaining alternate ways of being, taking responsibility to inquire, and being reflective. In this chapter, we address the question of how the arts can support teachers and students in developing a critical stance.

Disrupting the commonplace. Children's literature can support students in becoming aware of the underlying systems of meaning that are operating in texts. These systems are usually taken for granted by readers. Readers have a tendency to see them as given, or something that is beyond questioning. In the children's book *Willy and Hugh* (Browne, 2000), for example, the topic is bullying. Few readers question the fact that Hugh is shown in the illustrations as a big male who looks like a bully because, for most of us, he fits our stereotype of bullies. At this point in the story, the illustration perpetuates this stereotype by not making the assumed bully character a smaller male or a female. As we read on, we learn that Hugh is not a bully, so the stereotype does get challenged in terms of suggesting that not everyone who looks like a bully really is one. One part of becoming critically literate is to learn to question underlying assumptions and stereotypes such as these. This is a mindset that has to be learned.

Kate Kuonen's eighth graders used drama to disrupt several commonplace beliefs as part of an instructional strategy called ***Interpretive Stances*** (Bleich, 1993; Lewison et al., 2008). Kate introduced the short story *The Lady and the Tiger* (Stockton, 1982) and assigned small groups of students to design a transmediation for one of the interpretive stances this strategy describes: philosophical, aesthetic, critical, analytical, metaphorical. This classic tale tells the story of an unfortunate princess who is forced by her father to end her relationship with the man she loves. The king gives her a choice for how she wants the end to come, but both options are unappealing. She can watch as her lover gets ripped apart by a vicious tiger or she can watch him marry a "lovely maiden" and ride off joyfully to start his new life with her instead of with the princess. The group that was assigned critical stance used drama to show jealousy, love, rage, and other emotions they thought characters in this story would have felt. One part of their dramatization featured a student in role as the princess criticizing her father for treating her so unfairly and arguing passionately for the freedom to make her own life choices. In another scene, the boy who was acting as the tiger charged out of his cage looking fierce, but then sat innocently licking himself and making no attempt to harm anyone. In this one instance of drama, students challenged dominant cultural beliefs about vicious animals and parent/child relationships (Leland, Ociepka, & Kuonen, 2012).

In working with teachers in Toronto, Jerry brought in what the teachers thought looked like innocent children's books and asked them to unpack the underlying systems of meaning that were operating. The result was that teachers learned consciously to engage and question what others might take for granted. Peggy Albers later initiated a similar project with teachers in Georgia. Instead of concentrating on the language of the text, Peggy asked teachers to identify only those stereotypes that were illustrated in the pictures accompanying the text (Albers, Harste, & Vasquez, 2011). What was interesting was that the dominant stereotype in each book was reinforced both in the text as well as in the illustration. In no case is this more obvious than in *Woolbur* (Helakoski, 2008), the story of a sheep who marches to the beat of a different drummer. It builds on assumptions—sheep are followers; artistic types are weird. All of the stereotypes of a free spirit are here. Woolbur is off on his own. Woolbur dresses unconventionally. Woolbur hangs out with a very different "flock." Table 7.1 lists two books that were used in this study and some of the stereotypes that were questioned.

Interrogating multiple viewpoints. An easy way for teachers to support students in considering multiple viewpoints on a topic is through the use of ***Text Sets***, an instructional strategy we introduced earlier in this volume. For example, a text set on war might include some books that show the futility of war and others that glorify the weaponry of war and our national achievements. In this case, students are offered alternate viewpoints and have to make their own decisions.

Another way that teachers can support students in taking an alternate look at a topic is by inviting them to think about the topic through the perspective of art, music, dance, or any number of different sign systems, including mathematics. The teachers at the Center for Inquiry in Indianapolis opened one school year with a focused study called Celebrating Indianapolis. This study invited students to explore two important questions: What does Indianapolis look like from the perspective of art? What does Indianapolis sound like from the perspective of

TABLE 7.1.   Examples of Unexamined Stereotypes Found in Children's Literature

Children's Literature Book	Stereotypes in Need of Interrogation
Sister Anne's Hands (Lorbiecki, 2000)	Being a minority member in a dominant culture causes problems. Teachers should be of the same ethnicity as the students they teach. Parents don't have to worry about what they say in front of children.
Into the Forest (Browne, 2004)	Intact families give children security; single-parent families, absent father families, or broken families are associated with fear, anxiety, and insecurity. Girls need protection; boys can be left on their own. Mothers stay at home; fathers don't. Boys ignore rules. Women (girls) are nurturers; men (boys) are not. Old women (grandmothers) are both weak and fragile. Children are lost and rather helpless without an adult around.

music? Teachers were amazed to find that student responses to these questions gave almost every viewer a new take on what Indianapolis as a city had to offer.

Fortunately there are several children's books that teachers can use to support readers in thinking about their world in terms of the arts. Bob Raczka's book, *No One Saw* (2001) invites students to explore ordinary things through the eyes of artists. *Art Is* (Raczka, 2003) expands what students might consider or not consider to be art. *More than Meets the Eye* (Raczka, 2003) invites students to rethink their world by using all five of their senses.

Seeing things in a sociopolitical context. One way to address this topic is to ask students how they might use art to change the world in positive ways. A French artist who simply goes by the name of J.R. had a project entitled Face to Face, in which he went to nations in conflict with each other, like Israel and Palestine. J.R. took pictures of people from each nation performing the same jobs (cab drivers, telephone operators, waitresses, businessmen) and had these photographs blown up so they were huge (over 12' high). Then he hung them side-by-side on buildings, arenas and underpasses—anywhere that provided a viewing wall. Despite the fact that Israel and Palestine were at war, most citizens couldn't identify which of the people were Israeli and which were Palestinian. This was true in both countries. While he never got on a soapbox to berate anyone about the Israeli-Palestinian conflict, his art sent a powerful message that invited viewers to rethink their stance. For a video on his work see http://www.ted.com/talks/jr_s_ted_prize_wish_use_art_to_turn_the_world_inside_out.html).

Most of the children's literature we have listed online in our annotated bibliography raises important social issues. The secret is to find books that extend the conversations your students are having—whether they are about gangs, drugs, homelessness, racism, gender bias, bullying, or any other difficult issue. *I-Statement Charts* support the taking on of multiple perspectives as well as the identification of sociopolitical issues. Once such issues have been identified, students can be invited to address the political issues they see as important by writing their own protest songs, coming up with their own public art project, or even putting together their own public service announcement.

Taking social action. Children's books in this category tell the stories of people taking social action to make their world better. Many of these books feature adults like Martin Luther King, Jr. (Rappaport, 2001) who helped to organize the civil rights movement in the United States or

Rachel Carson (Paladino, 1999) who brought the dangers of pesticides and the need for a more sustainable approach to agriculture into the public debate. *One More Border* (Kaplan, 1998) recounts the social action of Sugihara, a Japanese diplomat stationed in Lithuania during World War II who saved the lives of many Jews by giving them visas to Japan. *The Butterfly* (Polacco, 2000) is another book about people taking action during the Nazi Holocaust. In this story, a French family protects a Jewish family that is hiding in their home.

There are also many books about children taking social action. In *The Day the Earth Was Silent* (McGuffee, 1997), some sixth graders make a flag honoring Earth Day. While the book ends with the flag being put away and people going about their daily business, the suggestion is there that a basic change in attitude worldwide has taken place. *The Streets are Free* (Kurusa, 2008) documents the story of children in the barrios of San Jose, Venezuela, coming together to advocate for a playground. Children take action in *Si, Se Puede!* (Cohn, 2002) by joining with striking workers to demand change. Books focusing on children advocating for civil rights include *White Socks Only* (Coleman, 1996) and *The Story of Ruby Bridges* (Coles, 1995). These stories feature African American children who take action by defying longstanding practices of segregation.

Both the texts and illustrations in all of these books lend themselves to further study. How do artists show determination and courage through both words and pictures? How can art be used to challenge injustice and change the world? Whenever possible it is important to take social action that extends outside the schoolhouse walls. It is important that children see their books addressing real world issues and showing that each of us can make a difference. Because children, for the most part, are natural born artists, art in all its various forms provides ways for them to get their voices heard.

Key Issues in Implementation

The arts take too much time. While it is true that making instruction multimodal takes time, it is also true that it is time well spent. In this age of accountability it is easy to get caught up in covering the curriculum rather than uncovering curriculum. Just remember, you learn more from one good quality language encounter than from a hundred poorly designed language encounters.

The arts not only add enjoyment, they add a depth that is impossible, we believe, to reach without including them. While process drama and most other art-based engagements do take time, it is important to remember that students often are learning strategies they will use again when they encounter new texts. One criterion we use to judge our own teaching is to ask ourselves if what we are teaching is generative, that is, will it lead to further use another day or allow us to explore an upcoming issue even more deeply?

But I'm not comfortable teaching the arts. Many teachers feel intimidated by the arts. *Ish* (Reynolds, 2004) is a picture book every teacher should read. It tells the story of an artist who doesn't like his work and throws it away. His sister, however, retrieves his pieces and hangs them on the wall in her bedroom. When he goes to look, he finds that his vases do look "vase-ish," his flowers look "flower-ish," and his sunsets look "sunset-ish." Not only can this book help you get over your fear of the arts, but it can help your students get over whatever artistic blocks they too may have. Reynolds' book, *The Dot* (2003) works similar magic except, in this instance, the art work begins by making one simple mark, a dot!

For teachers, one starting point is letting children sketch in response to a book. Lorraine Spiteri, one of the teachers we worked with in Toronto, wrote on her blog that just allowing children to draw rather than write about the book they had read heightened interest in her reading program. Introducing clay as a medium to work with might be a harder step for you to take, but once you see how excited the children are to have some new kind of material to work with, you will be sold on it.

After first using what is readily available, we next recommend that you take stock of what talents you personally have. So often our own talents are never shared with students. Change this. Make sure that you bring your art into the classroom regardless of what that art is. If you play a musical instrument, bring it in and use your talent to extend a book discussion that involves music or dance. If you like to dance, find some books that have dance as a theme and share your love of this art form with the students. If you are a cook, share your cooking. If you knit, bring in your knitting. If you scrapbook, bring in your scrapbook. If you collect folk art, bring in your collection. The possibilities are endless. And remember, once you have tapped your own artistic talents, tap those of your students, their parents, and other teachers in your school.

Our last piece of advice is to give yourself and your students time. As Carolyn Burke reminds us, "No one became a professional without first being an amateur" (Harste, Short, w/ Burke, 1988, p. 186). This sound advice is worth posting on your white board!

Working With Linguistically and Culturally Diverse Learners

One of the big breakthroughs in our understanding of literacy was that there is no one universal definition of literacy or one universal way of becoming literate. Different groups of people define literacy differently just as different communities have their own ways of inducting their children into literacy (Street, 1995). This is evident even in picture books. Take a look at the children's book, *Pictures by Chinese Children* (NECA, 1976), which contains copies of the pictures that were on display at the National Exhibition of Children's Art in New York City. They are very different from what children in the United States would produce under similar circumstances. As is evident in these children's drawings, we now know that different cultural groups have different ways of knowing. While Europeans value language as a primary way of knowing—that is why some argue that our schools are "too verbocentric" (Siegel, 1995)— other cultural groups value art, music, dance and movement as dominant ways to mean. *The Cello of Mr. O* (Cutler, 1999) addresses this issue as does *The Harmonica* (Johnston, 2004). Both books tell stories of how important music is in their respective cultures during times of little hope.

Winnie the Witch (Thomas & Korky, 1990) is one our favorite curriculum books. Winnie keeps trying to get Wilbur, her cat, to fit with her home décor, much like we continue to think that children should fit into the way school currently is being conducted. Once Winnie decides to change her color scheme and support Wilbur in being the cat he is, they are able to live happily ever after. Similarly, the arts can help us reach students not currently being well served in schools.

Because public schools are meant to serve all students, it is important that we use a variety of communication forms to reach the wide variety of students we teach. Picture books are ideal as they give children new to English an opportunity to use their visual knowledge to propel their growth in language. Equally important, perhaps, is the variety of books now available.

Our experience tells us that no one becomes literate without first seeing himself or herself in literacy. Extending stories by inviting children to use technology, art, music, drama, dance, and mathematics not only gives students the opportunity to think deeply, but insures access to literacy for more students.

Technology Extensions and Electronic Resources

Along with music, drama, and art, technology also provides multimodal ways to support quality learning. Today's students bring a different set of experiences to school than their teachers did at their age. Technology has changed and continues to change the world in many ways. The question of how educators might redefine literacy to make it relevant for students in these changing times becomes urgent. "We must ask ourselves, what are the everyday literacies that learners bring into the classroom? How can I value and integrate these literacies into my own practice?" (Albers & Harste, 2007, p. 8).

In answer to these questions we think it's important to provide opportunities for students to use these new literacies in their daily work, including their responses to literature. For example, teachers who want their students to write about the book(s) they are reading might set up a protected online site and invite their students to blog, create web pages, and exchange messages about these books. One such site is Think.com, a protected online learning platform that allows individual classroom teachers to set up and monitor a global social networking site that is open only to them and other teachers and students who have joined the site. Think.com is a creation of the Oracle Educational Foundation, a nonprofit corporation (http://www.oraclefoundation. org/). In terms of new technologies, Think.com has numerous interactive components. Users can send messages to each other, set up a personal page, and post art, music, and video. There is also a tool for setting up surveys and keeping track of both the vote count and who has voted. One of the teachers Jerry worked with read parts of *The Best Art You've Never Seen: 101 Hidden Treasures from Around the World* (Spalding, 2010) to her class and used Think.com to invite students to contribute examples of off-beat art they thought had failed to receive the acclaim they deserved. Students contributed everything from pictures of their favorite skateboard to outfits they had designed themselves.

Fan fiction. Rebecca Black (2008) describes fan fiction as a growing Internet genre that involves readers taking stories and rewriting them, adding details, characters, and new adventures. Readers post their extensions of stories to fan fiction sites. Their postings are read by others who are interested in extending their own reading of the book. Black reports that extensions are worked over so often that they take on a life of their own. She also reports that students who explore fan fiction sites often find books they simply must locate and read. *The Hunger Games* series (Collins, 2010) is very popular among teenagers and has spawned a great deal of speculation as to sequels despite the fact that Collins has said that the three books making up this series, *The Hunger Games, Catching Fire,* and *Mockingjay* are more than enough.

Pop culture remixes. Knobel and Lankshear (2008) describe how students are using a process called remix to take cultural artifacts and manipulate them into "new kinds of creative blends" (p. 22). When working with literature, students might use remix to include music, visual images, YouTube videos, sounds, and animations in their responses. Using computers to blend any of these elements provides an opportunity for expressing ideas and making meaning. Teachers can easily make their own remixes, or have students make them, by using the Internet to search for a topic and then creatively combining the images found.

Vivian Vasquez put together a remix of *Little Red Riding Hood* images from books and advertisements (see our website). She put A-Moe's *Beauty and the Beast* soundtrack to the images using iMovie software. The results were fascinating and demonstrated how a literary cultural image was being used to manipulate consumers in critical ways. Pepsi presents *Little Red Riding Hood* as a hooded vampire and in so doing suggests that there is something really sexy and seductive about their product. Vampire books were the best sellers on the 2009–10 list of adolescent books, so Pepsi is also using knowledge of literature and the population they wish to reach by remixing and, in the process, getting consumers to remake their image.

While these are only a few examples of how technology might be used to support quality learning and instruction, it is important to notice that in each instance the teacher began by building off what children already knew. The technological literacies students bring to school are too important to be ignored. They are the basis upon which teachers create powerful instructional experiences. In each instance, teachers also helped students make connections as well as put together materials that would encourage them to explore what didn't make sense. By making the students' questions the focus of inquiry, everyone was able to expand their knowledge base and learn.

Teachers often argue that they are not comfortable using technology. While there are skills involved in mastering any art form or any new technology, our advice is that you not wait for the opportunity to make art and technology happen in your classroom. Suggest what you wish to learn to your school administrator as a possible inservice topic, take a workshop or, better yet, a course. Search the Internet, as there is a growing number of videos available which you can use by yourself or with your students. Rather than think about mastery, think about learning a new technology as expanding your communication potential and that of your students. Technology allows teachers to tap into the students' world by making learning new, current, and fun.

Assessment

One of the easiest ways to document the contributions that the arts are making to your literature program is to have children keep a *Sketchbook*. While a very inexpensive composition book works, we particularly like the 8 ½ × 11" bound black sketchbooks available at art stores and hobby shops. Children can use their sketchbooks to make written as well as visual responses to books. While a sketchbook can be divided into different sections (strategy lessons, personal responses to literature, group responses to literature, etc.), we have found it easier to use it as a daily running record. Digital photographs of work completed by groups involved in Sketch to Stretch, for example, can be included as well as students' reflections on that activity. Photographs taken during process drama can be added as well as digital printouts of blog sites and videos used or developed. If students are asked to record initial reflections on an activity, they later can be asked to revisit that experience once the digital photographs of their work or their group activities have been reproduced. *Picture This* is a strategy that asks students to reflect on a curricular engagement based on digital photographs taken while they were involved in the experience. These reflections capture ephemeral moments in curriculum, allowing students to monitor their own growth while also helping teachers fine tune future instructional experiences.

Even 3 × 5" cards such as those that might be produced by such strategies as *Quotable Quotes* and *Post Cards of the Mind* can be taped on adjoining pages in the Sketchbook for purposes of evaluation. We encourage children to use their artistic talents to make these books as attractive as possible and use them regularly for documenting growth as well as for sharing this growth with parents and administrators. Students, we have found, cherish their sketchbooks. We also use sketchbooks in our children's literature classes at the college level. Prospective teachers find their sketchbooks to be handy resources since they serve as reminders of how they might invite students to respond to books and of the curricular goals literature addresses.

Invitation: Through the Cracks

This invitation (see Textbox 7.1) asks you to read *Through the Cracks* (Sollman, 1994) to your class. While this book was written to encourage conversations about the potential effects of cuts in music and the arts on student learning, no real student voices are heard. This invitation not only brings students into the conversation, but also invites them to help you in your efforts to support everyone's learning in your classroom.

Textbox 7.1. Invitation: *Through the Cracks*

How do we create classrooms where everyone succeeds? How might the arts support alternate ways of knowing as well as a more inclusive school environment? While these are the kinds of topics professionals reserve for themselves to think about, *Through the Cracks* invites students to explore these important issues and contribute to this much needed conversation.

Materials & Procedures

- A copy of *Through the Cracks* (Sollman, 1994)
- Large sheets of paper
- Colored markers

1. After reading the book, form small groups and distribute markers and large sheets of paper. Ask students to:
   1. Describe some of your best learning moments.
   2. Discuss what these moments tell us about how we learn.
   3. Identify what sign systems (language, art, music, mathematics, drama, movement) were involved in the best learning moments.
2. Share student responses and discuss what can be concluded about creating a classroom where no one falls through the cracks.
3. End by having each student talk about what he or she might do to support everyone's learning in your classroom.

Professional Development

Totally tangled. Teachers can't do for students what they can't first do for themselves. This professional development activity is meant to challenge you as well as make you a bit uncomfortable. Our belief is that we have lots to learn by working in a sign system that is not necessarily our strength.

For this engagement you will need:

- art supplies (we recommend good watercolor paints and good watercolor brushes, but any art materials will do including markers, colored pencils, tempera paints, charcoal or pastel sticks, etc.);
- a stack of blank Art Trading Cards (2 ½ by 3 ½ on art paper, one for each participant);
- black, fine, felt-tipped pens or markers (one for each participant);
- Bob Raczka's book, *Here's Looking at Me: How Artists See Themselves* (2006). (Or any of the art books mentioned in this chapter can be substituted.)

Raczka presents 14 artists and their self-portraits, just enough to whet your appetite as to how you might represent yourself in portrait. Using the blank art trading cards provided, do a self-portrait without doing any preliminary drawings first. All you are going to do is lay down different colors side by side in the shape of a face.

Most likely you and your colleagues are not going to be totally happy with the results. To save this piece of art you are going to add a second layer of art on top of what you already have. Putting a new layer of art on top of an initial piece adds depth and often helps to clarify meaning. "Zentangles" is an art form created by artists Rick Robers and Maria Thomas as a tool to be used by artists and non-artists alike (Bartholomew Steen, 2010). Zentangles are very popular with

FIGURE 7.3. Totally Tangled—Watercolor Overlaid with Zentangles.

teens on the Internet. This art form involves creating complicated felt-tip line drawings (here is where the black, fine, felt-tipped pens come in) over the original images one line at a time. Simple tangles or complex patterns are combined in unplanned ways that take off in amazing directions. While there are stylized forms, they are easy to create on your own. Jerry maintains that he has saved many pieces of art by adding Zentangles around, over and on top of a first attempt. See Figure 7.3 for finished examples as well as a close up of basic Zentangle patterns.

In working with teachers in Toronto, Jerry had students sketch in response to a social issue picture book that was read. The next day he read the story again and this time asked teachers to add Zentangles to enhance and deepen their meaning. Adding art to art allowed him to read a good book a second time and gave his students time to think deeply about what they wanted to say. Vivian Vasquez worked with first graders exploring how best to grow tomatoes—the old fashioned way or the "topsy turvy" way (2011). After reading books and conducting experiments, she provided children with blank art trading cards and had them sketch their questions and concerns. As a culminating experience to this professional engagement, share the cards you have created and decide how you wish to use them to position yourself differently in the world. Table 7.2 provides a list of articles for further reading and is meant to support you in your efforts to keep multiple ways of knowing an ongoing topic of conversation in your school.

TABLE 7.2. Suggestions for Further Reading

Harste, J. (2011) Seamlessly art. In R.J. Meyer & K.F. Whitmore (Eds.), *Reclaiming reading.* Mahwah, NJ: Erlbaum.	Leland, C.H., & Harste, J.C. (1994) Multiple ways of knowing: Curriculum in a new key. *Language Arts,* 71 (5), 337–345.	Harste, J. (2008a) Visual literacy. In Lewison, M., Leland, C.H., & Harste, J., *Creating Critical Classrooms.* Mahwah, NJ: Erlbaum.
This article describes a seamless curriculum in which there is constant movement across various sign systems throughout the day. After reading this article, plan a day in your classroom in which you and your students move seamlessly across sign systems.	Try replicating the engagement that is discussed in this article in your own classroom and share your findings with colleagues.	Try to analyze some of your students' art using the visual discourse procedures described in the article.

eight

Language Study
Lingering in Text

As a teacher in a multiage fifth/sixth grade classroom, Latosha Rowley knows that her students are well on their way to becoming critical readers. Many of them can describe the types of books they prefer and can talk about their favorite authors and why they like them. While this is a good start, Latosha also knows that being a critical reader entails more than being articulate about one's reading preferences. Being a critical reader means that one is consciously aware of how authors use language to privilege certain perspectives and marginalize others. It also means that readers are able to recognize multiple perspectives and consider how they affect the meaning-making process. Being aware that there are different lenses for seeing characters and interpreting the actions they take makes it less likely that readers will accept the first point of view they encounter.

Language study provides opportunities for students to dig deeply and develop as critical consumers of text. While we prefer to use social issues texts for these discussions, any text can be used for this purpose. Even folktales that address ethical issues provide a rich context for multiple perspectives to emerge. For example, the seemingly simplistic picture book *One Fine Day* (Hogrogian, 1971) is an Armenian folktale that can be the starting point for sophisticated conversations about fairness and violence. The story is told as a fantasy with talking animals and the expectation that severed body parts can be sewn back on with no problem. Through a sparse text, readers are introduced to a thirsty fox that comes upon a pail of milk. Although this milk belongs to an old woman who is gathering wood, the fox laps it up before she notices. Upon realizing this, the woman becomes very angry and chops off the fox's tail. The fox cries and begs her to sew his tail back on so that his friends won't laugh at him. The woman agrees to do this, but only after the fox replaces the milk in her pail.

Unfortunately for the fox, what appears as a simple task turns into a chain of events that becomes increasingly harder to resolve. First, the cow won't give him any milk unless he brings her some grass. But the field won't give him grass unless he brings it some water, and the maiden won't let him use her bucket to carry water to the field unless he first brings her a blue bead. The fox finds a peddler who has a blue bead but the peddler demands an egg in exchange and the hen wants some grain before she will give up an egg. Finally the fox meets a miller who feels sorry for him and gives him some grain without demanding something in return. Now the fox is able to meet all the demands and the old woman sews his tail back on.

While the story ends on a positive note with everyone getting what he or she wants, the ending can be seen as the starting point for conversations about how the author portrayed the different characters and the actions they took. Was the fox justified in drinking the milk he found since he had traveled a long way? Or was he just stealing? Was the old woman justified in cutting off the fox's tail to make up for the lost milk? Or was this an instance of cruelty to animals? Critical language study is a good way to approach tough questions like these. The goal is to prepare readers who know how to unpack texts for purposes of seeing different perspectives—and possibly repositioning themselves in the world.

Latosha read *One Fine Day* aloud to her fifth and six graders and then asked them to talk about the story in groups of three. At first the students did not appear to be invested in any particular point of view. They might have thought that a story about talking animals was babyish and not worthy of their time or attention. This quickly changed, however, when Latosha started asking questions about justice and morality. How did the author create this text to justify some characters' actions and question others? As the discussion progressed, it became evident that many students had strong feelings about the actions taken by both the fox and the old woman. As it also became clear that everyone in the class did not agree, they began to comb through the text to find evidence and supporting arguments for their positions. As the time for this discussion came to an end, support groups for the fox and the old woman had formed and students were engrossed in the discussion. Class members who had been paying attention but not talking were recruited by both sides to get involved in the conversation and they were happy to jump in. The debate continued in hushed tones as students lined up and left the room to go to their next class. Clearly this discussion was not over.

Principle #1: There Is Always Another Perspective

Much has been written about the importance of readers understanding that meaning is not literally "in" a text, but is transacted (or interpreted) by readers as a result of their background knowledge and what they bring to the text (Rosenblatt, 1987). As Kucer (2008) puts it, "We know that transactions with any meaningful text involve making connections with what is known, and are enhanced by hearing what others have been thinking about any given text" (p. 188). At the same time, it is important for readers to understand that "texts are social spaces" (Fairclough, 1995, p. 6) and as a result, are never neutral. Moje, Young, Readence, and Moore (2000) suggest that students who become aware of how texts manipulate them "can become critical consumers and producers of text who challenge dominant meanings and realize that there is more than one way to read texts and their world" (p. 408).

In the case of *One Fine Day*, the fifth and sixth graders went from being not very interested to becoming highly engaged as they discussed the story and answered questions that their teacher asked. These questions, developed by Mitzi and a group of teachers working with the Junior Great Books Program (Will, 1986), don't have easy answers:

- Did the fox steal the milk or did he have the right to drink it?
- Was the old woman cruel or justified in chopping off the fox's tail?

- Was the fox clever?
- Did the fox get his tail back because of luck, his cleverness, persistence, or some other reason?

In response to the question about whether the fox stole the milk, most students replied affirmatively, but a few argued that the fox had a valid reason for drinking it. They noted the text never said he stole the milk. It simply said that he saw a pail of milk and lapped it up. Students in this group pointed out that according to the text, the fox had "traveled through a great forest" and was "very thirsty" (unpaged) and this meant that he needed the milk to survive. They saw this situation as different from "stealing something for fun." They also argued that the fox didn't attack the old woman or scare her away to get the milk. He saw it sitting there and lapped it up. Their pets at home would do the same thing and shouldn't get their tails cut off. Other students insisted that stealing is stealing, regardless of the circumstances, and maintained that the fox deserved to be punished.

This led to a conversation about the fairness of the punishment and many students expressed the opinion that the old woman overreacted when she cut off the fox's tail in retribution. For example, Isaiah stated that the woman was cruel because "she hurt him really bad" and all she had to do was to go get some more milk. Dairon agreed that she was cruel and said she should have "found a different solution." Anna also thought that cutting off the fox's tail was mean. "Licking up milk is not that bad and tails will never grow back. She could have cut his whiskers instead." Annele summed up this sentiment with the pronouncement "Violence is never the answer!" Another group of students disagreed and maintained that the fox deserved the punishment he got—especially if it was possible to sew the tail back on after he replaced the milk.

The question of whether the fox was clever also led to multiple perspectives being expressed. Some class members held staunchly to the view that he couldn't have been very clever because (1) he took the milk without asking permission and (2) he got caught doing it. Several argued that he just should have told the woman how thirsty he was and probably she would have given some milk to him. Sarah noted that most of his attempts to "sweet talk" the other characters in the story by referring to them as "dear cow," "beautiful field," and "sweet maiden" didn't work since they made him go look for other things. The fox also told the peddler that a pretty maiden would be pleased with him if he gave the fox a bead for her, but that didn't work either and the peddler demanded an egg in exchange for the bead. If the fox had really been clever, they argued, he would have talked the old woman into giving him some milk. Or he would have lapped up the milk in a sneaky way so she didn't notice him.

Others called attention to the fact that the author must have thought the fox was clever because the text said that the peddler was "not taken in by the promise of a pretty smile or the cleverness of the fox." Students with this perspective brought up the idea that the fox knew how to talk to people in a way that would make them feel sorry for him. Kaylee noted that the fox knew that crying was a good way to get sympathy because he cried when he got to the miller and the text said that the miller did feel sorry for him. She also suggested that the fox's flattery (he called the miller "kind") worked that time even though it hadn't worked with the other characters. She wondered if that was because the text said "the miller was a good man" and maybe the other characters were more selfish.

While there was little agreement on whether the fox was clever, there was consensus that he was persistent. Sarah looked the word up online and shared the meaning of "continuing on and not giving up." Anna thought this described the fox well since "he just wouldn't stop." She went on to suggest that the fox was also "really lucky that the miller at the end was nice and didn't ask for anything." Kira wondered if the story would ever have ended if the miller hadn't been in it. She noted that the fox was desperate to get his tail back and would have done anything to avoid having his friends laugh at him. She observed that the fox was like kids in this regard since they are also very concerned about getting laughed at by their friends and will do whatever it takes to avoid it. The fox's persistence in attempting to get back to his friends without getting laughed at was totally plausible for many students.

In each of these examples, students were encountering multiple perspectives and building their awareness of how language can be used to achieve one's goals. As Gee (1999) suggests, we "actively use spoken and written language to create or build the world . . . around us" (p. 11). For example, the students who brought up the fox's purposeful use of flattery and tears to get his tail back did that to support their particular view of him as a deliberate and not so innocent character. At the same time, the teacher's use of open-ended questions provided a context for students to make judgments about the characters and come to the realization that it was acceptable to disagree with each other. Questions similar to those Latosha used for *One Fine Day* can be asked about any story to support readers in unpacking multiple perspectives. Textbox 8.1 provides a list of generic questions that might be used with any story as a way to bring out diverse responses and push everyone's thinking.

Textbox 8.1. Unpacking Multiple Perspectives

- Which character(s) do you want to defend?
- Which character(s) do you want to criticize?
- How did the author's use of language influence your decision to defend or criticize any of them?
- Who might agree or disagree with your perspective?
- Why should readers consider different views?

We recommend providing students with a copy of the text being discussed and encouraging them to underline or circle any specific instance of language they see as influencing their interpretation of the story. If the text being discussed is in a book that cannot be marked up, students can use post-it notes to keep track of their thoughts about how the language in the text is positioning the characters. Like Latosha, we would structure this activity by starting with students working in groups of two or three to talk about the story and answer the questions and then move to a whole class discussion.

Mitzi regularly uses the more formal Junior Great Books and Socratic Seminar configurations. On the first day, she reads the text aloud with students following to make sure all students, even the least proficient readers can participate and have a basic understanding of the story. On the second day, students read quietly with a partner and at the end of each paragraph or page, they jot down questions, note things that puzzle them, make observations about the way the author uses language, and/or talk back to the author in writing. On the third day, students move the tables and chairs into a big circle (like a seminar table). She then starts the discussion with an open-ended question and acts as a facilitator, not a participant in the discussion. Mitzi videotaped some seminars she led and analyzed how she facilitated. This analysis showed that her role was to help students clarify the reasons behind their responses, direct their responses to peers, bring

TABLE 8.1.   Great Books and Socratic Seminar Discussions

There are many similarities between Junior Great Books and Socratic Seminar discussions. Here are resources for each.

Junior Great Books

- Article on the implementation and outcomes of the Junior Great Books Program in third grades in the Chicago Public Schools. Criscuola, M.M. (1994). Read, discuss, reread: Insights from the Junior Great Books program. *Educational Leadership*, *51*(1), 58–61.
- Information on materials and training for Junior Great Books at the Great Books Foundation website: http://www.greatbooks.org/

Socratic Seminars

- Article on the implementation and response of seventh graders to Socratic Seminars. Mee, M. (2007). Enough about you, let's talk about me: Student voice in the classroom. *Middle Ground*, *10*(1), 37–38.
- Information about procedures guidelines and books on Socratic Seminars at the StudyGuide.org website: http://www.studyguide.org/socratic_seminar.htm.

more students into the discussion, and keep the discussion on track by occasionally summarizing ideas or perspectives. On numerous occasions, Mitzi tried leading discussions when the desks were not in a circle or when students' chairs were in a circle and they used lapboards. She felt that the quality of the discussions always went down without the seminar desk configuration. For more information on leading these discussions see Table 8.1.

Principle #2: Critical Readers Recognize Frames and Stereotypes

Jim Gee (1999) uses the idea of cultural models to describe how texts endow characters with particular identities: "One way to look at cultural models is as images or storylines or descriptions of simplified worlds in which prototypical events unfold" (p. 59). Citing the work of Fillmore (1975), Gee describes how the cultural model of a bachelor goes further than the image of an unmarried man. For example, the Pope is not thought of as a bachelor, even though he is not married. Another way to consider why we don't think of the Pope as a bachelor is through the concept of "frames," which Lakoff (2004) defines as "mental structures that shape the way we see the world . . . the goals we seek, the plans we make, the way we act" (p. xv). We see frames as very similar to Gee's notion of cultural models. Going beyond cultural models, Gee also introduces the idea of Discourses (1999). He explains them as a type of identity kit that includes ways of talking, ways of dressing, and ways of acting. For example, the Discourse of being a fan at a football game is very different from the Discourse of being in the audience of a symphony orchestra. Membership in one of these Discourse groups doesn't mean that one can also demonstrate membership in the other unless there is an opportunity to participate and become part of it. (See ***Discourse Analysis for Kids*** in Chapter 10.)

In reading *One Fine Day*, Latosha's students encountered the frame of a fox as a crafty and less than noble animal. This frame is common in literature; the fox that lured Henny Penny and her friends to his den and devoured them is a good example. Jane Wattenberg's (2000) version of this old story refers to Foxy-Loxy as "that mean ball of fur" (unpaged). But as Janks (2010) reminds us, we can choose to read both "with a text" and "against a text" (p. 96). In other words, we don't have to accept the frame or Discourse that the text provides.

Reading against a frame. According to critical theorists, the idea of "teaching against the grain" involves "engaging in processes and practices that are transformative" (Martin,

2007, p. 343) in that people with little power begin to derive power from the local knowledge they produce. For example, Delbridge (2008) describes an eighth grader who demonstrated what it means to take a critical stance when she read "against an author" (p. 164) she perceived to be stereotyping the residents of a community where she once lived. She used her knowledge of that community (Fresno, CA) to talk back to the text that described its residents in ways she found problematic. "I could not believe what I was reading because I never saw any of that . . . I thought it [the book] was stereotyping people. Like putting it out there that they weren't very smart, weren't capable of going through life without getting in a lot of trouble" (p. 164). Instead of simply going along with the author's assumptions about the residents of Fresno, this student used her local knowledge as a source of power to challenge them.

Similarly, in Latosha's class, some students read against the predominant frame of foxes and argued that as a wild animal, the fox in this story was simply doing what he had to do to survive. Others compared the fox to their pets at home and concluded that animals shouldn't be blamed for eating food when it has been left unattended. Kaylee dramatically pronounced that what happened here was an example of "animal cruelty." Other students read with what might be a more common frame and argued that foxes are bad animals. Jaylin, for example, disagreed with Kaylee and stated that foxes are real pests to farmers and cause them to lose a lot of money. Even so, he still thought that the old woman's choice of punishment was not appropriate.

While the frame or stereotype of old women as helpless or senile was not addressed by the students directly, the fact that this character didn't notice the fox drinking from her pail might suggest that she was out of touch with reality and not capable of taking care of herself. Kira wondered why the old woman in this story just happened to be carrying a big knife with her. This might suggest a frame of old women as being unpredictable or even dangerous. In this case, however, Kira read against this frame and said she didn't think of old women as carrying weapons or hurting animals. A number of students argued that the old woman overreacted and responded with unnecessary violence. What kind of person, they asked, would hack off the tail of an offending animal without first asking some questions about why the animal acted as it did?

Examining frames in multiple texts. In both cases, it will be helpful if students are invited to examine the positioning of foxes and old women in other texts. *Fox* by Margaret Wild (2001) is the story of a fictional fox that supports the frame of foxes as crafty and untrustworthy animals. In this story of friendship and betrayal (also discussed in Chapter 2), Dog and Magpie have formed a close relationship based on the fact that each of them is handicapped and needs the other. Fox is jealous of their friendship and uses lies and deceit to break it up. The story ends with Fox shaking Magpie "off his back as he would a flea" and saying, "Now you and Dog will know what it is like to be truly alone" (unpaged). Then he goes on his solitary way, having gained little more than the satisfaction of knowing that Dog and Magpie will suffer from the same loneliness he knows. A similar unflattering perspective on foxes is evident in *The Tale of Tricky Fox* (Aylesworth, 2001) because the title character is depicted as bragging about his ability to "fool a human" (unpaged) and then telling a string of lies to achieve his goal.

A more sympathetic view of foxes is portrayed in non-fiction and realistic fiction books about foxes. For example, *City Foxes* (Tweit, 1997) is a photo-documentary of a fox family living in a Denver cemetery. This book shows how the mother and father fox work together to care for their newborn kits. The frame here is that of a loving family struggling to survive in a dangerous and unforgiving environment. The frame of the fox as a self-sacrificing parent struggling to feed his family is also evident in Eve Bunting's *Red Fox Running* (1993). The book begins with the image of a fox running over the frozen ground in a desperate search for food to take to his den.

The line "Hunger runs beside you" emphasizes the grim situation and a reference to the animal's paws as "raw and bleeding" (unpaged) makes the fox seem noble indeed as he continues his quest to feed his family in spite of his own suffering. These two books provide a counter narrative to the frame of the fox as a selfish animal that lives only for itself.

A similar inquiry might be pursued to identify common cultural frames for old women. Cynthia Rylant (2000), for example, portrays *The Old Woman Who Named Things* as a lonely character who is unable to form attachments to living things because she is afraid she will end up losing them. So she names her car, her chair, and other inanimate objects and treats them as her friends. The stereotype of old women as solitary and slightly crazy might fit with the portrayal of the old woman in *One Fine Day*. This frame is also found in Barbara Cooney's *Miss Rumphius* (1985). This book tells the story of "the Lupine Lady" who was "little and old" and was on a quest to "do something to make the world more beautiful" (unpaged). Her decision to walk through the town and countryside scattering lupine seeds earned her the nickname "That Crazy Old Lady" but that didn't stop her. In this case, what seemed like craziness to some turned out to lead to something quite wonderful: "The next spring there were lupines everywhere. Fields and hillsides were covered with blue and purple and rose-colored flowers." This story situates the idea of what it means to be crazy as a cultural perspective and challenges the stereotype of crazy old women.

A ***Counter Narrative*** to the stereotype of old women as lonely and afraid to form attachments can be found in Patricia Polacco's *Mrs. Katz and Tush* (2009). In this story Mrs. Katz is lonely but she reaches out to Larnel, a neighborhood child from a different ethnic group, and to Tush, a kitten no one wanted. On the last page of the book we find evidence of her success in forming lasting attachments and resolving her loneliness: "As the years passed, Mrs. Katz, Tush, and her descendants became part of Larnel's family" (unpaged).

Comparing different versions of old women or foxes as they are portrayed in a variety of texts helps readers dig deeply and understand that there is not one "right" perspective and each reader must use evidence from the text to form his or her own opinions about old women, foxes, and all the other characters in any particular text. In this case, Latosha began the study of *One Fine Day* by assuming that her students could take a critical perspective. She did not treat them as "blank slates" and begin by explaining what it means to be treated unfairly. In reality, she had noticed that her students frequently talked about equity issues. Indeed, this is a common topic in most elementary and middle school classrooms. Children are eager to point out why they think something is not fair and tell anyone who will listen what they think needs to be done to correct the problem. As it turned out, Ms. Rowley's students didn't let her down. They read both with and against the frames embedded in the text. The questions in Textbox 8.2 are offered as suggestions for beginning conversations about framing and frames.

Textbox 8.2. Unpacking Frames

- How does the author portray the characters as certain types of people or animals?
- Is this portrayal believable?
- How does the author use language that influences your perspective?
- Can you identify any stereotypes?
- Can you read against the stereotypes?

Principle #3: Language Study Helps Readers Unpack Texts

The concept of language study sounds like it might be technical or boring. Readers might wonder if they will be asked to diagram sentences or engage in other sorts of grammar exercises. As the vignette from Latosha Rowley's classroom shows, this is not the case. The type of language study we are talking about invites readers to consider texts critically as they look for evidence that authors are privileging certain perspectives and messages. Readers are encouraged to judge how specific word choices and the use of particular grammatical features show who is doing what and whether these are the actions of someone who has power. Critical readers are able to understand how authors position them and what the effects of this positioning might be. "Critical reading, in combination with an ethic of social justice, is fundamental in order to protect our own rights and the rights of others" (Janks, 2010, p. 98).

As we demonstrate in the ***Language at Work*** strategy described in chapter 10, texts are filled with embedded meanings that readers need to figure out. Consider the opening sentences in *Piggybook,* a seemingly "cute" picture book by Anthony Browne (1986):

> Mr. Piggott lived with his two sons, Simon and Patrick, in a nice house with a nice garden, and a nice car in the nice garage.
> Inside the house was his wife. (unpaged)

Fairclough's (1995) theory of Critical Discourse Analysis (CDA) provides a helpful tool for identifying the different messages in this text. CDA requires readers to ask questions about the experiential value of specific words. In this case, we can ask what difference it makes that all of the "nice" things (the house, the garden, etc.) are associated with the father and two boys. We might also ask what difference it makes that Mrs. Piggott is never mentioned by name at all and is only described passively as "his wife" who is "inside the house." CDA encourages us to ask the question "Whose interest does this text serve?"

In this case, it seems that Mrs. Piggott is being marginalized and there are some power issues at play here. The words tell us that the males in this story have agency: they "live" in the house. The author's use of the passive voice when he refers to Mrs. Piggott as the wife who is "inside the house," on the other hand, implies that she has no agency. We wonder why she was not included in the list of people "living" in the house. Does the author want us to think that she exists (as opposed to "lives") inside a house that might not be very "nice" for her? The author's choice of verbs supports this hypothesis. At the beginning of the story, the father and sons continually "call out" to Mrs. Piggott, giving her orders to "hurry up" with whatever meal they are ready to eat. She does not appear in the picture of the family eating breakfast, which makes us wonder if she was too busy serving them to get anything for herself. The verbs used for Mrs. Piggott show that she is doing a lot of work. The author reports that after this meal, Mrs. Piggott "washed all the breakfast things, made all the beds, vacuumed all the carpets, and then went to work." After serving the evening meal, she "washed the dishes, washed the clothes, did the ironing, and then cooked some more." Indeed, as we read on, we begin to suspect that the author was positioning us to see inequities in the Piggott household. The illustrations in the book also add to our suspicions since the face of Mrs. Piggott is not shown until the final page when she finally asserts herself and achieves a more equitable relationship with her husband and sons.

As the story progresses, Mrs. Piggott disappears and the father and sons literally turn into helpless pigs. Their verbs change to match this transformation. Instead of "calling out" to Mrs. Piggott to wait on them, they now squeal, grunt, and snort. Again, Browne's illustrations are very important since they show the male Piggotts becoming pigs and fitting the frame of pigs as messy, gluttonous creatures. Most readers see this transformation as a fair consequence for their actions without thinking too much about whether the author set them up to respond this way. If we think about it, however, we might come to the conclusion that the story was not told in an unbiased way. This is not an unusual occurrence since "someone is always attempting to position us in a specific way. We can follow along docilely, or we can bring up other perspectives and challenge what is being presented" (Lewison et al., 2008, p. 78). In short, it is the reader's responsibility to be aware that language and power weave together in a purposeful way.

The idea that texts are not innocent can be unsettling. After all, many of us have grown up believing that if we read something in a book or see it on a TV news show, then it must be true. Fortunately it is never too late to learn about the work texts do and how they do it. Comber (2001) argues that this is a necessity for effective citizenship in the 21st century. In the case of *Piggybook*, for example, we can see that the male Piggotts were shown as not doing anything to assist in the running of the household. This frame resonates with many women who feel that they never get a fair deal since they are responsible not only for their jobs outside the home, but ultimately for jobs like cleaning and cooking inside the home as well. This frame might not present an accurate picture since there are men who do take responsibility for household tasks just as there are women who don't. But it's easy to buy into the stereotype of men who can't (or won't) take care of themselves or anyone else while reading this story. It's also easy to buy into the stereotype of over-worked women who have a hard time advocating for their own interests and wait until the situation reaches a boiling point before taking action. Being aware of the author's word choices and grammatical forms (like active or passive voice) can help readers identify what Shannon (2002) refers to as the myths that are embedded in all stories. Textbox 8.3 provides suggestions for helping readers attend to the implicit messages in texts by examining word choices and grammatical features.

Textbox 8.3. Unpacking Implicit Messages in Texts

- How are grammatical forms used to express messages?
- Who has agency and/or voice? Who doesn't?
- How do word choices support underlying messages?
- What verbs are used for each character? What do they show about him or her?
- Do any words have meanings that might be questioned?
- Which words are used repeatedly and for what purposes?
- What does this author want you to believe?

Key Issues in Implementation

While we see language study playing an important role in supporting comprehension and the growth of flexible readers, we also know that it can seem like something that is too difficult or too controversial to be of benefit. To counter this perspective, we will describe three main obstacles to language study and suggest ways to respond to them.

Language study encourages readers to talk back to texts and challenge the interpretations they and others make. Sumara (2002) argues that literature should involve "reformulating the already formulated, interrupting certainty, [and] making trouble" (p. 46). This type of close analysis provides an opportunity to disrupt students' commonplace beliefs as they explore other ways of seeing and interpreting the world around them. If we put all of these characteristics together, we get a list that includes talking back, making trouble, and disrupting beliefs. These behaviors are not usually seen as what we want to encourage in our young people. More often than not, our cultural messages to them focus on the need to be respectful and obedient. We ask them to answer the questions at the end of the story and often imply that there is one right answer and we should all agree on what it is. This stance fits with the traditional frame of kids being "seen and not heard," a view that is still held by some parents and educators. Adults in this group might see a curriculum that encourages children to talk back to what is perceived as cultural wisdom as a threat to their power. Encouraging kids to talk back also challenges the traditional teacher/student relationship that privileges what Cazden (2002) and others have referred to as the I-R-E model. In this model the teacher initiates ("I") a question, the student responds ("R") and the teacher evaluates ("E") the response. Since this model privileges "official" knowledge and "right answers" over the knowledge constructed by learners, it cannot coexist with a critical approach to language study that focuses on analyzing and deconstructing text.

An example of language study that might cause trouble focuses on the adolescent novel *The God Box* by Alex Sanchez (2007). The story features Paul, a born-again Christian who is fighting a growing realization that he is gay. When a homophobic peer in Paul's Bible study group says that all gay people should be killed and cites the story of Sodom and Gomorrah in Genesis Nineteen as evidence, there is a lengthy discussion among the group members about the actual words in the biblical text and the different ways they might be interpreted. This is exactly the kind of language study we have been talking about in this chapter. Paul continues to study the language used in other biblical references to the two ill-fated cities when he gets home that night. He reports finding many references to "the Sodomites as prideful, unjust, unwelcoming, and inhospitable to strangers, to the point of violence" (p. 86) but no references to anything about homosexuality. Language study is important in this story because it helps Paul come to the conclusion that it is possible for him to be both gay and Christian. Some readers will see language study in this context as a threat to their religious beliefs and will argue that this discussion does not belong in schools. Others, however, might think it is more productive for young people to learn how to discuss different perspectives than to wait for them to issue statements about killing those who are perceived as going against the norm.

Encountering disagreement on what should be read or discussed in schools is nothing new. As Kincheloe (2007) points out, "all educational spaces are unique and politically contested" (p. 16). It is never easy to figure out how to respect multiple perspectives when they are so dramatically opposed to each other. Sometimes it helps to provide more information about the school context and why teachers think conversations about controversial topics like homophobia are needed in the first place. We once worked with some teachers who were finding the school climate becoming increasingly dangerous for their gay and lesbian students. They shared their concerns with parents and sought their help in deciding what to do to protect all students from violence. In this case, most of the parents agreed that it made sense to discuss these issues in school and said that their children might benefit from reading books that addressed them. For example, in *The God Box* (Sanchez, 2007), a gay student gets attacked by a classmate and almost dies. The harm this act brings to both boys is irreparable. One goes to prison and the other faces a long recovery and permanent physical damage.

The teachers we worked with also found that some parents remained opposed to having their children read books about homophobia, so these students were provided with alternate materials. While it was problematic that potentially violent students missed out on conversations that might have helped them to gain more empathy and understanding, the teachers believed it was important to respect the wishes of parents as far as they could without changing the curriculum for everyone.

Critical language study challenges the traditional focus on discrete skills. As stated at the beginning of this chapter, many of us remember language study in terms of learning grammar and parts of speech. According to this view, students study prepositions by memorizing a list and then showing that they can identify them in sentences. Instead of attempting to figure out what language and grammar might be doing to people or making them believe, students simply analyze the mechanics of the text. We see critical language study as accomplishing both the traditional goal of grammar study and the newer and more urgent goal of helping students understand how language can be used to privilege or marginalize them and others. As we demonstrated in Principle #3, critical language study requires readers to pay attention to the actual words being used and decide how those words show how much power and agency a character has. What is even more important is that students engaging in critical language study are expected to take an active role in their learning while students engaging in traditional grammar study can be quite passive as long as they absorb the required material and repeat it back to the teacher.

Critical language study is not commonly found in existing curriculum materials. While we have seen some lessons focusing on "fact and opinion" or "point of view" in commercial literacy materials, we have found few examples of lessons focusing on talking back, disrupting, or digging into alternate interpretations. More often than not, curriculum materials and teaching practices reinforce the idea of coming to a consensus. Children and teachers alike are encouraged to be nice people who go out of their way to find a point on which they can agree. Finding materials that were designed to push a more critical perspective can be difficult since there are fewer of them available. *Creating Critical Classrooms* (Lewison et al., 2008) and *What If and Why?* (Van Sluys, 2005) offer ideas for moving curriculum in this new direction.

What might be most unsettling about approaching language study from a critical perspective is that it leaves us with a sense of uncertainty as to how to teach. Not having a set of prepackaged materials that some supposed expert has recommended means that the game plan will change for teachers who have come to rely on scripted lessons that are purported to be the best ways to teach. Advertisements for commercial programs that approach language study in a mechanical way often claim to be based on "scientific" evidence that answers all questions and leaves no space for uncertainty. But as both Harste (2008) and MacGinitie (1983) have argued, educators make better decisions when they allow uncertainty and their knowledge of individual children to guide their thinking. Harste (2008) expresses this perspective cogently: "I see this 'programs over people' mentality as a professional hazard, and, even more alarming, it seems to be growing" (Lewison et al., 2008, p. 36). The antidote to this type of programmed teaching is to find out what children know and what interests and questions they have before deciding to go with a program that assumes every student has the same needs.

Working With Linguistically and Culturally Diverse Students

Linguistically and culturally diverse students are often labeled as "struggling" or "remedial" readers. Franzak (2006) uses the wordless picture book *Zoom!* (Banyai, 1995) to make the case that context affects how we see and understand everything we think we know. "By zooming out into ever-larger views, the reader understands that phenomena are always framed by a bigger picture" (Franzak, 2006, p. 209). The *Zoom!* metaphor can help us to see how diverse students are negatively positioned by the very language we use to describe them. Referring to them as "at risk" or "struggling" positions them as having something wrong with them. However, the fact that some students bring a different set of experiences and background knowledge could be seen as an asset instead of a deficit. If we zoom out and see the bigger picture, we might recognize the deficit perspective as a social construction. Diverse students often bring knowledge and experiences that are valued in the real world, but not in the world of school. Therefore, it is more accurate to refer to them as "marginalized readers" (Moje, Young, Readence, & Moore, 2000, as cited in Franzak, 2006).

We think it's important for marginalized students to recognize and value their strengths and capabilities—and for educators to start valuing these capabilities in school. Introducing them to books in which characters who don't look "smart" in school look very capable at home is a good place to start. Karen Hesse's chapter book *Just Juice* (1998) tells the story of a nine-year-old girl who comes from a culture of illiteracy and is seen as a failing student in school. A close reading of the book, however, shows her taking care of younger siblings and helping her parents in a number of important ways. A similar theme of a child taking on adult responsibilities in ways that don't count in school runs through *The Circuit* (Jimenez, 1998), an adolescent novel about migrant workers from Mexico.

Linguistically and culturally diverse students often look like more successful students when their teachers tailor the curriculum to meet their needs instead of maintaining a "one size fits all" focus. In *Locomotion* (2003), Jacqueline Woodson directly challenges the dominant view of culturally diverse and poor children as deficient. Readers are introduced to Lonnie, an African American child who was orphaned when his parents were killed in a fire. Although the living conditions in the foster home he ends up in are not ideal, he is seen by his teacher as a capable student, especially when it comes to writing. Her high expectations for him and the frequent opportunities she gives him to write about important things in his life position him as a successful student. Instead of putting Lonnie into a remedial reading class, his teacher invites him to use writing as a vehicle for making sense of the world and talking about what's on his mind.

Another book that challenges dominant views about successful students is *Bronx Masquerade* by Nikki Grimes (2002). In Mr. Ward's English class "Open Mike Friday" is everyone's favorite period. After Wesley writes a poem, 18 of his classmates clamor to use poetry to express frankly what is on their minds. The novel demonstrates the power of teaching as well as how teachers might use writing to celebrate the lives of their students. This book echoes the work of Duncan-Andrade and Morrell (2000) who argue that hip-hop music is an effective way to reach marginalized urban youth and teach them the critical and analytical skills necessary for succeeding in school. They discuss how students are more likely to develop literacy skills if they have cultural frames that help them link class material to their own lives. Similar to Mr. Ward in this book, Duncan-Andrade and Morrell see hip-hop as a way to bring popular culture into the classroom to help all students become successful literate beings.

Technology Extensions and Electronic Resources

James Damico's Critical Web Reader (2010: http://cwr.indiana.edu/) provides a set of tools for teachers and students to evaluate web-based resources. The home page for this site lists its goals as helping readers to:

- determine if a website aligns with their purposes;
- discern the credibility and reliability of a website;
- pose investigative questions to guide their own inquiry;
- identify, evaluate, and corroborate claims and evidence;
- evaluate techniques authors/creators use to influence readers (loaded words, provocative images, links to other sites, etc.);
- consider how their own beliefs, values, perspectives, or biases affect their reading;

- consider how people with different backgrounds, beliefs and experiences might read the site;
- synthesize information across sites;
- communicate findings to different audiences.

The "Resources" tab provides suggestions for selecting a search engine, choosing keywords, identifying credible sources, and identifying useful sources. This section offers the following advice:

> Not all of these results will be related to your topic. Some may be pages which appear to be related to your topic, but are not of a high quality. Once you have entered keywords into a search engine and it has returned a list of results, choose the ones which are most credible and useful for your purpose.
>
> (Retrieved July 22, 2010 from: http://cwr.indiana.edu/Resources/CWRResources/SearchingforWebsites/tabid/12081/Default.aspx)

Clicking on the words "credible" and "useful" takes the reader to additional links that provide questions for judging the credibility and usefulness of a site. There is also practical advice like "try, try again" when the first search doesn't work. Other tabs include descriptions of current and past projects and a list of related references.

Michele Knobel and Colin Lankshear (2009) recommend a site called NewLits.org. This site provides professional articles commissioned from leaders in the field as well as a wiki space where participants post contributions and edit everyone's work. This includes "remixes of the commissioned papers, accounts of using new literacies in classrooms" (p. 632) and artifacts like lesson plans, video clips, and examples of student work. There are also links to other useful sites like fictionpress.com, where kids are encouraged to "let the words flow" and write their own stories and books. While the content of NewLits.org is constantly being updated, we found a number of useful resources like a unit on fan fiction for fourth graders and a set of electronic sources for teaching with graphic novels.

Assessment

Assessing students' ability to engage thoughtfully in language study might be done informally as we listen to their literature discussions and more formally if we give them particular texts to analyze and deconstruct according to the frames they see in them. Noting examples of students asking some of the same types of critical questions being modeled by the teacher also can provide evidence of their development in this area. Textbox 8.4 provides a list of things to look for if teachers are interested in assessing their students' ability to use language study effectively.

Textbox 8.4. Assessment

We know that language study is happening when we see these sorts of things happening:

- We observe students going back to the text to find evidence for their statements about what they think an author is trying to get them to believe.
- Students are able to explain why specific words and constructions (for example, use of passive voice rather than active) help to frame characters in specific ways.

- Frames and stereotypes are being identified and analyzed in terms of what readers would have to believe to accept them.
- Discussions are characterized by competing discourses and talking back to texts. In other words, we see students reading both with texts and against them.
- Students can articulate how they see specific texts privileging or marginalizing different people or groups.

Invitation: Frames & Stereotypes

This invitation (see Textbox 8.5) focuses on helping readers to recognize frames and stereotypes. A selection of picture books provides different frames for both foxes and old women. Some frames are quite positive and some are equally negative. Students are invited to read the different books and identify the frames they see in them. A graphic organizer (Table 8.2) is provided to encourage participants to take notes on the language being used and to think about how this language can be seen as evidence for how authors are positioning different characters. Instead of pushing readers to come up with a set of *right answers*, this engagement attempts to complicate things by pushing for a set of *different answers*. While the idea of complicating things might seem counterintuitive, it introduces a new social practice and that's what this book is all about.

Textbox 8.5. Invitation: Frames & Stereotypes

Frames are images or storylines that position us to see events in predictable ways with characters playing familiar but often stereotypical roles. The "big bad" wolf that devoured Red Riding Hood and her grandmother is a good example of a frame that positions wolves as dangerous animals. This invitation focuses on identifying competing frames for foxes and old women.

Materials & Procedures

- A copy of the children's book, *One Fine Day* (Hogrogian, 1971)
- Copies of the *Frames & Stereotypes Organizer* (see Table 8.2)
- Copies of children's books that feature foxes and old women, framed both positively and negatively. Some possibilities include:

Books with foxes
City Foxes (Tweit, 1997). Positive frame
Red Fox Running (Bunting, 1993). Positive frame
The Tale of Tricky Fox (Aylesworth, 2001). Negative frame
Fox (Wild, 2001). Negative frame
Henny Penny (Wattenberg, 2000). Negative frame

Books with old women
Miss Rumphius (Cooney, 1985). Positive frame
Mrs. Katz and Tush (Polacco, 2009). Positive frame

The Old Woman who Named Things (Rylant, 2000). Negative frame
The Tale of Tricky Fox (Aylesworth, 2001). Negative frame

1. After distributing a copy of the *Frames & Stereotype Organizer* to each student, take turns reading *One Fine Day* (Hogrogian, 1971) aloud.
2. While reading, ask students to pay special attention to the fox and the old woman. How are the characters framed? Have students record their decisions on the *Frames & Stereotype Organizer*. Why do you think the author chose to frame the characters in this way?
3. Ask students to look through the other books provided for this invitation and try to identify the ways that foxes and old women are framed in these texts. How are they similar or different from what you found in the first book?
4. How can you explain the different frames employed by the authors? Which ones do you see as the most believable?

TABLE 8.2. Frames and Stereotypes Organizer

Foxes are . . . what kind of animals?	**Old women are . . .** what kind of people?
What characteristics do they have? Provide evidence for each frame you find.	What characteristics do they have? Provide evidence for each frame you find.
Book: *One Fine Day* **Frame:** Foxes are. . . **Evidence from text:**	**Book: *One Fine Day*** **Frame:** Old women are. . . **Evidence from text:**
Book: **Frame:** Foxes are. . . **Evidence from text:**	**Book:** **Frame:** Old women are. . . **Evidence from text:**
Book: **Frame:** Foxes are. . . **Evidence from text:**	**Book:** **Frame:** Old women are. . . **Evidence from text:**
Book: **Frame:** Foxes are. . . **Evidence from text:**	**Book:** **Frame:** Old women are. . . **Evidence from text:**

Professional Development

Study groups of teachers and prospective teachers will find it useful to engage in doing language study together. It's much easier and more fruitful when done in collaboration with others. We suggest sharing a seemingly "innocent" picture book like *One Fine Day* (Hogrogian, 1971) or *Piggybook* (Browne, 1986) and then talking about possible underlying messages and frames. We had a rich discussion with teachers about *Pete & Pickles* (Breathed, 2008), a cartoon type of picture book Jerry had purchased for his grandchildren. As it turned out, the teachers did not find all of the messages they perceived as being sent by this book to be as "cute" as the cover illustration. They also noted some stereotypes like women who can't accept reality and keep engaging in outrageous imaginary stunts to make themselves feel better, and men who are so dragged down by reality that they can't imagine anything. These teachers talked about the need to discuss the stereotypes with children as part of the read aloud experience. Participating in this type of critical discussion is good preparation for doing language study later with students. Textbox 8.6 provides a brief list of focusing questions that study groups might use to get started. Table 8.3 summarizes some professional articles that provide more information about language study and examples of what it looks like in action. These articles can serve as resources for study groups.

Textbox 8.6. Questions to Support Readers in Unpacking a Text

1. Who wrote this text?
2. Who might benefit from this perspective or these ideas?
3. Who might be hurt by this perspective or these ideas?
4. What other perspectives or ideas might be taken from this text?

(adapted from Luke & Freebody, 1997; Kucer, 2008)

TABLE 8.3.   Suggestions for Further Reading

Shannon, P. (2002) The myths of reading aloud. *The Dragon Lode*, 20(2), 6–11.	Baildon, M. & Damico, J. (2006) "We have to pick sides": Students wrestle with counter claims on websites. *Social Education* 70(3), 156–160.	Leland, C. & Harste, J., with Huber, K. (2005) Out of the box: Critical literacy in a first-grade classroom. *Language Arts*, 82(4), 258–268.
This article provides examples of underlying messages in picture books. Shannon includes testimonials from authors like Dr. Seuss and offers his perspectives on why famous people like Presidents Clinton and Bush might have selected specific books to read aloud when they visited schools.	The authors describe how middle school students attempted to deal with conflicting information found on different websites. They provide a list of questions for teachers to use to help students evaluate websites more effectively. Some of the questions focus on the importance of locating evidence for the various claims being made.	This article describes the professional journey of a first grade teacher who decided to begin using critical literacy practices in her rural classroom. Examples of the children's writing, art, and discussions about authors' intent document the success of young children engaging in language study.

nine
Challenging the Challengers

I have met thousands of children now, and not even one time has a child come up to me and said, "Ms. Rowling, I'm so glad I've read these books because now I want to be a witch."—J. K. Rowling, *Harry Potter* author

(ALA Banned Books Week Poster, 2005)

Lisa Hannon is a first grade teacher at a Catholic school. She has been teaching for fourteen years and doesn't think of herself as a person who censors books or approves of censorship. She does recall picking up books to read to her class and then putting them down because of her own discomfort. Lisa owned a copy of *Feathers and Fools* (Fox, 1989), an allegory about war that makes some teachers uneasy because a group of swans and a group of peacocks become suspicious of each other and use the weapons they've collected to kill each other. Lisa owned the book for quite a while, but never read it aloud because of the references to the birds fighting and the mention of blood and weapons. While taking a class with Chris that focused on children's books and critical literacy, Lisa decided to take a chance and read *Feathers and Fools* aloud to her first grade students. The kids had a lively conversation and talked about the violence among the birds, but they didn't connect the meaning of the book to people or war. *Feathers and Fools* ends on a hopeful note—two eggs remain, and the new swan and peacock hatchlings notice their similarities instead of their differences. Lisa's students noticed the eggs and hatchlings and discussed how they hoped that the "kid" birds would do better than the parents and not fight with each other. When reading this "troublesome" book aloud to her first graders, the world didn't fall apart and Lisa realized the discussion they had was really an important one. Had she not enrolled in a class where difficult issues were discussed, she might have left the book on the shelf and this important conversation would never have happened. The experience of reading

Feathers and Fools and other risky books to her first graders had such a significant impact on Lisa that she talked to her principal about buying more social issues books for the school library. She also volunteered to do a webinar on critical literacy for the Archdiocese of Indianapolis.

Lisa's story is a familiar one. As we've worked with teachers over the years, we've heard stories of so many books that seem too violent, too graphic, too realistic, or too uncomfortable to read to students. As we discussed in Chapter 4, time after time once the books are read, amazing conversations happen. There seems to be a hunger among students to dig deeper and talk about important real life issues. At times, we teachers seem too afraid to let this happen.

Principle #1: Why Censorship Threatens Democracy

Similar to the picture book *Feathers and Fools*, *The Great Gilly Hopkins* (Paterson, 1987) is a chapter book that some teachers are unsure about reading with their students. *The Great Gilly Hopkins* is a moving book about the seemingly incorrigible eleven-year-old Gilly who has been placed with one foster family after another until she goes to live with the Trotters. This book won the Newbery Honor Book prize, the National Book Award for Children's Literature, Best of the Best Children's Books, and at least nine other awards. What charms readers most is gum-chewing Gilly's bold, angry, irreverent, and eventually lovable character. We use this book in a number of places in this chapter to illustrate the complicated issues around banned and challenged books.

Challenged and banned books. A few years back, Mitzi found herself on a school district committee that was reviewing a parent's request to have *The Great Gilly Hopkins* taken off school shelves. The complaint was similar to the scores of challenges to this book that made it one of the 100 most challenged books in the country for two decades (1990–2009) (American Library Association, 2011). The complaint focused on the use of profanity by Gilly (*hell* and *damn* were artfully used to show Gilly's anger and frustration) and the low moral standard in the books (Gilly talking back to adults). The theme is one of transformation, allowing readers to witness the diminishing of Gilly's anger and the change in her language and attitudes toward her troubling situation as a child who was dumped into the foster care system by her mother. In Mitzi's case, the school board took the committee's recommendation and did not ban the book.

Unfortunately, this was not the case in many schools and libraries across the country. For example, *The Great Gilly Hopkins* was banned in school libraries in Albemarle County, Virginia. Here the school board convened a panel of educators who recommended that the book remain on the shelves, similar to what happened in the district where Mitzi worked. But in Albemarle County, "the school superintendent ordered it removed anyway" (Staples, 1996, p. 2). In a response to the Albemarle County School Board, Katherine Paterson wrote, "Though Gilly's mouth is a very mild one compared to that of many lost children, if she had said 'fiddlesticks' when frustrated, readers could not have believed her and love would give them no hope" (Staples, 1996, p. 2). Paterson's words were echoed in the voices of "at-risk" seventh and eighth graders when Laura Robb read the book aloud.

> Katherine Paterson's novel had a powerful impact on these students, many of whom said they couldn't get Gilly out of their minds and dreams. Keysha, in a letter to Gilly's mother, chastised Courtney for abandoning her daughter [Keysha's spelling is as she wrote it originally]. "If you had any sence, you would know that you just broke a young girl's heart, somethings thats hard to replac," she wrote. Gilly's story struck a deep, responsive chord within these troubled adolescents and helped them to talk and write about powerful feelings. They begged me to read another Paterson book. Gilly opened this group to the world of story. (Robb, 1992, p. 2)

In an analysis of *The Great Gilly Hopkins*, Cairns (2008) points out another reason we might want to use this book with young people. She notes how Gilly's

> emotional and psychological development can be charted through her changing relationship to the imaginative and expressive potentialities of language. Most importantly, literacy becomes not a basis for illusory control and manipulative power, but for the kind of human relationships that make possible the building of a self. Language becomes a rich inner resource, not simply a means for power over others. (p.9)

This book is a wonderful volume to use for language study, where students can examine how Paterson crafts Gilly's language through the course of the book and the many changing ways Gilly uses language not only to get things done in the world, but to discover a kinder, more thoughtful Gilly.

Some say, why worry about *The Great Gilly Hopkins* being banned? It's an old book anyway. We worry because there are scores of books being challenged and banned each year. In 2009 there were over 490 attempts to ban books (Brunner, 2010) and this number reflects only incidents reported. The American Library Association estimates that for each reported book challenge, four or five remain unreported. The following list reports the top ten challenged books in 2009 (Brunner, 2009):

- *TTYL; TTFN; L8R, G8R* (series) by Lauren Myracle;
- *And Tango Makes Three* by Justin Richardson and Peter Parnell;
- *The Perks of Being a Wallflower* by Stephen Chbosky;
- *To Kill a Mockingbird* by Harper Lee;
- *Twilight* (series) by Stephenie Meyer;
- *The Catcher in the Rye* by J.D. Salinger;
- *My Sister's Keeper* by Jodi Picoult;
- *The Earth, My Butt, and Other Big, Round Things* by Carolyn Mackler;
- *The Color Purple* by Alice Walker;
- *The Chocolate War* by Robert Cormier.

It's remarkable that these "top ten" lists, no matter which year you look at, usually include some of the classics like *To Kill a Mockingbird*, as well as newer volumes like the picture book *And Tango Makes Three,* which is based on a true story of two male penguins in New York City's Central Park Zoo who raise a baby penguin on their own.

But possibly of more concern than the scores of books that have been challenged year after year is a "type of censorship that involves books quietly disappearing from libraries" (Staples, 1996). Adults can simply walk into a library and pull a book off the shelf. This "stealth censorship" and the self-censorship we exercise as teachers may be even more distressing than the top ten banned book lists.

Self-censorship in classrooms. In a study comparing how middle school teachers and students reacted to reading and discussing *I Hadn't Meant to Tell You This* (Woodson, 1994), Freedman and Johnson (2001) give us a comprehensive view of teacher self-censorship of books and how it can silence and short-change students. This book is the story of two girls who form an unlikely friendship—a white, poor, abused girl and a black, popular, suburban girl—both without mothers. The book includes issues of friendship, racism, child abuse, class prejudice, abandonment, hope, and courage. The book has won many awards including the "Coretta Scott King Honor, ALA Best Book for Young Adults, ALA Notable Book, a Booklist Editor's Choice, and a Hornbook Fanfare" (Freedman & Johnson, 2001, p. 359).

The 15 female teachers and 11 middle school girls who read and discussed this book in separate groups all enjoyed the book. They understood and remarked about the power of the book, made personal connections to characters, and alluded to the importance of discussing current societal issues including racism, classism, and the compelling dilemmas adolescent girls encounter. Although both groups were deeply touched by the book, their responses differed. The girls saw the book as helpful to understanding the difficult and troubling issues that affect their own lives. For example, one girl noted:

> This book makes me think in a lot of ways. Look on the inside, not just on the outside. And it's just saying that it doesn't matter what color you are to have friends. About blacks and whites I think they're saying there's always going to be that little wall, and so how are we going to break it? And I think they broke it right there by standing up for their friendship. I think friendship is more important than color. (p. 362)

Although the teachers also found the book compelling, Freedman and Johnson's study demonstrates the "self-censorship paradox." The teachers demonstrated a keen awareness of the pedagogical power literature has to engage young people in deliberate questioning, genuine dialogue, and critical reflection, yet their feelings of insecurity pressured them into opting for a less provocative piece (p. 358). All of the teachers except one said they wouldn't use the book because it was too controversial, that they lacked or were unsure of support from their administrators, and that although the topic of sexual abuse was discussed in school it would be a problem if it was presented in a novel. One teacher's disturbing response points out how she became even more of a self-censor after reading this book.

> I would most definitely *not* use this book in my classroom, but it sure has awakened me to the importance of censoring my own books before using them in my classroom. I suppose I could use bits and pieces of this book to teach lessons about racism, classism, and interpersonal relationships. The parts of the book about sexual abuse are very sensitive issues and should not be addressed with an entire class . . . The book is very much related to what a lot of students go through especially with more and more fathers as the sole parent. (p. 364)

So even though this teacher sees that this book "reflects the world" in which her students live, she is more concerned about protecting herself than "informing" and "arming" her students (p. 368). Freedman and Johnson are clear that, "the practice of simply substituting a less controversial book solves nothing . . . As teachers, we must take our professional responsibilities seriously and make proactive decisions on behalf of our students" (p. 368). We strongly agree.

Self-censorship in libraries. One would imagine that librarians would be less likely to feel the pressures of self-censorship, but that isn't the case. In a study conducted by the *School Library Journal* of 654 media specialists, 70 percent reported they have not purchased books because they were concerned about possible negative reactions from parents (Whelan, 2009a). That's a frightening percentage. When asked what topics they were likely to self-censor, the results were not surprising: sexual content (87 percent), language (61 percent), violence (51 percent), and homosexuality (47 percent) (Whelan, 2009a, p. 28).

> A trained media specialist is expected to choose a range of titles that best suits the curriculum and meets the reading needs of students—and involves making judgment calls. "But if you reject a book just because of the subject matter or you think that it would cause some problems, then that's self-censorship," says Scales [a First Amendment advocate and former school librarian], "And that's going against professional ethics." (Whelan, 2009a, p. 28)

Both teachers and media specialists have an ethical and moral commitment to have books on shelves that students would benefit from reading. We live in difficult times and self-censoring books out of fear seems like a coming-to-life of Ray Bradbury's futuristic America in *Fahrenheit 451* (1987). Although we don't have "firemen" burning books, we don't want our schools to become places where trivial information is seen as *good* and complicated or controversial knowledge is seen as *bad*. Standing up for students' right to read is not an easy task for teachers or media specialists, but we have a professional commitment to take action so books that have the potential to change kids' lives are available to them.

Help if a book or other media is challenged. Both the American Library Association and the National Council of Teachers of English (NCTE) provide advice, documents, and support to teachers faced with challenges to books, film, and other media. Table 9.1 presents a variety of resources from these two organizations.

TABLE 9.1. Resources to Help Teachers with Issues of Banned or Challenged Books

Resource	Description	URL
NCTE: Guidelines on The Student's Right to Read	Gives model procedures for responding to challenges, including "Citizen's Request for Reconsideration of a Work."	http://www.ncte.org/positions/ statements/ righttoreadguideline
NCTE: Guidelines for Selection of Materials in English Language Arts Programs	Presents criteria and procedures that ensure thoughtful teacher selection of novels and other materials.	http://www.ncte.org/positions/ statements/ selectingelamaterial
NCTE: *Rationales for teaching challenged books*	Rich resource section includes table of contents of NCTE's Rationales for Commonly Challenged Books CD-ROM, an alphabetical list of other rationales on file, the SLATE Starter Sheet on "How to Write a Rationale," and sample rationales for *Bridge to Terabithia* and *The Color Purple*.	http://www.ncte.org/action/ anti-censorship/rationales
NCTE: *Guidelines for dealing with censorship of nonprint materials*	Offers principles and practices regarding challenges to nonprint materials.	http://www.ncte.org/positions/ statements/ censorshipofnonprint
ALA: *Banned Books Week materials*	*Banned Books Week* (BBW) is an annual event celebrating the freedom to read and the importance of the First Amendment. Held during the last week of September, *Banned Books Week* highlights the benefits of free and open access to information while drawing attention to the harms of censorship by spotlighting actual or attempted banning of books across the United States. There are lots of materials for teachers.	http://www.ala.org/ala/ issuesadvocacy/banned/ bannedbooksweek/index.cfm

It's often thought that challenges come only from conservative groups, but challenges to books come from both the right and the left (McClure, 1995; Nilsen & Donelson, 2009), which you will read about in the next two sections. As teachers, we have found that most parents are reasonable and if they don't want their child to read a particular book, we have another ready for the student to read. We believe strongly in a parent's right to have control over what his or her child reads, but not what the class reads or what is in a school library. The book described in the next section *I'm Glad I'm a Boy! I'm Glad I'm a Girl!* (Darrow, 1970), is one that has the potential to be challenged by liberal parents, but the way it's used can prevent challenges from occurring.

Principle #2: Even Troublesome Books Have Potential

Jerry was gleeful when he found a particularly obnoxious book written in the 1970s called *I'm Glad I'm a Boy! I'm Glad I'm a Girl!* (Darrow, 1970). The book is filled with stereotypical illustrations and text such as "Boys can be policemen. Girls can be meter maids." When Jerry reads this book to classes, or better yet has a male read the "boy" pages and a female read the "girl" pages, he is greeted with booing and hissing. What's interesting to us are the many important conversations about gender issues in children's literature that spring up after reading this book. Questions like "Is it really better now?" and "What groups are still being stereotyped?" open up new inquiries for the class.

We hold "the more books the better" philosophy. With this stance comes the possibility of using books that are not only dull, but books that are especially disturbing—those old sexist and racist books that we occasionally still find stuck in a back cupboard of a classroom or on the shelves of our libraries (or new ones where the racism and sexism are less explicit). We have found these books have the potential to start important conversations that might never occur if we hadn't dragged them off the shelf. So instead of self-censoring these texts, we now collect them for use with students.

Against popular wisdom, we believe that nearly all books, even books like *I'm Glad I'm a Boy! I'm Glad I'm a Girl!*, belong in classrooms. What's critical is how we use these books. If they are read and never interrogated for stereotypes or hurtful descriptions, school becomes a place where racism, sexism, and many other "isms" are simply reproduced. On the other hand, by only using books that have been evaluated as "stereotype free," students never get the chance to spot, discuss, and challenge representations that privilege certain groups while marginalizing others. By engaging students in strategies that help them read with a critical edge (see Chapter 8) we have seen many young people become critical consumers of books, TV, and other media. With this in mind, we use the principle *even troublesome books have potential* to challenge commonplace assumptions about book choice.

Being able to choose the right book for the right child has long been seen as an important attribute of great reading teachers (Mooney, 1990). When we encounter a reluctant reader and find an author or book whose topic grabs her interest, we nearly fall over ourselves in a rush to bring out related books in the hope of propelling this reader from a reluctant to a passionate consumer of books. While we see the value of this perspective and have placed many books in the hands of children, we also are aware of its limitations. We believe that it is important to be knowledgeable about books, so when an issue comes up in a child's life we can hand an appropriate book to that child, but the concept of the reader-as-individual and the essentialized idea that there is a right book for each child can go too far.

As long-time classroom teachers and teacher educators who have spent much time in classrooms, we are convinced that creating passionate readers goes way beyond matching particular children with particular books. Just picture what happens at a book-share after sustained silent reading time when students are presenting 30-second informal book talks. After Miguel sheepishly admits to his fourth grade class how he almost cried a number of times while reading *Shiloh* (Naylor, 1991) and how it was the best book he ever read, all of a sudden there's a run on *Shiloh*; it's flying off the shelves at school and public libraries. This Newbery Award winning book about a boy's ethical dilemmas over what to do about a mistreated beagle pup becomes one of those books you can't keep out of kids' hands. We strongly believe that the culture of the classroom can have more to do with *how* kids read and *what* kids read than our attempts to pair particular books with individual students.

We find a similar phenomenon occurs when kids find seemingly transgressive books like *Everyone Poops* (Gomi, 1993). As the title suggests, this book is about bodily waste and defecation, starting with an elephant and moving to a host of creatures including humans. Many of us have witnessed similar situations to what Mitzi saw one day in a second grade classroom. A small group of youngsters was in the back corner of the classroom snickering over what they believed to be an illicit piece of literature. The smart teacher stays away from that corner and the "naughty" book eventually gets enjoyed, giggled over, and read repeatedly by nearly every child in the class. This may sound like we are abdicating responsibility by turning over book choice entirely to students, but although kids are often much better booksellers than we are, we *still* have critical roles to play in choosing books. To illustrate this, we discuss books that have traditionally been considered trashy or inappropriate for use in classrooms and how not all books are equal.

Trashy books. Another stereotypical characteristic of a great reading teacher is someone whose shelves are filled with carefully chosen literature for independent reading, read aloud, and content instruction. Administrators often ask teachers to make sure they have a purpose in mind for each book they use in the classroom. To help you with rationales for using books, Table 5.1 in Chapter 5 gives ten principles for using literature that can easily be applied to individual books. While the principle of knowing why you are using a particular book is important if a parent or administrator asks why you are using it, it also has limitations unless you have a wide range of what's acceptable for kids to read. The *careful choice of books model* implies that we'd better be really cautious before we put a book on our shelves, which often results in self-censorship and keeping some books out of the kids' hands. It's true there are a few books we would not put in our classrooms based on the age of our students, but we strongly believe in *the more books the better,* even those we think are horrible. Many of us have shuddered, but have also seen the incredible power of "less-than-enthusiastic" readers sailing through book after book of "trashy" series like *Captain Underpants* (Pilkey), the ninth most challenged of all books from 2000–05; *Goosebumps* (Stine), the sixteenth most challenged of all books from 1990–2000; or *The Stupids* (Allard), the twenty-sixth most challenged of all books from 1990–2000 (American Library Association, 2009). The controversies surrounding these books are evident in the pervasive way they are taken off shelves in libraries and classrooms across the country. In addition, we regularly hear opposing viewpoints on what to do with "these books" during debates in teachers' lunchrooms, in newspaper articles, and in interactive conversations on the Internet. As an example, here's a small segment of a typical exchange from the archives of the Children's Lit. Listserv (1995) that illustrates a range of viewpoints on *Goosebumps*. It starts with a librarian who admits that even though kids love the books, she doesn't want them in her library.

> As an elementary librarian in a public school, I would not choose to spend my limited funds on *Goosebumps*. The kids do love them. I have read them and find them uninteresting, not at all engaging. When I took this job in the fall, there were a total

of 6 copies of *Goosebumps* in the inventory. They are always checked out and I keep hoping that they will be lost. One has been . . . hooray! I will not replace them, nor do I intend to buy more. This is not to say that I do not have controversial books nor books which are "junk" but that while I am there I will spend my funds on what I consider quality literature. The trash can be bought out of their own funds! (Originally posted on March 2, 1995)

It's worthy to note that although this librarian (and others we know) can't keep *Goosebumps* books on her shelves because the kids love reading them so much, many believe these books have no place in the library. We see this stance as counterproductive to creating readers by positioning students and librarians as opponents rather than collaborators. We also wonder why she finds some "junk" books acceptable, but *Goosebumps* definitely are not. In contrast, the following response from children's literature scholar Perry Nodelman details some of the expected and surprising things he found when he actually read 18 Goosebumps books.

Here's my experience of *Goosebumps*. I got interested in them after I read that *NY Times* piece last summer about best-selling books. I figured that any series whose sales almost equaled the combined sales of the fifteen next most popular series was worthy of my attention. I expected real junk. I found some undeniably simplistic writing and characterization, but some very ingenious situations—many borrowed from adult films and novels, but handled in interesting ways. And in some cases these books evoke all sorts of subtle psychological issues—never directly: they have the understatement of fairy tales. I was also surprised to find out how un-formulaic they are: the main characters are sometimes underdogs who triumph, sometimes underdogs who lose—and sometimes, underdogs who triumph by turning into monsters. I can't say that all 18 of the Goosebumps I've read are equally interesting—but many of them are. (Excerpt from an email by Perry Nodelman distributed on the Child-Lit Listserv on March 2, 1995. Reprinted with permission from Perry Nodelman.)

We love the way Nodelman really digs deeper and finds out what draws students to the *Goosebumps* series rather than just dismissing it as trash. We are not book police, deciding which books are appropriate for which students to read. Rather, we are committed to respecting kids' choices, *but* on the other hand, we strongly believe in negotiation and persuasion. We try our darndest to make the books we love so attractive that kids want to read them just as much as they want to read *Captain Underpants*.

Not all books are equal: Starting important conversations. One of the main reasons we feel comfortable allowing students to read so-called trashy books in our classrooms is because our rooms and those of the teachers we work with are filled with lots of great children's and adolescent literature, which we believe has the power to start important conversations that can move kids from *The Stupids* (Allard, 1977–89) to *Stargirl* (Spinelli, 2000). This quality literature serves as a backdrop or criterion from which kids can engage in text analysis the way Nodelman did in his study of *Goosebumps* books.

As an example, we present Lori Norton-Meier's story of how her kindergarten class analyzed a set of books they had ordered with book money from the school's parent/teacher association (2009). The class ordered *The Story Box* book set, because it contained a book they loved, *Mrs. Wishy-Washy* (Cowley, 1980). When the books came, Norton-Meier spilled them on the rug to the oooohs and aaaaahs of the children gathered around in a circle. She picked up one of the books, *The Bicycle* (Cowley, 1991), and started reading. "The clown got on and the lady got on, and the boy got on, and the girl got on, and the bear got on . . ." (Norton-Meier, 2009, p. 189).

Norton-Meier described the unusual silence that followed her reading, and how both she and the children were stunned by the mind-numbing quality of the text. "Then Jeffrey pops to his knees with his hands firmly planted on his hips, exclaims, 'Now, wasn't that a crappy piece of literature!?'" (p. 189).

This starts an amazing conversation among the kindergartners about how "crappy" is a perfect way to describe the book, how awful it was, how it didn't have a good ending, and how nothing happens in the text. One child queried, "It doesn't really have a happy ending—or a sad ending—does it have an end?" (p. 189). This moved the conversation away from simply talking about how terrible the book was to digging deeper and analyzing why it was so disappointing and what the author might have done to make it better. The kids talked about how it reminded them of other books they read and liked, but these other books had plots (our words not theirs)— something actually happened in the story. They talked about how maybe the author didn't use enough words to include a plot. Meier-Norton describes the variety of responses students had from reading *The Bicycle*, including "an emotional response (crappy literature), a critique about the structure of text, a comparison of two texts, and a wondering about how the text could be more intriguing to the audience" (p. 192). Norton-Meier attributes the presence of some crappy literature in her classroom as an impetus to her students becoming better readers, responders, and critics.

But if Norton-Meier had only read "crappy" books to her class and had not spent lots of time discussing quality literature with students, the incredible conversations around *The Bicycle* probably would have never taken place. So from our perspective, bring on the books—all books, any books, but make sure to create spaces where students know a good book when they hear it or read it and can talk about what makes it a good one. We believe important conversations can start as a response to any book as long as the foundation of our literature program helps students appreciate good literature and gives them many occasions to try on the identity of a critical reader.

Sometimes we might be tempted to believe that if we have mainly award-winning books in our classrooms, all of our problems of *choosing the right book* will be solved. The next section challenges that assumption.

Principle #3: Book Awards Are More Complicated Than They Seem

Lee Heffernan taught third grade for years. When she changed grade levels to sixth grade, Lee looked forward to working with young adolescents. She had her sixth-graders engage in the regular beginning-of-the-year curriculum—reading books that have been nominated for the state book award. The theme for this part of her curriculum was *Keep Your Eyes on the Prize*. Students started the school year by reading titles from the list of Young Hoosier Book Award nominees. Like many states, Indiana presents a book award to an author each year. The award is designed to "stimulate recreational reading among middle school students" (Indiana Library Federation, 2008) and is chosen by a committee composed of members of the Association for Indiana Media Educators, a subgroup of the Indiana Library Federation. Students who read five or more books on the list get to vote for their choice of the winning title, with the award being announced in the spring of each school year (Heffernan & Lewison, 2009).

Because the current Young Hoosier Book Award (YHBA) list did not contain many titles that focused on social justice issues, Lee anticipated that inviting students to question the notion of book awards, and awards in general, would bring a critical lens to the class literacy work, with students investigating how awards influence and shape us as consumers and creators of texts.

Work during this unit was guided by the question, "How do book prizes, and prizes in general, work and why do we have them?" The year began with a discussion about the criteria for choosing books for the YHBA and the purpose of the award. During the discussion, many students noted the arbitrary nature of the criteria. Why did the books have to be published within the last five years? And why couldn't foreign-born authors have their books nominated? Students began understanding that these criteria had real impact on the types of books that were nominated. Many felt it was unfair that J.K. Rowling's Harry Potter books could never be nominated for the state award (Heffernan & Lewison, 2009).

In order to learn more about book awards, students read descriptions of awards on the American Library Association website and found out that book awards have a wide range of purposes. While some book awards promote reading generally (YHBA), others promoted specific genres (Edgar), reading for older kids (Prinz, Newbery), and younger kids (Caldecott). Others promoted awareness of specific underrepresented social groups (Rivera, King, Schneider). Students worked during their computer lab time to research specific book awards and to design a book award with a purpose and criteria of their own (Heffernan & Lewison, 2009). They ended up by studying all kinds of awards and how they affect people. In this chapter, like Lee's kids, we ask what are book awards and what is their purpose?

Complicating book awards. There are hundreds of book awards given every year. Here we focus on the major children's book awards or those that we feel are especially important. The awards on the website (www.routledge.com/cw/leland) are all given by divisions or affiliates of the American Library Association (ALA). This listing on the website is meant to be a reference, a way to familiarize yourself with some of the major book awards. We've included the criteria for each award, so you and your students can interrogate different awards the way Lee's students did.

Controversies around award winning books. Although many teachers and librarians use book awards as criteria for choosing books for classrooms, these awards are steeped in controversy. First, there is lots of disagreement about the *cultural authenticity* of award winning books (see Chapter 4). We use the extensive research of Smolkin and Suina (1997) throughout this section as one complex example of the multiple perspectives that Native Americans hold regarding the Caldecott award winning book *Arrow to the Sun: A Pueblo Indian Tale* (McDermott, 1974). After extensive interviews, Smolkin and Suina found that different Pueblo groups read and interpreted the book very differently. The Eastern Rio Grande Pueblos, who were the victims of very repressive policies under Spanish colonial rule (Smolkin & Suina, 1997, p. 310), are more traditional than Western Rio Grande Pueblo groups. One of the major controversies in McDermott's book is the image of the Kachina figure, sacred in the Pueblo tradition. Members of the Eastern Pueblos believe that "women, girls, and uninitiated young boys . . . are not allowed to see Kachinas out of the context of their own community's ceremonies" (p. 312). So, you can imagine how offensive it was for them to see these images in a children's picture book. On the other hand, Smolkin and Suina spoke with two teachers from the Western Pueblos who "felt comfortable having the book in their homes and sharing the book with the children in their classrooms" (p. 312). In short, there is no "monolithic Pueblo world" that can rate the book as culturally acceptable or not. Smolkin and Suina urge us to get beyond simplistic dichotomies when we consider multicultural books like *Arrow to the Sun*.

They call for a move toward "multiple pedagogies" to decrease censorship and so do we. Once we start censoring books, the opportunities for multiple perspectives to be examined diminish. We understand that some of the Eastern Pueblo people will not have *Arrow to the Sun* in their homes or classrooms, but that doesn't mean the book should be banned from other settings. What we find especially important is sharing complicated viewpoints such as those about *Arrow to the Sun* with our students to start critical conversations that don't have easy answers. For example, after reading *Arrow to the Sun* aloud to students and then sharing the contradictory results of Smolkin and Suina's study, students can then examine the criteria for choosing Caldecott books, found on the website (www.routledge.com/cw/leland), and decide if they think the criteria are appropriate or should be changed. We expect no consensus on an inquiry like this—just very meaningful and significant conversations around books.

Stereotypes in award winners. A second complicating issue around award winning books is that they may *perpetuate racial and gender stereotypes.* Albers (1996) examined twelve years of Caldecott winning books and found the representations of females and people of color to be limited and stereotyped. Taxel (1986) points out that one big issue around books with inaccurate or hurtful representations of characters is our belief in the power of literature, the power it has to impact our lives. He discusses the complexity of weighing the artistic excellence of award winning books in light of books that are blatantly sexist or racist (p. 248). We have found some of the questions that arise from Taxel's inquiry to be great discussion starters for classroom conversations:

- How much do we soak up when we read a book? Do inaccuracies and stereotypes matter?
- Can the content of a book be dangerous to children (who are passive consumers of texts) or do children change, transform, or reject stereotypical images in books?
- How important is it that characters in books are believable by the groups they represent?
- Does who is telling the story make a difference in whether negative stereotypes are acceptable?
- How do we judge award-winning books that have literary merit but include inaccurate or hurtful representations of particular groups of people?
- Are aesthetic criteria alone sufficient to judge books for children?
- Should racial and gender representations be fully examined before a book can receive an award? If so, who can be the judge of these representations?
- Can you think of any justifiable reasons for including representations of characters that may be viewed as hurtful by certain groups?

These are not easy questions—ones that we still struggle with as adults. But, when we read books that we know are stereotypic like *I'm Glad I'm a Boy! I'm Glad I'm a Girl!* (Darrow, 1970), we also read books like *Piggybook* (Browne, 1986), and others that challenge commonplace gender representations of characters. Multiple perspective text sets allow students to examine complex questions and come to important insights about how characters are portrayed in books. They can examine questions such as:

- How are female (black, Latino, Asian, poor, rural, etc.) characters portrayed in each of the books?
- What does each author want us to think about girls and women?
- What is the relationship between female characters and other characters in each of the books?
- Which of the books in this text set would you recommend for friends to read? Why would you recommend these books?

What are the consequences of book awards? A third complicating issue around award winning books is the *work they do in the world.* For example, Sibert Award winning author Marc Aronson (2001) notes that many librarians don't read books carefully before they order them if they have won awards. We have noticed this ourselves—if a book has won an award we are more likely to buy it without reading as many reviews as we might for other non-prize winning books. In addition, Kenneth Kidd (2007) asks us to consider the market ramifications of books winning awards in terms of sales. His article made us think of the "Oprah Effect," where books that she recommended on her TV show became bestsellers. Kidd points out that although there is no cash prize associated with awards such as the Newbery, "it can double the sales of a book, as well as increase sales of the author's other books" and getting the award "keeps the titles and authors in circulation for decades" (p. 168). Kidd notes that these award-winning books also are likely to be showcased in prominent places in libraries and bookstores. So another aspect of awards that students may want to consider is their economic impact. It could be interesting for groups of students to look at book sales numbers in relation to awards. They could also conduct an inquiry into what books are prominently displayed in local bookstores and other retail establishments where books are sold.

It was our intention by exploring the principles of *Censorship Threatens Democracy*, the *Potential of Troublesome Books*, and the *Complicated Nature of Award Winning Books*, to bring to the surface the idea that the books we choose to use with our students are never neutral. Whatever we choose, there can be unexpected issues. This makes having a sound rationale (even in the back of your mind) for why you are using particular books in your classroom an important part of teaching practice. Pure enjoyment of reading is a fine rationale for having particular books in your classroom. Being able to discuss why you think a book is important for your students to read can circumvent most problems that arise. Table 5.1 in Chapter 5 is a great resource to use for creating justifications for using particular books as it delineates ten principles that explain why we use literature in classrooms. And remember, the vast majority of teachers have not had the experience of having a book they are using challenged.

Key Issues in Implementation

One of the biggest stumbling blocks to using important books, or "trashy" books, or whatever books we want in classrooms are district mandates for basal reading programs or leveled book collections. There have been reading series in schools for many years, but in the past, teachers were viewed as professionals who knew what students needed in terms of reading development. In Mitzi's first teaching experience she was given a basal reader, but used only a portion of the stories from those books. The majority of reading that students did came from the classroom and school libraries. We acknowledge that some reading programs can be helpful to novice teachers, as they were to Mitzi, while she slowly added a wide range of books and activities such as sustained silent reading, partner reading, and other strategies to promote the love of reading in her students. The difference today is that many teachers are told that they can only use prescribed curricula in ways that show fidelity to the programs, many of which take so much time during the day that there is no flexibility or opportunity for using quality children's literature. In some cases, these mandated programs have resulted in a reduction in time or in extreme cases, elimination of content area subjects such as social studies and science. This stands in opposition to our own experience where we found social studies curricula greatly enhanced by using social issues, multicultural, and international books.

The National Council of Teachers of English has a helpful brochure on its website, *Guidelines for Defining and Defending Instructional Methods*, http://www.ncte.org/positions/statements/defendinginstrmethod. "Increasing questions about and attacks on various methods used in teaching English language arts led to a 1994 NCTE Resolution on the right to teach (reaffirmed in a 1996 resolution) calling for the identification, definition, and defense of methods which are most often attacked. A joint subcommittee of the NCTE/SLATE (Support for the Learning and

Teaching of English) and the NCTE Standing Committee Against Censorship was formed to develop a document to implement that resolution."

The committee's work produced a brochure that is available on our website: www.routledge.com/cw/leland. No permissions are required to photocopy and distribute this document. If students are to receive high quality instruction, it is essential that teachers have the freedom to select appropriate methods and materials for teaching. This NCTE website would be helpful to some teachers we know who have an administrator surveilling their classrooms to make sure the mandated materials, often leveled books, are being used at a particular time of the day.

Working With Linguistically and Culturally Diverse Students

Books about sensitive or difficult issues are often self-censored and never shared with students. A survey was conducted in 2008 by the *School Library Journal* on self-censorship (Whelan, 2009b, see Figure 9.1). School librarians reported they didn't purchase books because of troubling content.

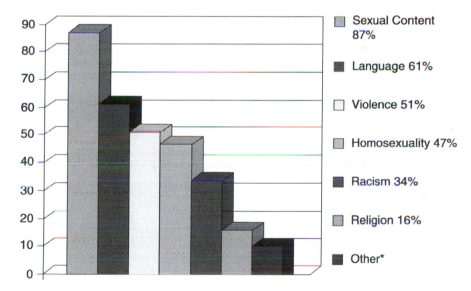

FIGURE 9.1.   Self-Censorship of Books by Librarians.

*Including drug use and inappropriate pictures (Whelan, 2009b). Used with permission of School Library Journal. Copyright © 2011. All rights reserved.

The chart shows that books addressing issues that touch kids' lives in important ways may never get into the hands of students who could benefit from reading them. We worry that kids who are struggling with issues of racism, gender identification, violence, physical abuse, verbal abuse, or religious persecution may not have access to books that can provide images of other kids who are in similar circumstances to their own. In other words, those students who are most vulnerable have the least chance of reading books that could be helpful in dealing with difficult issues that are present in their lives.

This self-censorship doesn't just affect individual students, but also the class as a whole. If we never read books about homosexuality related to the age group we teach, how are we ever going to create tolerant, caring classrooms? In short, although we give lots of lip service to the importance of diversity and say we support difference in our teaching, there are some topics that lie outside of our comfort zones.

An example comes from Coe Booth, the author of *Tyrell* (2007), an ALA best Book for Young Adults. This book is about an African American 15-year-old boy whose father is in jail and whose mother's joblessness has left his family homeless and living at a roach-infested shelter. Trying to escape the poverty he finds himself in and make a better life for his brother, Tyrell has to make hard decisions about whether to take the easy money that can come from drug dealing or stick to the ideals he has for his family. Booth commented that she has seen her book in locked cases in libraries instead of with the rest of the books in the teen section (Whelan, 2009a).

> Even more frustrating, says Booth, is labeling. [She notes that] It seems that any book with an African-American character on the cover is quickly being labeled as street-lit, regardless of the subject matter or the setting of the book. Meanwhile, books about Caucasian characters in urban settings don't get lumped into this genre. (Whelan, 2009a, p. 28)

We are not saying it's easy to bring books with controversial themes into your classroom. It takes courage. But as professionals, we have a responsibility to all of our students, not just the one's who fit into "safe" categories of difference. What if the student who lives with two moms never sees anyone like himself in books, even though there are a number of wonderful picture and chapter books on the subject? What if we don't let other students in our class know that there are all kinds of families, none better than others, just different? If we want to walk the walk and not just talk the talk about diversity, then we need to be professional and open up the often-narrow definition of what diversity means in our classrooms.

Technology Extensions and Electronic Resources

The web has great resources for having your class explore issues related to challenged or banned books. The American Library Association's *Frequently Challenged Books* webpage is one of the best and is easily found on any search engine. It includes information about banned and challenged books; a listing of challenged books by year, by author, by decade, or by statistics; a link to the *Banned Books Week* site and associated classroom resources; and much more (ALA, 2011b, http://www.ala.org/ala/issuesadvocacy/banned/index.cfm).

A site we especially like is by Jim Trelease, author of *The Read-Aloud Handbook* (2006). Trelease has a helpful website on www.trelease-on-reading.com called Censors and Children's Lit. There are multiple sections on this site including the topics shown in Table 9.2. Through his research, Trelease powerfully calls attention to some of the absurdities of censorship.

TABLE 9.2.   Jim Trelease on Censorship

• Religion, Harry Potter, and the Taliban	• The Great Textbook War
• The Vatican weighs in on Harry Potter	• Book-lynching in Indianapolis High School
• "Forbidden Fruit" concept in censorship	• Test and textbook censors
• Banning "Bridge to Terabithia"	• Capt. Underpants and Junie B. Jones
• Censoring Red Riding Hood's grandma	• When is it "inappropriate"?
• Censoring Thomas Merton, Judy Blume— even Bill Martin Jr.	

Another useful resource comes from the Book and Periodical Council of Canada. This organization has created a document called *When the Censor Comes* (Bernstein, 1996, http://www.efc.ca/pages/chronicle/whattodo.html). This guide for teachers, librarians, and booksellers starts with a definition of all the different types of censorship that might affect a teacher (challenges, public attack, written complaints, and probably our biggest enemy—self-censorship). We particularly like a number of sections in the guide including:

- How to spot a would-be censor.
- Heading them off at the pass.
- Who ya gonna call?

In short, there are hundreds of websites that address the issue of challenged or banned children's books. The three we highlighted here are just a sampling of what's available electronically as resources in your classroom.

Assessment

There are a number of ways to assess whether we are providing students with a wide range of literature and accepting our professional responsibility to have children read books that are important to their lives, even if they are controversial. The following questions are helpful in assessing classroom libraries and reading programs.

- Do you have a wide range of books on your classroom shelves including great literature; books that you may not like, but those that the kids do; controversial books; books that are important for students gaining multiple perspectives on topics of your curriculum?
- When you use books that contain stereotypes, do you have a range of strategies to use with students to help them unpack problematic images of others?
- If a parent questions a book you are using, can you provide a rationale for using the book, and if necessary, an alternate book for the child to read?
- Have you used a questionable book this year?

Invitation: Mini-Inquiries Into Challenged or Banned Books

It is important that all of us educate ourselves relative to censorship. This invitation (see Textbox 9.1), *Mini-Inquiries into Challenged or Banned Books*, invites students to enter the conversation by asking them to re-examine books they plan to read as well as some they will have already read at an earlier age.

Textbox 9.1. Invitation: Mini-Inquiries Into Challenged or Banned Books

This strategy asks students what it is they think about books that have been challenged or banned. While we may think of our right to read as a fundamental right, there are many in our country who believe they are in a better position than we are to judge what is appropriate or is not appropriate reading material. This invitation asks students to make up their own mind.

Materials & Procedures

- A range of books that have been banned. Examples include:

  And Tango Makes Three (Richardson & Parnell, 2005)
  In the Night Kitchen (Sendak, 1970)
  Sylvester and the Magic Pebble (Steig, 1969)
  Rose Blanche (McEwan, 1987)
  Nappy Hair (Herron, 1977)
  The Lorax (Seuss, 1971)
  Smoky Night (Bunting, 1994)
  Where the Wild Things Are (Sendak, 1963)
  The Story of Babar (De Brunhoff, 1937)
  Red Riding Hood (Marshall, 1993)

- Printouts of why each of these books has been banned (see the American Library Association and the National Council of Teachers of English website for a list of challenges brought by various groups against these books)

1. Explain to students that all of these books have been banned by individuals or groups who think they don't belong in schools or libraries.
2. Invite students to pick a book and read it.
3. Read the materials that explain why the book was challenged or banned.
4. Make a mini-book (see One-Page Stapleless Books in the Literature Response Strategy section of this book), poster, or write a poem that:

a) Explains whether or not you like the book and why.
b) Tells why this book was challenged or banned.
c) Reports whether you agree or disagree with the challenge and justifies whether you think this book should be used or not used in our classroom.

Other Notes

Rather than provide materials as to why particular books have been banned, students might be invited to do their own web searches.

Professional Development

Since we all have had instances where we have seen books and said, "I'd never use that in my classroom," we think it's important to meet with colleagues and discuss those books that we've self-censored. In class or study group meetings, have everyone bring in two books they decided not to use with students. The following questions can guide these conversations.

- What about this book made you decide not to use it in your classroom?
- What worries do you have about what would happen if you read the book to your students or let a student read it?
- Has anyone else in the group used the book or thinks they might use it? If so, what makes you comfortable using this text?
- How can we support each other to use more risky books with our students?
- What are the benefits of using risky books in our classrooms?

TABLE 9.3.   Suggestions for Further Reading

Whelan, D.L. (2009a) A dirty little secret: Self-censorship is rampant and lethal. *School Library Journal, 55*(2), 26–30.

This article starts with the story of a young adult novelist who was sure his new book *Boy Toy* (Lyga, 2007) would spark controversy when it hit the bookstores and libraries, but nothing happened. The book was getting rave reviews and Awards despite its controversial content. Then Lyga heard stories about how school librarians loved the books but were afraid to buy it for their libraries for fear of complaints. This article describes how many wonderful children's and young adult books are being kept out of school libraries and what we can do about it.

Norton-Meier, L.A. (2009) In defense of crappy literature: When the book is bad but the literary thinking is rich! *Language Arts, 86*(1), 188–195.

This article begins with the story of Norton-Meier's kindergarten class and how one child proclaims, "Now, that was a crappy piece of literature!" This rather shocking statement provides an opportunity for an examination of literacy, identity, agency and power. Critical issues and provocative questions emerge about the importance of "crappy" literature and how we create spaces in our classrooms for students to question, examine, respond, and think in a variety of ways about all types of texts.

Heffernan, L. & Lewison, M. (2009) Keep your eyes on the prize: Critical stance in the middle school classroom. *Voices from the Middle, 17*(1), 19–27.

This study focuses on ways that sixth graders reacted to the question of book awards and awards in general, positioning themselves as reflective inquirers as they engaged in the regular sixth-grade beginning-of-the-year curriculum—reading books that have been nominated for the state book award. The article focuses on how students examined book awards from four types of critical stance—conscious engagement, trying on alternate ways of being, responsibility to inquiry, and reflexivity.

ten
Literature
Response
Strategies

Art Trading Cards

Art Trading Cards began as business cards among artists. Each one was an original piece of work with the artist's contact information on the back. When used as part of the reading program, students design cards that express what they see as the main meaning of a book. This process requires readers to figure out what is most important and then represent it symbolically. Finished cards serve as testimonials for great books once students begin trading them. Figure 10.1 shows an Art Trading Card recommending the adolescent novel *Call Me Hope* (Olson, 2008) to other readers.

Materials & Procedures

- Art trading cards—2½" × 3 ½" pieces cut from 140 lb. watercolor paper (also available precut at hobby stores)
- Watercolor, oil, tempera, or acrylic paints and brushes
- Black fine-tipped markers (e.g. Micron .05 or .08)

1. Distribute blank cards and work with students to generate a list of all of the things they might do with them to support reading literature. Remind them to "Think Artistically."
2. Invite students to think about the books they have read and design Art Trading Cards for their favorites. The title, a brief synopsis, and what they liked about the book are included on the back of the card.
3. Students trade finished cards with classmates.

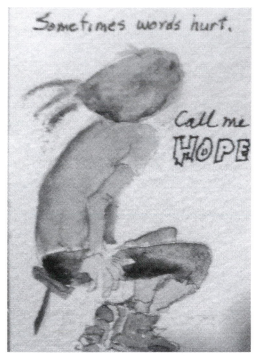
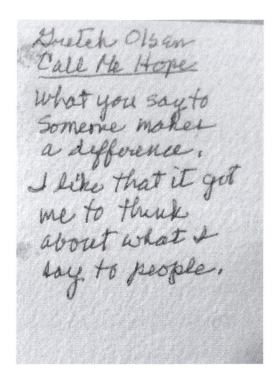

FIGURE 10.1.   Using Art Trading Cards to Recommend Books.

Other Notes

Art trading cards can be part of a focused study. When exploring important social issues, our students developed art trading cards that depicted the social issue they were most interested in working on and exchanged cards with others who were interested in the same issue.

Extensions

Zentangles (Bartholomew Steen, 2010) involves using a fine tipped pen to decorate an existing piece of art with repetitive and intricate patterns. Since it takes patience to create Zentangles, the practice is thought to promote meditation. Zentangles can add another layer of meaning onto art that initially the artist may not have thought was successful. Figure 10.2 shows a picture of two children working on a computer. The artist wanted to highlight the importance of multiple ways of knowing in a digital world; Zentangles allowed her to focus on what she saw as most important.

Author Wall of Fame

When engaged in an author study, it's helpful if students have a variety of ways to share their investigations of particular authors. One option is an author wall of fame (Fox, 2006), where students create visual representations of the work they've done.

Materials & Procedures

- Poster board
- Markers
- Glue

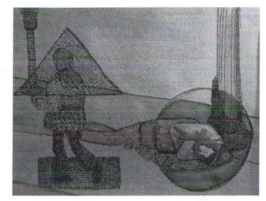

FIGURE 10.2. Using Zentangles to Highlight Social Issues (used with permission of the artist, Alice Sanborn).

1. After conducting an author study, individuals or small groups of students create a graphic and visual representation of the author studied.
2. Students can include photos, drawings, writing, titles of texts, and other information they've gathered.
3. Remind students that this will be up on a bulletin board or in a hallway, so it will be most effective if they design their posters to be seen from a distance and pull in readers.

Other Notes

Although this strategy is designed to be used with author studies, it can just as easily be used with genre or focused studies. All you need to do is change the title of the wall. Even though students will usually be sharing what they've learned in class discussions and presentations, posters that represent the most important aspects of their inquiries are a good way to leave material documentation of the work they have done. When students spend a lot of time on one project, it's valuable for them to be able to see evidence of their work on the walls as part of the classroom or school environment.

Becoming a Text Analyst

Allan Luke and Peter Freebody (1997) believe that readers need to go beyond being proficient code breakers, meaning makers, and text users and also become text analysts. Text analysts not only gain personal and social meanings from texts but also examine how the text is trying to position them. Luke and Freebody's four resources model is one of the foundations of critical literacy, helping students interrogate the authors' intentions and what they want readers to believe.

Materials & Procedures

- All works of children's or adult literature can be used. (There are a number of questions that can be asked of any text being read.)

1. For characters and perspectives:
   Whose voices are represented and whose are missing in this text?
   Why is _____ (character) so prominent in this text?
   What would _____ (missing character) say if he/she had a voice in this text?
2. For plot and meanings:
   Which stories are privileged and which are marginalized in this text?
   How would this story be different if it was told from the perspective of _____ rather than _____?
   What views are represented in this text? Not represented?
3. For positioning:
   In what ways am I positioned within this text?
   What did the author want me to believe after reading the text?
   What are the ways this text could be rewritten to reposition the reader?

Big Books

Big books (Holdaway, 1999) are over-sized copies of easy to read books that emergent readers enjoy. While commercially available, they can also be made by teachers or groups of students. Big books allow students to follow along and see the print and pictures as the text is read aloud. Teachers typically invite students to read along and engage them in conversations about various semantic and graphophonic elements in the story.

Materials & Procedures

- A class favorite book
- Over-sized sheets of newsprint
- Markers

1. After identifying a book that emergent readers enjoy, a teacher or parent prints the words of the text on large sheets of newsprint, leaving ample room for illustrations on each page.
2. While teachers or parents may try to replicate the illustrations in the original text in the big book, these books often take on special meaning when students make their own illustrations.
3. Once illustrated and stapled together, the book is placed on an easel and read to the entire class. Individual students sometimes use pointers to follow the text.

Other Notes

1. Once shared with the whole class, big books are put into the class library. Students pair up and read them during buddy reading or free reading time.
2. Teachers sometimes make big books out of the nursery rhymes, jump rope jingles, or songs that young children come to school already knowing by memory.
3. Some teachers use post-it notes to cover words or phrases in big books, thus encouraging students to use their knowledge of language, the story, and their world to predict the words and phrases underneath. On other occasions only the initial letter of a word

or the first word in a phrase is shown, while the rest of the letters or phrases are covered by notes that are removed as the reading progresses and predictions are confirmed.

Book Brochures (See Chapter 4: Invitation)

Buddy Reading (See Literature Circles: Extensions)

Chart-a-Conversation

Powerful literature discussions happen when readers have opportunities to talk about books. Pat Smith, a professor from Australia, developed the chart-a-conversation strategy to support readers in considering multiple perspectives as they engage in extended conversations about books.

Materials & Procedures

- A reading selection
- A response sheet with four columns: I Like; I Dislike; Patterns/Puzzles; Problems

1. Read the selected text aloud. We often use a familiar text like *Where the Wild Things Are* (Sendak, 1963) for the first experience.
2. Form groups of students with one designated as the recorder. Each group gets a response sheet. Students discuss the book in terms of the four columns: Things they like, things they dislike (which might be difficult as children rarely talk negatively about books), patterns or puzzles they see (in the illustration as well as the text), and problems they have with the book (like scary monsters in the book or how the book might be used or advertised).
3. Once groups have something in each column, they select new recorders. All groups come together and take turns reading from their response sheets until all items have been shared. As groups share one thing they liked, disliked, patterns, and problems, the recorders write new items on their group's individual worksheet. A different writing implement is used to keep track of what's new.
4. Reform the original groups and talk about one of the new items on their response sheet.
5. As a culminating activity, students spend several minutes reflecting in writing on this experience. What new insights do they have about the role that discussion plays in the reading process? Share these reflections.

Conscience Circle (See Process Drama)

Counter Narratives (See Emancipatory Fairy Tales)

Cultural X-Rays

Gertz (1973) defines culture as a set of social practices within a group of people. These social practices go beyond external characteristics, like language, food, and clothing, to include basic values and perspectives. It is important for children to understand that everyone has a culture. Cultural x-rays is an instructional strategy designed by Kathy Short (2009b) to support children in seeing people in terms of values and beliefs rather than in terms of surface differences such as race, gender, or nationality. The metaphor of an x-ray highlights the need to understand what is on the outside as well as the inside of each person as a cultural being.

Materials & Procedures

- Literature in which characters explore their cultural identities. (Some examples are *A Day's Work* [Bunting, 1997], *Grandfather's Journey* [Say, 1993], *Ruby's Wish* [Bridges, 2002])
- Paper and colored markers

1. Have children create two personal cultural x-rays (one for themselves and one for the main character in the book being read) using an outline of a body shape with a heart inside.
2. After reading, have students place the values and beliefs they have in the heart of one of the cultural x-rays (What is important to me?) and the values and beliefs the book character has in the heart of the other cultural x-ray (What is important to the character in the book?). Surface differences between themselves and the character in the book are listed outside of the heart on each cultural x-ray.

Other Notes

Students often struggle with the notion of values and beliefs. Many list things that they value like families, rather than why they value these things. If this happens, ask students to think about what values and beliefs they have gained from the things they have listed in their heart. What values did you gain from your family? What do they add to your life? Why is this significant to you?

Deconstructing Fairy Tales (See Chapter 2: Invitation)

Developing a Miscue Ear (See Chapter 3: Invitation)

Discourse Analysis for Kids

Jim Gee's discourse analysis strategies (1999) can be simplified and used with all students. It's a way for students to begin to pay attention to language, the work it does in the world, and how it can shape perception. This is best done a few times as a whole class and then students can work in small groups to do an analysis. We start with a greeting card because it has brief text, and move to picture books and poems.

Materials & Procedures

- Greeting cards for a particular holiday (Valentine's Day, Halloween, Birthdays). Cards designed specifically for boys, for girls, or cards that respond to a topic of interest like Barbie, NASCAR, etc. work especially well. (See Table 10.1 for an analysis of a typical girl's birthday card)
- List of discourse analysis questions

1. Examine the *situated meanings* of the card:
   What are the key words in this card?
   What do these words mean here?
   How do the fonts impact the meaning?

TABLE 10.1.   Sample Discourse Analysis

	Girl's Birthday Card
	Cover: Pink with glitter and illustrations of clothes, shoes, make-up. Cover Text: Pink and glitter and girly stuff. Inside Text: This day is so cool. Hope your birthday is dazzling!
Situated Meanings	Key words: Pink, Glitter, Dazzling. Meanings: Glitter and Dazzles mean flashy, attention-getting, glowing. Fonts: Curly and feminine.
Social Languages	Text: This day is so cool. Teen grammar and language. You hear this among friends, on TV, on radio. Signifies one is a member of a particular group.
Cultural Models	Simple story line: Girls like the color pink, flashy stuff, and consumer goods. Beliefs: If you have a lot of "girl" consumer goods you'll have a great birthday. All girls buy into this conception of femininity. Symbols: Actual glitter, pink color, illustrations of stereotypical consumer goods for girls.
Discourses	Rules: In order to have a good birthday you need to adhere to stereotypical notions of femininity. Purpose: To make a particular kind of girl appreciate the person who sent such a "cool" card. Indicates the sender knows what's important to this girl. Discourses: Teen TV shows, movies, commercials.

2. Examine the *social languages* of the card:
   How are nouns, verbs, and other words used?
   Whose language is this?
   Where do people speak in this way?
3. Examine the *cultural models* of the card:
   What simple story does this card tell?
   What would you have to believe for this card to make sense?
   What symbols are important to the meaning of the card?
4. Examine the card's *discourses* by looking at the situated meanings, social languages, and cultural models together:
   What are the rules of this card?
   What is this card trying to make you think?
   How do these discourses relate to your life?

Other Notes

Once students have become proficient in analyzing greeting cards, we move on to examining the discourses in children's literature. Picture books are a good place to start because of their length and the careful use of language.

Draw and Write in Role (See Process Drama)

Emancipatory Fairy Tales

It is important to support students in learning to critique texts and construct counter-narratives. One way to do this is to provide opportunities for them to produce their own texts that "talk back" to dominant cultural stories. Since many fairy tales depict characters in stereotypical ways, we introduce emancipatory fairy tales (Lewison et al., 2008) as a way of challenging them.

Materials & Procedures

- Any fairy tale
- Standard writing materials

1. After reading the fairy tale students are invited to think about the underlying messages that are being communicated as well as whose story this is and who has been left out or not heard from. For example in *Little Red Riding Hood* some of the underlying messages that one group of students identified were: "girls should stay on the path," "young girls and old women are vulnerable," "children should mind what their parents say," "children should not talk to strangers," and "men are wolves and not to be trusted." Readers never hear the wolf's side of things nor explore how the story would change if the main character were a boy rather than a girl.
2. Students rewrite the story by altering one of the elements of literature (setting, plot, characters). While the results are often hilarious, what is more significant is that participants begin to identify and challenge some of the larger systems of meaning that are taken for granted in our society.

Extensions

What If? After reading a piece of literature students are invited to generate and respond to What if? questions. For example, what if Red Riding Hood had been taking karate lessons before she met the wolf? What if she was taking a basket of goodies to her grandfather rather than her grandmother? What ifs are meant to help students see how unexamined cultural assumptions position readers in particular ways.

Environmental Print Books (See Literature Logs: Extensions)

Frames & Stereotypes (See Chapter 8: Invitation)

Graffiti Board

While the familiar practices of doodling and jotting down random thoughts are often seen as off-task behaviors, the graffiti board strategy (Short & Harste, w/ Burke, 1996) recasts these everyday behaviors as productive ways to make connections and build new understandings. This strategy invites participants to record their initial thoughts about a book or a theme through writing or sketching in a public forum. They are told beforehand that there are no right or wrong answers.

Materials & Procedures

- A large sheet of unlined chart paper
- Markers

1. Post a large sheet of unlined chart paper in a place that is easily accessible to all students and invite them to share their thoughts on a particular book or topic by writing short notes or drawing pictures.
2. Allow time and opportunity for everyone to make an anonymous entry.
3. As a group, review the completed graffiti board and discuss any issues, patterns, and surprises that participants see as important.
4. If desired, this information can be used as the starting point for a more organized web or for generating a list of new questions.

Other Notes

A graffiti board has multiple benefits. First, it can help teachers in planning curriculum by allowing them to see what their students already know about a topic. It also makes them aware of some of the misconceptions students might have. The strategy supports students by providing a low-risk way for them to get their ideas into a more public forum where they will get feedback. It also motivates them to consider a variety of other ideas. Some teachers use a graffiti board to introduce a new study and then bring it back at the end of the project to celebrate what has been learned.

Hot Seat (See Process Drama)

Illustrator Study (See Chapter 6: Invitation)

Ink Shedding (See Say Something: Extensions)

Interpretive Stances

Being critically literate entails developing an awareness that there are different ways of responding to texts and that how we respond positions us in specific ways. David Bleich, a reading response theorist, developed this strategy to support readers in responding to texts in new ways. His research showed that most readers have a preferred way of responding and do so without considering other stances they might take.

Materials & Procedures

- Handout: *Different Interpretive Stances* (adapted from Bleich, 1993; Lewison et al., 2008; Leland et al., 2012)
- Any text can be read

1. Each student gets a copy of the handout (see Table 10.2) and joins one of six groups.
2. Read the book aloud.

TABLE 10.2.   Interpretive Stances

Different Interpretive Stances	
Stance	**Definition**
Metaphorical	Responds by making analogies (connections) to prior events and life experiences.
Philosophical	Looks for universal truths or messages that go beyond the text.
Aesthetic	Responds to the emotional experience of reading. Tracks highs and lows during the roller coaster experience of reading.
Analytical	Responds to how the text works and why the author wrote it in a particular way. Takes a close look at texts and considers why certain words (characters, settings, etc.) were chosen and how they create the effects they do.
Intertextual	Makes sense of the text in terms of other texts, movies, books, etc.
Critical	Looks for instances of unfair treatment in everyday events. Points out the stereotypes that the text perpetuates; helps us see the big issues that lie just beyond the text.

3. Each group is assigned a particular stance they use to develop a response to the book.
4. Groups share their stances, what they see as defining characteristics, and the kinds of responses to the text that they see as typical.
5. Students reflect on their own reading practices by identifying the stance they typically take when responding to books.

Other Notes

Extend this engagement by asking students to "try on" a stance they don't normally take when responding to a new book. Or ask them to try on all six stances for a particular book.

I-Statement Charts

Readers sometimes find it challenging to explain how different characters in a story view the world. I-statement charts challenge readers to identify the different positions being taken by selected characters in any book. This strategy was developed by Kim Huber, a first grade teacher (Leland & Harste with Huber, 2005) but we have found that it works well with all ages. Students use both language and art to explore multiple perspectives and extend their meaning-making potential.

Materials & Procedures

- Unlined paper, writing tools
- A story (read independently or aloud)

1. Read a story and choose three characters to analyze.
2. Fold paper into three sections; list a different character at the top of each section.
3. For each character, write one or more I-statements to show what that person was thinking during the story. For example, one character might say, "I feel happy because. . ." while another might say, "I feel sad because. . ."
4. Make a sketch of each character to show how he or she was feeling.

Other Notes

Expectations can be more complex for older readers. For example, instead of writing a few words in each column, they might be asked to provide more detailed explanations for their conclusions about what the characters were thinking or feeling. While younger students might focus on facial expressions in their sketches, more sophisticated readers might be challenged to show body language.

Key Ideas (See Quotable Quotes: Extensions)

Language at Work

Norman Fairclough's discourse analysis strategies (1989) can be simplified and used with elementary and middle school students. It's a way for students to begin to pay attention to language, the work it does in the world, and how it can shape our perceptions. This is best done a few times as a whole class and then students can break up into partners and small groups to do this analysis.

Materials & Procedures

- Newspaper headlines on a common issue ("*Gaddafi Strikes at Rebels,*" "*Rebels are Attacked,*" "*Gaddafi Is Dangerous,*" "*War Erupted in the Middle East,*" "*May Peace Reign,*" "*Peace Might Come After Talks,*" "*Followers Bowed as Gaddafi Passed,*" "*Please Work for Peace*")

1. Examining *words*:

   What formal or polite language is used? (*Please Work for Peace*)

   How is respect for status or position shown? (*Gaddafi* as opposed to *Rebels; Followers Bowed as Gaddafi Passed*)

   Do words express positive or negative values to readers? (*Gaddafi* is dangerous; *Rebels* signals non-conformists)

2. Examining *grammatical features*:

   How are grammatical forms used to express certain messages?

   Active voice (taking responsibility): (*Gaddafi Strikes at Rebels*)

   Passive voice (concealing responsibility): (*War Erupted*)

   What types of agency predominate?

   Direct Action: (*Gaddafi Strikes at Rebels*) an agent acts on something

   Non-Directed Action: (*Rebels Are Attacked*) they just happened to be there with no part in this action

   Attributions: (*Gaddafi is Dangerous*) involves one participant + an attribute after the verb

   Is agency unclear?

   What choices are made to highlight or background *agency*? (*War Erupted*—agency unclear, hidden)

   Is the agent an inanimate object? (*War, Peace*)

   What is the authority of one character in relation to other? (*Gaddafi* is singled out as a leader; the *Rebels* as a mass of non-conformists)

   How are *modal auxiliary verbs* used—may, might, should, could, can, can't, ought? (*Peace Might Come After Talks*—the key agents needed to create the state of peace are not named or being considered)

Other Notes

1. These three headlines, taken from *The Scotland Herald*, *BBC News*, and *The Guardian*, report the same story. Below each headline are key issues in understanding how language does the work it does.

   "*Teachers Must Spend Longer in School*"
   - Hidden agent who has power over teachers
   - "Must"—teachers have no agency

   "*Shake-Up for Teaching Conditions*"
   - Agent is inanimate object (teaching conditions)
   - Who is acting on "teaching conditions" is concealed

   "*Teaching Unions Reject Call for More 'Flexible' Working Practices*"
   - Agency is clear (Teaching Unions reject)
   - Active Voice
   - Teaching Unions have power

2. Once students have become familiar with Fairclough's framework using headlines, teachers should move on to using short stories and poems.

Learning Wall (See Chapter 6: Assessment)

Literature Circles

Readers need time to read both extensively, for enjoyment and information, and intensively, to deepen and enrich the reading experience. Just using literature isn't enough. It is what we do with literature that counts. Researchers have found that reading instruction is improved when students are given time to talk to each other and tie what they have read to their life experiences. When teacher-led questioning decreases and the focus is on inquiry, students take their discussions in directions that are important to them, thus increasing the potential for enjoyment and digging deeper into books (Harste et al., 1988).

Materials & Procedures

- Multiple copies of literature that supports discussion
- Spaces where groups gather to meet, plan, and discuss what they have read
- Writing materials and pens for taking notes, setting goals, and scheduling meeting times
- Bulletin board space for literature circle groups to post their plans for all to see

1. Students select a book or text set they wish to read (see text sets).
2. Remind groups that there are multiple ways to respond to texts including discussing reactions to the book, pointing out favorite parts, raising questions about puzzling aspects, or sharing surprises. Students can also use strategies such as say something, sketch to stretch, quotable quotes, save the last word for me, or taking inventory. We suggest posting a list of possible text responses to support alternate ways of talking, writing, and drawing about texts.
3. Groups meet to decide how much they will read before their next meeting and whether they will read on their own with partners using any of the strategies they find supportive. These plans are posted.
4. The teacher's role is to visit each group and see how the discussions are going, offering suggestions if necessary. It is important that all group members understand that they are responsible for everyone's success in their group.
5. After reading and discussing the entire book, students decide what big idea it conveys and how they will present their book or text set to the class. Options include making a chart, presenting a book talk, writing a drama, doing a readers' theater, making a game, creating a display, making a mural, or reading their personal responses to the book from their literature logs.

Extensions

Roles in Literature Circles. Some teachers begin literature circles by assigning roles for group members to play, such as:

- Discussion Leader—keeps classmates focused on the big idea in the story
- Questioner—asks questions and keeps the discussion going
- Wordsmith—identifies important words or phrases in the story and checks the meaning in a dictionary or online
- Connector—connects events in the story to real-life experiences
- Story Mapper—draws pictures/sketches to help classmates keep track of characters and visualize events in the story

While assigning roles can be helpful when initiating literature circles, what is problematic is that students tend to play their role rather than listen to the conversation. Our advice is to stop using the roles as soon as possible and not institute roles as an ongoing social practice in your classroom (see Chapter 5: Technology Extensions).

Partner Reading. An easy way to prepare children for success in literature circles is to have them partner up and take turns reading and discussing what was read. Many teachers use partner reading (sometimes called **Buddy Reading**) the first couple of months of school before they introduce literature circles. Teachers argue that it is much easier for a child to share his or her thoughts with one person than with a group of people.

Literature Logs

Learners need time to reflect on their reading experiences and the processes they used to understand what they read. Recording thoughts, feelings, images, and ideas in the form of words or sketches is not simply a representation of what one knows, but an extension of that knowing. Literature logs are a great way for students to keep track of responses to the books they read independently, hear read aloud, or prepare for literature circles.

Materials & Procedures

- Writing materials
- Spiral notebooks or homemade books made by stapling sheets of paper into a cover

1. Encourage students to write their reactions, connections, and questions rather than a summary of the story.
2. Entries can be webs, sketches, charts, favorite quotes, and diagrams as well as written reflections.
3. Literature logs can also take the form of bookmarks or little books that are placed in the book to record the student's thoughts while reading.

Extensions

Environmental Print Books. Paper stapled into a cover can become an environmental print book when students are asked to bring in labels of things they see in their homes that they can read. After these are pasted into the books, they dictate what they want to say about each label to a teacher or other adult who writes it next to the label. Environmental print books are easy to read, predictable books for students new to reading. Homemade books are also useful when students take environmental print walks and identify things they can read in school and around the playground. These books are later taken home and shared with families.

Literature Response Little Books
(See One-Page Stapleless Books: Extensions)

Little Books (See One-Page Stapleless Books: Extensions)

Mantle of the Expert (See Process Drama)

Mini-Inquiries Into Challenged or Banned Books (See Chapter 9: Invitation)

Mini-Inquiry Books (See One-Page Stapleless Books: Extensions)

Musical Conversation (See Written Conversation: Extensions)

One Observation, One Connection, One Question, One Surprise

Students need to know how to prepare for having a literature discussion. Jennifer Story, a middle school teacher at Dole Middle School in Hawaii, tells her students that they need to bring one observation, one connection, one question and one surprise. Lee Heffernan, a teacher from Bloomington, Indiana, has expanded on this strategy. While she uses many of Jennifer's original categories, she often adds new items: "Identify one thing you want to remember for always," "What things could you write about from your own life that this story makes you think about?" and, if it is a picture book, "What one illustration do you think captures the essence of this book that we might photocopy and place on our Learning Wall?"

Materials & Procedures

■ Post-it notes (a minimum of four per student)

1. As students are reading their trade book or text set, they jot down one observation, one connection, one question, and one surprise on separate notes.
2. To start the literature discussion students choose one note they created that they think will lead to the best conversations and shares it with the group.
3. As time permits, students take turns sharing their remaining observations, connections, questions, and surprises.

Other Notes

Teachers sometimes collect all the "question" notes that students have generated and type them into a list. During a second literature discussion, this list is distributed and groups discuss what they see as possible answers.

As an alternative, after a read aloud, students work in small groups to generate one observation, one connection, one question, and one surprise.

One-Page Stapleless Books

A one-page stapleless book can be a classroom resource with many uses. Students might make a book to respond to a story they have read or heard, conduct a mini-inquiry, write their own story, or create a small graphic novel.

Materials & Procedures

■ Unlined paper (one sheet per student)
■ Scissors (optional)

1. Figure 10.3 provides directions for how to make a one-page stapleless book (Lewison et al., 2008).
2. Walk students through the process of making stapleless books so that each has one.
3. Generate a list of ways these books might be used. Give students ownership by letting them decide how they want to use the one they made.

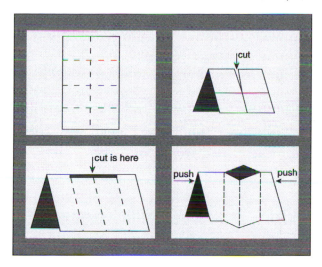

FIGURE 10.3. One-Page Stapleless Book.

Extensions

Little Books. Primary teachers often use stapleless little books to record nursery rhymes the children already know. Children then illustrate the books and use them as initial reading material. Later students use little books to write their own predictable or patterned books, e.g. "I like candy. I like going to the movies. I like school. I like having fun."

Literature Response Little Books. Teachers of elementary and middle school students often use Little Books as a bookmark and ask students to record things they wish to talk about on each page. These literature response little books are brought to literature study meetings and used to start conversations.

Mini-Inquiry Books. Teachers at all levels use little books as mini-inquiry books. Students are asked to jot down questions they might like to research as they pursue books and other materials at the beginning of a new unit of study. Some teachers call them "Wonderful Questions Booklets" when they are used for this purpose.

Partner Reading (See Literature Circles: Extensions)

Patterns & Surprises (See Quotable Quotes: Extensions)

Picture This (See Sketchbooks: Extensions)

Postcards of the Mind (See Say Something: Extensions)

Process Drama

Process drama invites participants to step into the text world and use their life experiences and ways of knowing to make sense of what is happening as a text unfolds (Edmiston & Enciso, 2002; O'Neill, 1995; Medina, 2004). Process drama uses a variety of techniques such as role playing, creating a still-life tableau, and conducting mock courtroom dramatizations in which key characters are put on trial. Participants think off the page as they re-enact scenes that might have occurred prior to the story or after the story took place. Drama strategies are great for readers at any level. We think they are especially helpful for learners who have difficulty comprehending, who seem to be detached from the reading, or who find it hard to imagine themselves in texts.

Materials & Procedures

- Any literature selection (although we recommend the use of books that raise important social issues and present problems and issues that merit deep thinking and discussion)
- Markers and large sheets of paper
- Simple props that might be used to identify key characters

1. Before beginning, read through the book and mark points where you will ask students to engage in particular drama strategies.
2. For example, after reading the first section of the book, stop and ask students to recreate a scene from the book in "frozen" form (*Tableau*). Tell them that when you tap their shoulder, they will become that character and say what they are thinking (*Tapping In*). Ask students what sounds they would hear in the setting where the story is happening. Practice putting these sounds together (*Soundscape*) and talk about how that affects the story.
3. Read another section of the book and try other dramatic forms (Table 10.3).
4. As a culminating experience, students pretend they are a character in the story and draw and write about how they feel and what they are thinking now that the story

TABLE 10.3. Process Drama

Drama Form	Description
Conscience Circle	A character who has a difficult moral decision or choice to make walks in one direction around the inside of a circle composed of classmates. As the character passes by classmates, they offer their advice about the decision.
Draw or Write in Role	Students pretend to be a character in the story and reflect deeply on some experience through drawing and writing.
Hot Seat	Students move into role as specific characters in order to answer questions from the class about their actions in the story and why they acted as they did.
Mantle of the Expert	"Special powers" are bestowed upon students to enable them to become experts in key jobs that relate to the story. Possibilities include forensic crime specialist, police officers, property damage assessors, criminal court judges, guidance counselors, doctors, etc. For example, if children are dramatizing the trial of the wolf in *The Three Little Pigs*, individuals might play lawyers on both sides, the judge, property damage assessors, etc.
Student in Role	Students use their imaginations to enter the pretend world and play the role of a character in a particular context.
Sculpting	Teachers ask students to sculpt or "mold" themselves into positions that physically represent abstract thoughts and feelings, e.g. What does it look like to be irate, cool as a cucumber, mellow?

Soundscape	Students orchestrate sounds using their voices, available musical instruments, found objects, etc., to express the mood of a particular place. Also called a "sound picture."
Tableau	Students use facial expression, body position, posture, gestures, and space between them to create a "frozen" picture representing their understandings of a scene.
Tapping In	When students are "frozen" (in a tableau) or silent (when drawing or writing in role), the teacher moves among them—touching one student's shoulder at a time—thus releasing them to move and/or speak their thoughts.
Teacher in Role	The teacher participates in the drama, often as a character or in another role that would make sense in the story. In role the teacher can assess, support, and guide students (who may or may not themselves be in role) as they explore their understandings of a story character or what is happening in the story itself.

is over (***Draw or Write in Role***). If a moral decision is left hanging, form a circle to hear what everyone is thinking (***Conscience Circle***) or become a character and invite students to question you (***Hot Seat***).

Other Notes

For a detailed description of how Wayne Serebrin and Pauline Broderick (2009) used *The Teddy Bear* by David McPhail (2002) to enact various elements of process drama with second graders, see www.routledge.com/cw/leland.

Quotable Quotes

Reading is a social process of meaning construction. We often improve our understanding of texts by discussing them with other readers. For this reason, it is important to build in opportunities for students to talk about what they are reading and what they think it means. Discussing challenging texts with others brings out different interpretations and frequently leads to a deeper understanding of the material. The quotable quotes strategy invites students to jot down sentences they find particularly interesting as they are reading. They later come together to share these quotes with peers and find out if their interpretations were similar or different (Short & Harste, w/ Burke, 1996).

Materials & Procedures

- 3" × 5" note cards
- A challenging story or non-fiction text

1. Read the text independently.
2. While reading, look for phrases or sentences you find interesting or hard to understand. Write each quote (and page number) on one side of a note card. On the other side, briefly explain why you chose it.
3. Meet with peers in small groups and take turns sharing your quotes. Try to figure out why your peers chose their particular quotes. Why are they significant?
4. See Extensions (below) as possible ways to end.

Extensions

Save the Last Word for Me. When everyone has made comments about the quote, the person who contributed it gets the last word and explains why he or she chose it. The hard part is to insure that this person indeed has the last word!

Patterns & Surprises. After sharing the quotes in small groups, ask students to put all the cards for their group on the table and move them around to form categories. What patterns & surprises do they observe as they look across all the cards?

Key Ideas. Instead of finding quotes, students jot down seven key ideas they got from reading on note cards. They can express ideas with single words or simple phrases. Students look through their seven cards and identify the idea they see as most central. This card is placed directly in front of them and the other cards are arranged in groups that make sense. Once cards are placed, students turn to a neighbor and explain why they arranged the cards as they did. This is a supportive strategy when students are reading informational texts and need to synthesize what they have read.

Roles in Literature Circles (See Literature Circles: Extensions)

Save the Last Word for Me (See Quotable Quotes: Extensions)

Say Something

Say Something (Harste et. al., 1988) highlights the social nature of language and demonstrates that understanding develops and evolves from our interactions with others. By stopping periodically to talk to each other about a shared text, students learn to say what is on their mind, a key to having great literature discussions.

Materials & Procedures

- Multiple copies of a reading selection

1. Pairs of students receive one copy of the reading selection to read and discuss together.
2. After reading the first page or several paragraphs, they stop and "say something" to each other about what they read. They might make a personal connection, a prediction about what will happen next, or talk about something in the text they didn't understand.
3. Students continue reading and take turns "saying something" to their partners at predetermined intervals until they are finished.
4. As a culminating experience, teachers might ask students to reflect on how "say something" supported their reading.

Other Notes

Using the same format, pairs of students can be asked to write instead of say something to their partner (see ***Written Conversation***).

Extensions

Ink Shedding. One student writes a response to a reading selection and then circulates that response to others in the class who in turn respond in writing to the author.

Postcards of the Mind. Several days after the reading, students create postcards that highlight key concepts from the selection. After sharing their postcards, they discuss why they remembered the things they did (Manning, 2010).

Six-Box Literature Response Strategy (See Chapter 5: Invitation)

Sculpting (See Process Drama)

Sketchbooks

While learners need time to engage in many different reading, writing, and multimodal experiences, they also need time to reflect on what and how they are learning. Sketchbooks provide opportunities for students to draw or write briefly about a book, an activity, or an experience they had, thus creating a place to come back to later, if they wish to reflect further on it.

Materials & Procedures:

- An 8 ½ × 11" hard-bound sketchbook (or equivalent)
- Art supplies, tape, glue

1. Students make entries in their sketchbooks at the end of an activity or the end of the day as a reminder of what they did. Entries might include sketches, quotes, personal responses, or photographs of group products.
2. In addition to place holding the activities they engaged in, students can be asked to reflect on their classroom literature experiences. Questions might include: What did I understand about the work I did in class today? What didn't I understand? What do I know now that I didn't know when I got to school today? What can I do better tomorrow? What do I have questions about or wonder about?
3. Encourage students to make their sketchbook a treasure by decorating them with artwork and including artifacts that represent their most important experiences.

Extensions

Picture This. Carolyn Burke, a professor at Indiana University, took digital pictures of students as they were involved in activities like reading books, discussing books with friends, conducting experiments, listening to speakers, etc. She printed out the pictures and gave copies to the students for their sketchbooks. Having photographs supported students in reflecting later on what and how they were learning.

Sketch to Stretch (See Transmediation: Extensions)

Soundscape (See Process Drama)

Student in Role (See Process Drama)

Subtext Strategy

It can be hard to identify meanings that are not explicitly stated in texts. The subtext strategy was developed by Jean Ann Clyde and a group of teachers in Louisville, Kentucky (Clyde, Barber, Hogue, & Wasz, 2006). It asks students to think about the various characters in a book and write down what they say, as well as what they are thinking. More often than not, these are not identical. This strategy helps students step into the world of the story and develop a deeper understanding of the underlying tensions.

Materials & Procedures

- A literature selection
- Post-it notes in two colors

1. Read the story and identify the various characters.
2. Students get a note of each color for each main character. Designate one color for "saying" notes and the other color for "thinking" notes.
3. Students create two notes for each character. On one note they write what the character might be "saying" and on the other, what the character might be "thinking."
4. Use these "saying" and "thinking" notes to identify larger issues that are at play in the story world. Discuss how these larger forces impact the story.

Other Notes

1. Try introducing this strategy with a piece of art that shows various characters engaged in an activity like ballet or a music lesson. Students write notes for what each character might say as well as what each might be thinking.
2. After students are familiar with this strategy ask them to think about audiences not directly involved in the story itself, like parents and other teachers, even though the book was about a particular student in a particular classroom. Supposing parents and other teachers hear about what went on, what would they say and what would they be thinking?
3. Jean Ann and her colleagues use this strategy to support students in reading content area texts and newspaper articles, as well as to expand their own original stories.

Tableau (See Process Drama)

Taking Inventory

One of the keys to a good literature discussion is ensuring that all voices are heard. This is easier to do when these discussions involve small groups of students, since students who are reluctant to speak up in the whole group may feel better about speaking up in a small group. Gloria Kaufmann, a teacher from Goshen, Indiana, designed this strategy to make spaces for more voices to be heard. While this strategy does not guarantee that everyone will talk, it provides a structure that encourages wide participation.

Materials & Procedures

- A large sheet of paper
- Markers

1. Begin by asking group members to identify something that they wish to talk about during literature discussion. Record each topic on a large sheet of paper positioned so

that everyone can see the topics being added. Continue going around the group until everyone (including you) has had a chance to participate.

2. Read through the list orally and look for topics that were mentioned by more than one person. Which topics seem to be the ones group members are most interested in pursuing? One of these might be selected as a starting point.

3. Topics not addressed during the first literature discussion of a text can be used to start a second discussion of that text at another time.

Tapping In (See Process Drama)

Target, Perpetrator, Ally, Bystander

Readers new to critical literacy often need support in taking a critical stance. Linda Christensen (2009), a teacher from Portland, Oregon and an editor of *Rethinking Schools*, developed this strategy to highlight the different roles people can take in interacting with each other. We find that it works best with books that raise important social issues. After experiencing this strategy, readers discuss texts quite differently.

Materials & Procedures

- A social issue children's book. We recommend beginning with a book like *Ruth and the Green Book* (Ramsey & Strauss, 2010). Set in the 1950s, this story follows Ruth's family while traveling from Chicago to Alabama. Because many hotels and gas stations in the South refused to serve African Americans, they encounter many problems. Finally, a friendly clerk shows them The Green Book, a guide to businesses that welcome everyone. What gives this story depth is that it has a common surface structure (a family coping with everyday needs) as well as an underlying social issue (racial prejudice) that cannot be overlooked

- A response sheet with four columns: Target, Perpetrator, Ally, Bystander

1. Introduce the response sheet and discuss what the words mean. (What is a target, perpetrator, etc?)

2. Read the story aloud to the class or form small groups and give each a copy to read together.

3. In small groups, students discuss the story and fill out the worksheet in terms of how they saw the different roles being played.

4. Reconvene the whole class to share responses. These will vary, depending on the perspectives that were taken. The target, for example, is Ruth's family at one level, but black people at another, and minorities at still another level. Similarly, while specific characters might be labeled as bystanders, everyone who witnesses discrimination and does nothing to prevent it is a bystander.

5. As a culminating experience, students discuss whether it's possible for some characters to be mentioned in more than one column.

Other Notes

Rethinking Schools is a professional journal that is devoted to supporting teachers in creating critical classrooms. Strategies like this one are regular features.

Teacher in Role (see Process Drama)

Text Sets

A text set is a collection of books and other resources that provides many different perspectives on a topic. Since text sets are multimodal, they can include more than just books. Pictures, videos, songs, maps, diaries, and classroom visitors who have first-hand knowledge of the topic and are willing to share their personal experiences are valuable additions. Experiencing a text set provides multiple perspectives on a topic and supports deeper understanding. When readers share these different perspectives, they extend their comprehension of each text and begin to see the reading event as an experience in itself (see Harste et al., 1988).

Materials & Procedures

- Two or more texts that have similar themes, topics, etc. (see website)
- Two different procedures may be used to encourage students to share and extend their understanding of text sets.
1. Everyone reads or listens to someone else read the entire set
    - The group discusses similarities and differences among and between the texts.
    - After discussing, groups brainstorm ideas for extensions (making comparison charts, writing dramas, making games, displays, murals or dioramas).
2. Everyone reads different texts
    - Each person in the group reads one or two of the texts in the set.
    - Students share what they learned with other group members and answer their questions.
    - Students discuss similarities and differences across the texts.
    - If the discussion lasts over several days, students can read other books in the text set as they become interested in these books or as the group decides everyone needs to read a particular book for the next discussion.
    - After discussing, the group brainstorms ideas for sharing their text set with the class.

Other Notes

1. Text sets of three or four books can be put in book bags for students to check out to take home to read with and to family members.
2. Text sets are excellent to use in literature circles because they facilitate discussion, especially among students who are reluctant to talk (see literature circles).
3. Middle school teachers often select five or six different novels that students can select to read during a grading period. Five copies of each novel are made available for students to sign up for and read. Teachers often refer to these novel sets as text sets.

Three Pluses & a Wish

Encouraging students to give each other constructive feedback can be difficult. To keep the experience positive, we ask students to evaluate peers' work by listing three pluses (things they liked) and one wish (something that might be changed). Requiring more pluses than wishes highlights strengths instead of weaknesses. When evaluating student work, we find three pluses and a wish useful for ourselves too. It insures that our feedback is more positive than negative. Heidi Mills and Tim O'Keefe developed this strategy when they worked in a Head Start program in Michigan.

Materials & Procedures

- Something you want students to evaluate
- Brief "three pluses and a wish" forms for students to fill out (optional)

1. Identify some material or performance that students will assess. This could range from a commercial website to an individual presentation or read aloud.
2. Students doing the assessment jot down three points about what is working well (pluses) and note one point (a wish) about how it might be improved.
3. Depending on the context, pluses and wishes might be publicly shared across the class (if they are evaluating a website, for example) or used to provide private feedback.

Other Notes

We introduce this strategy by first having students use it to evaluate something that none of them produced. They might watch a video or spend time reviewing a website and then generate three pluses and a wish to share with the class. After applying the strategy to people or products outside of the class, we ask them to use it to provide helpful feedback to each other. For example, Chris asks her students to fill out three pluses and a wish forms as they watch classmates' presentations and then shares this feedback privately with students as part of the evaluation and grading process.

Through the Cracks (See Chapter 7: Invitation)

Transmediation

Transmediation (Leland & Harste, 1994; Siegel, 1984, 1995; Suhor, 1984) involves taking something that you know in language and moving that knowing to another sign system such as art, music, mathematics, dance, or drama. Moving across sign systems (from language to art, for example) has been shown to generate new ideas and new insights. Many teachers find that transmediation enlivens their reading program while also supporting students' comprehension.

Materials & Procedures

- A piece of literature
- Musical instruments, audiotapes of musical selections
- Scarves or other props to support interpretive dance and drama (optional)

1. Read the story aloud to everyone or form small groups and give each a copy to read together.
2. Form four groups. After reviewing the text, students discuss the messages they think the author wanted to convey. Group 1 expresses these messages through music, Group 2 expresses them through mathematics, Group 3 through interpretive dance, and Group 4 through drama.
3. Each group presents their interpretation using as few words as possible. Students in other groups try to explain what was expressed and how it connected to the book. Once these arguments have been made, members of each group talk about their interpretation of the story and how it relates to their presentation.

Extensions

Sketch to Stretch asks students to symbolize what the story means through a sketch. (This is different from drawing a picture of a favorite scene and entails deeper thinking.) Typically students meet in small group to talk about what the story means to them before drawing. Sketches are shared with the entire class using the procedure described above.

It is important to vary the medium so as to keep an edge on learning. Introducing new forms of expression like clay, collage, or puppets helps to achieve this goal. In addition, students might choose which sign system they want to use in subsequent experiences.

What If (See Emancipatory Fairy Tales)

Written Conversation

Students love to talk to each other so why not have them talk on paper? Written conversation (Harste et al., 1988) is just that. After reading a book, they partner up and begin a conversation by writing back and forth to each other.

Materials & Procedures

- A book that at least two people have read
- Writing paper
- Standard writing materials
- Musical instruments (optional)

1. Students who have read the same book pair up and have a silent written conversation about the book. Written responses can include observations, connections, questions, surprises, or anything. Student 1 writes a message and passes the paper to Student 2, who either adds something new or responds. The paper then goes back to Student 1 and in this fashion the conversation continues until neither has more to "say." Remind students that they may not talk aloud, only write.
2. Written conversation is a particularly useful strategy when students are upset over the outcome of a story or have very diverse opinions about an issue and are having a hard time listening to each other's points of view.
3. Written conversation also works well with a small group contributing comments to each other.

Extensions

Musical Conversation invites students to have a conversation about a book using whatever musical instruments they have available, including their own voices. Readers are invited to attend to the emotional or "lived through" experience of reading. A third student might read the text as the two musicians take turns talking to each other on their musical instruments. While any musical instrument will work, we find that Orff Schuluerk and Zuzuki Orff xylophones support students in producing harmonious compositions.

Zentangles (See Art Trading Cards: Extensions)

References

Children's and Adolescent Literature

Annotations of all titles can be found at www.routledge.com/cw/leland

Adams, Pam (2000) *This old man*. Child's Play International.

Allard, Harry G. (1977–89) *The Stupids* (Series). Illus. James Marshall. Sandpiper.

Altman, Linda Jacobs (1991) *Amelia's road*. Illus. Enrique O. Sanchez. Lee & Low.

Anzaldua, Gloria (1995) *Friends from the other side/Amigos del otro lado*. Illus. Consuelo Mendez. Children's Book Press.

Aristophane (2010) *The Zabime sisters*. Trans. Matt Madden. First Second Publishing.

Asch, Frank (1982) *Happy birthday, moon*. Simon & Schuster.

Aylesworth, Jim (2001) *The tale of Tricky Fox*. Scholastic.

Banks, Lynn Reid (1985) *The Indian in the cupboard*. Illus. Brock Cole. Doubleday.

Banting, Ernin (2003) *Afghanistan: The people*. Crabtree.

Banyai, Istvan (1995) *Zoom!* Viking.

Bartholomew Steen, Sandy (2010) *Totally tangled*. Design Originals.

Barwell, Ysaye M. (1998) *No mirrors in my Nana's house*. Illus. Synthia Saint James. Harcourt.

Bellairs, John (1973) *The house with a clock in its walls*. Perfection Learning.

Bellairs, John (1975) *The figure in the shadows*. Dial.

Benson, Kathleen & Haskins, Jim (2006) *Count your way through Afghanistan*. Illus. Megan Moore. Millbrook.

Berger, Barbara (1984) *Grandfather Twilight*. Philomel.

Booth, Coe (2007) *Tyrell*. Perfection Learning.

Bradbury, Ray (1987) *Fahrenheit 451*. Ballantine.

Bradby, Marie (1995) *More than anything else*. Illus. Chris Soentpiet. Scholastic.

Breathed, Berkeley (2008) *Pete & Pickles*. Philomel.

Bridges, Shirin Yim (2002) *Ruby's wish*. Illus. Sophia Blackall. Chronicle.

Browne, Anthony (1986) *Piggybook*. Knopf.

Browne, Anthony (1998) *Voices in the park*. DK Publishing.

Browne, Anthony (2000) *Willy and Hugh*. Red Fox.

Browne, Anthony (2004) *Into the Forest*. Candlewick.

Bunting, Eve (1993) *Red fox running.* Illus. Wendell Minor. Clarion.

Bunting, Eve (1994) *Smoky night.* Illus. David Diaz. Harcourt.

Bunting, Eve (1996) *Going home.* Illus. David Diaz. HarperCollins.

Bunting, Eve (1997) *A day's work.* Illus. Ronald Himler. Sandpiper.

Bunting, Eve (1998) *Your move.* Illus. James Ransome. Harcourt.

Bunting, Eve (2001) *Gleam and Glow.* Illus. Peter Sylvada. Harcourt.

Bunting, Eve (2006) *One green apple.* Illus. Ted Lewin. Clarion.

Carle, Eric (1997) *From head to toe.* HarperCollins.

Carle, Eric, Anno Mitumasa, & Blake, Quentin (Eds.) (2007) *Artist to artist: 23 major illustrators talk to children about their art.* Penguin.

Celenza, Anna Harwell (2006) *Gershwin's Rhapsody in Blue.* Illus. JoAnn E. Kitchel. Charlesbridge.

Chbosky, Stepen (1999) *The perks of being a wallflower.* Turtleback.

Chin, Charlie (1993) *China's bravest girl.* Illus. Tomie Aral. Children's Book Press.

Choi, Yangsook (2003) *The name jar.* Perfection Learning.

Cisneros, Sandra (1984) *The house on Mango Street.* Perfection Learning.

Cohen, Barbara (1983) *Molly's pilgrim.* Illus. Michael J. Deraney. Lothrop.

Cohn, Diana (2002) *Si, se puede! Yes, we can!* Cinco Puntos Press.

Coleman, Evelyn (1996) *White socks only.* Illus. Tyrone Geter. Albert Whitman

Coleman, Evelyn (1998) *To be a drum.* Illus. Aminah Brenda Lynn Robinson. Albert Whitman.

Coles, Robert (1995) *The story of Ruby Bridges.* Illus. George Ford. Scholastic.

Collier, Bryan (2000) *Uptown.* Holt.

Collier, James & Collier, Chris (1985) *My brother Sam is dead.* Scholastic.

Collins, Suzanne (2010) *The hunger games trilogy (The hunger games, Catching fire, Mockingjay).* Scholastic.

Cooney, Barbara (1985) *Miss Rumphius.* Puffin.

Cormier, Robert (1974) *The chocolate wars.* Laurel-Leaf Books.

Cormier, Robert (1977) *I am the cheese.* Laurel-Leaf Books.

Cormier, Robert (1983) *The bumble bee flies away.* Laurel-Leaf Books.

Cowley, Joy (1980) *Mrs. Wishy-Washy* (Box Set). Wright Group.

Cowley, Joy (1991) *The bicycle.* Wright Group.

Cronin, Doreen (2000) *Click, clack, moo: Cows that type.* Illus. Betsy Lewin. Simon & Schuster.

Crutcher, Chris (2004) *Ironman.* HarperCollins.

Cutler, Jane (1999) *The cello of Mr. O.* Illus. Greg Couch. Dutton.

Darrow, Whitney, Jr. (1970) *I'm glad I'm a boy! I'm glad I'm a girl!* Simon & Schuster.

Dayton, Brandon (2009) *Green monk.* Whistling Cloud.

De Brunhoff, Jean (1937) *The story of Babar.* Random House.

de Hann, Linda & Nijland, Stern (2003) *King & King.* Tricycle Press.

De Paola, Tomie (1979) *Oliver Button is a sissy.* Harcourt.

DiCamillo, Kate (2000) *Because of Winn Dixie.* Candlewick.

Dillon, Leo, & Dillon, Diane (2002) *Rap a tap tap: Here's Bojangles – think of that!* Scholastic.

Dillon, Leo & Dillon, Diane (2007) *Jazz on a Saturday night.* Scholastic.

Dorris, Michael (1992) *Morning girl.* Hyperion.

Dunrea, Olivier (2000) *Appearing tonight! Mary Heather Elizabeth Livingstone.* Farrar, Straus and Giroux.

Edwards, Richard (2005) *Petit Singe cherche son refuge/Little monkey's one safe place.* Illus. Susan Winger. Frances Lincoln.

Fierstein, Harvey (2002) *The sissy duckling.* Illus. Henry Cole. Simon & Schuster.

Figueredo, D.H. (1999) *When this world was new.* Illus. Enrique O. Sanchez. Lee & Low.

Fleischman, Paul (1997) *Seedfolks.* Illus. Judy Pedersen. HarperCollins.

Fox, Mem (1989) *Feathers and fools.* Illus. Nicholas Wilton. Harcourt.

Fox, Mem (1989) *Koala Lou.* Illus. Pamala Lofts. Sandpiper.

Fox, Mem (1989) *Night noises.* Illus. Terry Denton. Harcourt.

Fox, Mem (2006) *A particular cow.* Illus. Terry Denton. Harcourt.

Frost, Helen (2003) *Keesha's house.* Farrar, Straus & Giroux.

Gaiman, Neil (2008) *The graveyard book.* Illus. Dave McKean. Middle Grade Publishing.

Garden, Nancy (2000) *Holly's secret.* Farrar, Straus & Giroux.

Gardiner, John Reynolds (1992) *Stone fox.* Illus. Greg Hargreaves. HarperCollins.

Giovanni, Nikki (Ed.) (2008) *Hip hop speaks to children: A celebration of poetry with a beat.* Illus. Kristen Balouch, Michele Noiset, Jeremy Tugeau, Alicia Vergel de Dios, & Damian Ward. Scholastic.

Gollub, Mathew (2000) *The jazz fly.* Illus. Karen Hanke. Tortuga.

Gomi, Taro (1993) *Everyone poops.* Illus. Amada Mayer Stinchecum. Kane/Miller.

Gonzalez, Rigoberto (2005) *Antonio's card/La tarjeta de Antonio.* Illus. Cecilia Concepcion Alvarez. Children's Book Press.

Goss, Janet, & Harste, Jerome (1981) *It didn't frighten me!* Willowisp.

Grimes, Nikki (2002) *Bronx masquerade.* Putman.

Hague, Kathleen (1999) *Ten little bears: A counting rhyme.* Illus. Michael Hague. Morrow Junior Books.

Hague, Michael (1993) *Teddy bear, teddy bear.* HarperCollins.

Hakim, Joy (2007) *History of US* (11 Volume Set). Oxford University Press.

Hal Leonard Corporation (2001) *The lyric book: Complete lyrics for over 1000 songs from Tin Pan Alley to today.* Hal Leonard Corp.

Hannah, Johnny (2005) *Hot jazz special.* Candlewick.

Hearne, Betsy (1997) *Seven brave women.* Illus. Bethanne Andersen. Greenwillow.

Heide, Florence & Gilliland, Judith (1992) *Sami and the time of the troubles.* Clarion.

Helakoski, Leslie (2008) *Woolbur.* Illus. Lee Harper. HarperCollins.

Henkes, Kevin (1991) *Chrysanthemum.* Greenwillow.

Herron, Carolivia (1977) *Nappy hair.* Knopf.

Hesse, Karen (1998) *Just Juice.* Illus. Robert Andrew Parker. Scholastic

Hill, Eric (1980) *Where's Spot?* Putnam.

Hill, Laban Carrick (2010) *Dave the potter.* Illus. Bryan Collier. Little Brown.

Hoban, Tana (1983) *I read signs.* Greenwillow.

Hoffman, Mary (2002) *The color of home.* Phyllis Fogelman.

Hogrogian, Nonny (1971) *One fine day.* Simon & Schuster.

Holiday, Billy & Herzog, Arthur, Jr. (2003) *God bless the child.* Illus. Jerry Pinkney. HarperCollins.

Hoose, Phillip (2001) *We were there too!: Young people in U.S. history.* Farrar, Straus and Giroux.

Hurd, Thatcher (1985) *Mama don't allow.* HarperCollins.

Hutchins, Pat (1971) *Rosie's walk.* Aladdin.

Isadora, Rachel (1979) *Ben's trumpet.* Greenwillow.

Isadora, Rachel (2002) *Bring on that beat.* Putnam.

Iwaoka, Hisae (2010) *Saturn apartments.* VIZ Media LLC.

Jackson, Ella (1994) *Cinder Edna.* Illus. Kevin O'Malley. Lothrop.

Jimenez, Francisco (1998) *The circuit: Stories from the life of a migrant child.* University of New Mexico Press.

Johnston, Tony (2004) *The harmonica.* Illus. Ron Mazellan. Charlesbridge.

Joosse, Barbara (2001) *Stars in the darkness.* Illus. R. Gregory Christie. Chronicle.

Kaplan, William (1998) *One more border: The true story of one family's escape from war-torn Europe.* Illus. Stephen Taylor. Groundwood Books.

Khan, Rukhsana (1998) *The roses in my carpet.* Illus. Ronald Hunter. Holiday House.

Kim, Susan & Klavan, Laurence (2010) *Brain camp.* Illus. Faith Erin Hicks. First Second Publishing.

Kubler, Annie (2002) *Head, shoulders, knees and toes.* Child's Play International.

Kurusa (2008) *The streets are free.* Illus. Monika Doppert. Annick.

Layman, John (2009) *Chew Volume 1: Taster's choice.* Illus. Rob Guillory. Imagine Comics.

Lears, Laurie (1998) *Ian's walk: A story about autism.* Illus. Karen Ritz. Albert Whitman.

Lee, Harper (1960) *To kill a mocking bird.* Lippincott.

Lee-Tai, Amy (2006) *A place where sunflowers grow.* Illus. Felicia Hoshino. Children's Book Press.

Lester, Helen (1999) *Hooway for Wodney Wat.* Illus. by Lynn Munsinger. Houghton Mifflin.

Lester, Julius (1998) *From slave ship to freedom road.* Illus. Rod Brown. Dial.

Lionni, Leo (1969) *Alexander and the wind-up mouse.* Knopf.

Lionni, Leo (1995) *Little blue and little yellow.* HarperCollins.

Lobel, Arnold (1972) *Frog and Toad together.* Harper & Row.

London, Jonathan (2000) *Who bop?* Illus. Henry Cole. HarperCollins.

Lopez de Mariscal, Blanca (2001) *The harvest birds/Los pajaros de la cosecha.* Illus. Enrique Flores. San Val.

Lorbiecki, Marybeth (2000) *Sister Anne's hands.* Illus. K. Wendy Popp. Dial.

Low, William (1997) *Chinatown.* Holt.

Lowry, Lois (1983) *The one hundredth thing about Caroline.* Illus. Diane de Groat. Houghton Mifflin.

Lyga, Barry (2007) *Boy toy.* Houghton Mifflin.

MacHale, D.J. (2004) *Pendragon* (Boxed Set): *The merchant of death; The lost city of Foe; The never war.* Aladdin.

Mackler, Carolyn (2003) *The earth, my butt, and other big, round things.* Candlewick.

Marín, Guadalupe Rivera (2009) *My papa Diego and me: Memories of my father and his art.* Illus. Diego Rivera, Children's Book Press

Marshall, James (1993) *Red Riding Hood.* Turtleback.

Martin, Bill, Jr. (1983) *Brown bear, brown bear, what do you see?* Holt.

Martinez, Alejandro Cruz (1999) *The woman who outshone the sun/La mujer que brillaba aún más que el sol.* Photographs by Fernando Olivera. Turtleback.

McDermott, Gerald (1974) *Arrow to the sun: A Pueblo Indian tale.* Viking.

McEwan, Ian (1987) *Rose Blanche.* Illus. Roberto Innocenti. Lectorium.

McGovern, Ann (1997) *The lady in the box.* Illus. Marni Backer. Turtle Books.

McGuffee, Michael (1997) *The day the earth was silent.* Illus. Edward Sullivan. Inquiring Voices Press.

McNaughton, Colin (2005) *Once upon an ordinary school day.* Illus. Satoshi Kitamura. Farrar, Straus, & Grioux.

McPhail, David (2002) *The teddy bear.* Holt.

Meyer, Stephenie (2005) *Twilight.* Little Brown.

Milich, Zoran (2002) *City signs.* Kids Can.

Mora, Pat (1997) *Tomás and the library lady.* Illus. Raul Colón. Knopf.

Mora, Pat (2009) *Book fiesta! Celebrate children's Day/Book Day; Celebremos el dia de los ninos/El dia de los libros.* Illus. Rafael Lopez. Rayo.

Mortenson, Greg & Relin, David Oliver (2009) *Three cups of tea: One man's journey to change the world . . . one school at a time* (Young Readers Edition). Adapted by Sarah Thomson. Puffin.

Mortenson, Greg & Roth, Susan (2009) *Listen to the wind.* Illus. Susan L. Roth. Dial.

Moss, Lynn (1995) *Zin! Zin!, Zin! A violin.* Illus. Marjorie Priceman. Simon & Schuster.

Munsch, Robert (1983) *The paper bag princess.* Illus. Michael Martchenko. Annick.

Myers, Walter Dean (2006) *Jazz.* Illus. Christopher Myers. Holiday House.

Myracle, Lauren (2004) *Internet Girls Series: TTYL (Talk to you later); TTYL #5 (Camp confidential); TTFN (Ta-ta-for-now); L8R, G8R (Internet girls); BFF (A girlfriend book you write together).* Harry Abrams.

National Exhibition of Children's Art (NECA) (1976) *Pictures by Chinese children.* Foreign Language Press.

Naylor, Phyllis Reynolds (1991) *Shiloh.* Illus. Barry Moser. Atheneum.

Neri, G. (2010) *Yummy: The last days of Southside Shorty.* Illus. Randy Duburke. Lee & Low.

O'Brien, Tony & Sullivan, Mike (2008) *Afghan dreams: Young voices of Afghanistan.* Bloomsbury.

Olson, Gretchen (2008) *Call me Hope.* Little Brown.

Pak, Soyung (1999) *Dear Juno.* Illus. Susan Kathleen Hartung. Viking.

Paladino, Catherine (1999) *One good apple: Growing our food for the sake of the earth.* Houghton Mifflin.

Panahi, H.L. (2005) *Bebop express.* Illus. Steve Johnson & Lou Fancher. HarperCollins.

Paolini, Christopher (2008) *Inheritance* (Boxed Set): *Eragon, Eldest, Brisinger.* Knopf.

Park, Linda Sue (2002) *When my name was Keoko.* Clarion.

Paterson, Katherine (1977) *Bridge to Terabithia.* HarperCollins.

Paterson, Katherine (1987) *The great Gilly Hopkins.* Perfection Learning.

Perez, Amada Irma (2002) *My diary from here to there/Mi diario de aquí, hasta allá.* Illus. Maya Christina Gonzalez. Children's Book Press.

Peters, Julie Ann (2004) *Luna.* Little Brown.

Picoult, Jodi (2004) *My sister's keeper.* Atria.

Pilkey, Dav (2010) *Captain Underpants* (Multibox Set). Scholastic.

Polacco, Patricia (2000) *The butterfly.* Philomel.

Polacco, Patricia (2009) *Mrs. Katz and Tush.* Doubleday.

Raczka, Bob (2001) *No one saw: Ordinary things through the eyes of an artist.* Millbrook Press.

Raczka, Bob (2003) *Art is.* Millbrook Press.

Raczka, Bob (2003) *More than meets the eye: Seeing art with all five senses.* Millbrook Press.

Raczka, Bob (2006) *Here's looking at me: How artists see themselves.* Millbrook Press.

Ramsey, Calvin Alexander, & Strauss, Gwen (2010) *Ruth and the green book.* Illus. Floyd Cooper. Carolrhoda Books.

Rappaport, Doreen (2001) *Martin's big words: The life of Martin Luther King Jr.* Illus. Bryan Collier. Hyperion.

Raschka, Chis (1998) *Yo! Yes?* Scholastic.

Rawls, Wilson. (1974) *Where the red fern grows.* Yearling.

Recorvits, Helen (2004) *My name is Yoon.* Illus. Gabi Swiatkowska. Farrar, Straus, & Giroux.

Reynolds, Peter H. (2003) *The dot.* Candlewick.

Reynolds, Peter H. (2004) *Ish.* Candlewick.

Richardson, Justin & Parnell, Peter (2005) *And Tango makes three.* Illus. Henry Cole. Simon & Schuster.

Robinson, Aminah Brenda Lynn (1997) *A street called home.* Harcourt.

Robles, Anthony (2006) *Lakas and the Makibaka Hotel/Si Lakas at ang Makibaka Hotel.* Illus Carol Angel. Trans. Eloise D. de Jesus. Children's Book Press.

Rockwell, Annie (2000) *Only passing through: The story of Sojourner Truth.* Illus. R. Gregory Christie. Dragonfly.

Rohmer, Harriet, Chow, Octavio, & Viduare, Morris (1997) *The invisible hunters/Los cazadores invisibles.* Illus. Joe Sam. Children's Book Press.

Rosen, Michael (2003) *We're going on a bear hunt.* Illus. Helen Oxenbury. Margaret K. McElderry Books.

Rowling, J.K. (2009) *Harry Potter* (Boxed Set): *Harry Potter and the sorcerer's stone*; *Harry Potter and the chamber of secrets*; *Harry Potter and the prisoner of Azkaban*; *Harry Potter and the goblet of fire*; *Harry Potter and the order of the Phoenix*; *Harry Potter and the half-blood prince*; *Harry Potter and the deathly hallows.* Arthur Levine.

Ryan, Pam Munoz (2002) *Esperanza rising.* Perfection Learning.

Rylant, Cynthia (2000) *The old woman who named things.* Illus. Kathryn Brown. Sandpiper.

Sanchez, Alex (2007) *The God box.* Simon & Schuster.

Salinger, J.D. (1951) *The catcher in the rye.* Perfection Learning.

Satrapi, Marjane (2003) *Persepolis: The story of a childhood.* Pantheon.

Say, Allen (1993) *Grandfather's journey.* Houghton Mifflin.

Schulman, Janet (1976) *The big hello.* Illus. Lillian Hoban. William Morrow.

Scieszka, Jon (1996) *The true story of the three little pigs.* Illus. Lane Smith. Viking.

Sendak, Maurice (1960) *The sign on Rosie's door.* Trumpet.

Sendak, Maurice (1963) *Where the wild things are.* HarperCollins.

Sendak, Maurice (1970) *In the night kitchen.* HarperCollins.

Seuss, Dr. (aka Theodor Geisel) (1971) *The Lorax.* Random House.

Shannon, David (1998) *A bad case of stripes.* Blue Sky.

Sharra, Steve (1996) *Fleeing the war.* Macmillan.

Shiga, Jason (2010) *Meanwhile, pick any path: 3,856 story possibilities.* Amulet.

Shin, Sun Yung (2004) *Cooper's lesson.* Illus. Kim Cogan. Trans. Min Paek. Children's Book Press.

Sollman, Carolyn (1994) *Through the cracks.* Davis Publications.

Spalding, Julian (2010) *The best art you've never seen: 101 hidden treasures from around the world.* Penguin.

Spiegelman, Art (1986) *Maus: A survivor's tale: My father bleeds history.* Turtleback.

Spinelli, Ellen (1996) *Somebody loves you, Mr. Hatch.* Simon & Schuster.

Spinelli, Jerry (2000) *Stargirl.* Knopf.

Stamaty, Mark Alan (2004) *Alia's mission: Saving the books of Iraq.* Knopf.

Steig, William (1969) *Sylvester and the magic pebble.* Aladdin.

Steig, William (1982) *Dr. De Soto.* Farrar, Straus & Giroux.

Stine, R.L. (1995) *Goosebumps* (63 book series). Scholastic.

Stockton, F. (1982) *The lady and the tiger. The Century,* 25(1), pp. 83–86.

Tal, Eve (2007) *A new boy.* Illus. Ora Shwartz. Mike & Honey Press.

Tan, Shaun (2006) *The arrival.* Scholastic.

Telgemeier, Raina (2010) *Smile.* Graphix.

Tennapel, Doug (2010) *Ghostopolis.* Graphix.

Thomas, Valerie & Korky, Paul (1990) *Winnie the witch.* HarperCollins.

Thomas, Velma Maia (2001) *No man can hinder me: The journey from slavery to emancipation through song.* Crown.

Tran, Truong (2003) *Going home, coming home/Ve nha, tham que huong.* Illus. Ann Phong. Children's Book Press.

Tsuchiya, Yukio (1951/1997) *Faithful elephants: A true story of animals, people, & war.* Illus. Ted Lewin. Trans. Tomoko Tsuchiya Dykes. Houghton Mifflin.

Tweit, Susan (1997) *City foxes.* Photography by Wendy Shattil. Alaska Northwest Books.

Viorst, Judith (1987) *Alexander and the terrible horrible no good very bad day.* Illus. Ray Cruz. Antheneum.

Walker, Alice (1992) *The color purple.* Houghton Mifflin.

Wattenberg, Jane (2000) *Henny Penny.* Scholastic.

Weber, Valerie (2006) *I come from Afghanistan (This is my story).* Weekly Reader.

Weing, Drew (2010) *Set to sea.* Fantagraphics.

Weisner, David (2001) *The three pigs.* Clarion.

Wild, Margaret (2001) *Fox.* Illus Ron Brooks. Kane/Miller.

Wiles, Deborah (2001) *Freedom summer.* Illus. Jerome Lagarrigue. Atheneum.

Willard, Nancy (1983) *The nightgown of the sullen moon.* Illus. David McPhail. Harcourt.

Williams, Karen Lynn & Mohammed, Khadra (2007) *Four feet, two sandals.* Illus. Doug Chayka. Eerdmans.

Wilson, Nancy Hope (1997) *Old people, frogs, and Albert.* Illus. Marcy D. Ramsey. Farrar, Straus & Giroux.

Winter, Jeanette (2009) *Nasreen's secret school: A true story from Afghanistan.* Beach Lane.

Wolf, Bernard (2003) *Coming to America: A Muslim family's story.* Lee & Low.

Wolff, Virginia Euwer (1998) *Bat 6.* Scholastic.

Wood, Audrey (1984) *The napping house.* Illus. Don Wood. Harcourt.

Wood, Audrey (1998) *Quick as a cricket.* Illus. Don Wood. Child's Play International.

Woodson, Jacqueline (1994) *I hadn't meant to tell you this.* Putnam.

Woodson, Jacqueline (1997) *The house you pass on the way.* Delacourt.

Woodson, Jacqueline (2002) *Visiting day.* Illus. James Ransome. Scholastic.

Woodson, Jacqueline (2003) *Locomotion.* Putnam.

Yang, Belle (2004) *Hannah is my name.* Candlewick.

Yashima, Taro (1976) *Crow boy.* Perfection Learning.

Yolen, Jane (1996) *Encounter.* Illus. David Shannon. Houghton Mifflin.

Zimmerman, Frederick (2007) *Cool maps for curious kids #2: Afghanistan, an unauthorized tour of* The land of a thousand suns *and* The kite runner. Nimble.

References
Professional
Publications

Adomat, D.S. (2009) Actively engaging with stories through drama: Portraits of two readers. *The Reading Teacher, 62*(8), 636–642.

Albers, P. (1996) Issues of representation: Caldecott gold medal winners 1984–1995. *The New Advocate, 9*(1), 267–285.

Albers, P. & Harste, J. (2007) The arts, new literacies, and multimodality. *English Education, 40*(1), 6–20.

Albers, P., Harste, J. C., & Vasquez, V. (2011) Interrupting certainty and making trouble: Teachers' written and visual responses to picturebooks. In Pamela J. Dunston, Linda B. Gambrell, C.C. Bates, Susan King Fullerton, Victoria R. Gillis, Kathy Headley, & Pamela M. Stecker (Eds.), *60th Yearbook of the Literacy Research Association.* Oak Creek, WI: Literacy Research Association.

Allington, R. (1977) "If they don't read much, how they ever gonna get good?" *Journal of Reading. 21*(1), 57–61.

Allington, R. (2009) If they don't read much . . . 30 years later. In E. Hiebert (Ed.), *Reading more, reading better* (pp. 30–54). New York: Guilford Press.

American Library Association (ALA) (2009) *Banned and challenged books.* Retrieved October, 23, 2010 from: http://www.ala.org/ala/issuesadvocacy/banned/index.cfm.

American Library Association (ALA) (2010a) *Most frequently challenged authors of the 21st century.* Retrieved September 28, 2010, from: http://www.ala.org/ala/issuesadvocacy/banned/frequentlychallenged/challengeda.

American Library Association (ALA) (2010b) *Frequently challenged books.* Retrieved September 1, 2010, from: http://www.ala.org/ala/issuesadvocacy/banned/frequentlychallenged/index.cfm.

American Library Association (ALA) (2011a) *100 most frequently challenged books by decade.* Retrieved October, 1, 2010 from: http://www.ala.org/ala/issuesadvocacy/banned/frequentlychallenged/challengedbydecade/index.cfm.

American Library Association (ALA) (2011b) *Banned book week: Celebrating the freedom to read.* http://www.ala.org/ala/issuesadvocacy/banned/bannedbooksweek/index.cfm.

American Library Association (ALA) (2011c) *Best graphic novels for teens.* http://www.ala.org/ala/mgrps/divs/yalsa/booklistsawards/greatgraphicnovelsforteens/ggnt11_topten.cfm.

Aronson, M. (2001) Slippery slopes and proliferating prizes. *The Horn Book Magazine, 77*(1), 271–278.

Arya, P., Martens, P., Wilson, G. P., Altwerger, B., Jin, L., Laster, B., & Lang, D. (2005) Reclaiming literacy instruction: Evidence in support of literature-based programs. *Language Arts, 83*(1), 63–72.

Au, K.H. (2001) Culturally responsive instruction as a dimension of new literacies. *Reading Online, 5*(1). Available: http://www.readingonline.org/newliteracies/lit_index.asp?HREF=/newliteracies/xu/index.html.

Baildon, M.C. & Damico, J.S. (2006) "We have to pick sides": Students wrestle with counter claims on websites. *Social Education, 70*(3), 156–159.

Ballentine, D. & Hill, L. (2000) Teaching beyond once upon a time. *Language Arts, 78*(1), 11–20.

Banana Slug String Band (2011) *Dirt made my lunch*: http://www.ces.ncsu.edu/4hplantandsoils/Dirt%20Made%20My%20Lunch%20Song%20Lyrics.pdf.

Bargiel, S., Beck, C., Koblitz, D., O'Connor, A., Pierce, K.M., & Wolf, S. (1997) Bringing life issues into the classroom (Talking About Books). *Language Arts, 74*(1), 482–490.

Barnes, D. (1992) *From communication to curriculum.* Portsmouth, NH: Boynton Cook.

Beck, I. & McKeown, M. (2001) Text talk: Capturing the benefits of read-aloud experiences for young children. *The Reading Teacher, 55*(1), 10–20.

Beck, U. (2002) The cosmopolitan society and its enemies. *Theory, culture & society, 19*(1), 17–44.

Beers, K. (1996) No time, no interest, no way! The 3 voices of aliteracy. *School Library Journal, 42*(1), 30–33.

Begler, E. (1996) Global cultures: The first steps toward understanding. *Social Education, 62*(1), 272–276.

Berghoff, B., Egawa, K.A., Harste, J.C., & Hoonan, B.T. (2000) Planning for focused studies (pp. 88–92). *Beyond reading and writing: Inquiry, curriculum, and multiple ways of knowing.* Urbana, IL: National Council of Teachers of English.

Berkowitz, S. (2010) Focused study project reflection. Unpublished manuscript. Indiana University.

Bernstein, S. (1996) *When the censor comes.* Retrieved October 1, 2010 from: http://www.efc.ca/pages/chronicle/whattodo.html.

Bird, M., Libby, V., Rowley, L., & Turner, J. (2002) Plan for meaning making. *Primary Voices, 10*(1), 25–30.

Black, R. (2009) Online fan fiction, global identities, and imagination. *Research in the Teaching of English, 43*(4), 397–425.

Black, R.W. (2008) *Adolescents and online fan fiction.* London: Peter Lang.

Bleich, D. (1993) *The double perspective: Language, literacy, and social relations.* Urbana, IL: National Council of Teachers of English.

Bourdieu, P. (1986) The forms of capital. In J.G. Richardson (Ed.), *Handbook of theory and research for the sociology of education* (pp. 241–258). New York: Greenwood Press.

Brabham, E. & Villaume, S. (2002) Leveled text: The good news and the bad news. *The Reading Teacher, 55*(5), 438–441.

Brewster, J.C. (2008) Traveling the world with outstanding children's literature. *Early Childhood Education, 35*(1), 371–375.

Brozo, W. & Tomlinson, C. (1986) Literature: The key to lively content courses. *The Reading Teacher, 40*(3), 288–293.

Bruner, J. (1987) *Actual minds, possible worlds.* Cambridge, MA: Harvard University Press.

Brunner, B. (2009) *Banned books: From Harriet the Spy to Catcher in the Rye.* http://www.factmonster.com/spot/banned-kids-books.html.

Brunner, B. (2010) *Books under fire: Banned books week calls attention to the most challenged and banned books in the U.S.* Retrieved September 27, 2010 from: http://www.infoplease.com/spot/bannedbookslist.html.

Bunting, E. (2008) A day's work (Illus. Ronald Himler). In *Reading Street Indiana* (Grade 3). Indianapolis, IN: Pearson.

Burke, C. (1980) The reading interview (pp. 210–212). In B.P. Farr and D.J. Strickler (Eds.), *Reading comprehension: Resource guide.* Bloomington, IN: School of Education, Indiana University.

Burke, C. (1998) *A focused study as a curricular organization.* Bloomington, IN: Inquiring Voices Press.

Cairns, S.A. (2008) Power, language, and literacy in The Great Gilly Hopkins. *Children's Literature in Education, 39*(1), 9–19.

Calkins, L.M. (1994) *The art of teaching writing.* Portsmouth, NH: Heinemann.

Cambourne, B. (1988) *The whole story: Natural learning and the acquisition of literacy in the classroom.* Auckland, New Zealand: Scholastic.

Cambourne, B. (1995). Toward an educationally relevant theory of literacy learning: Twenty years of inquiry. *The Reading Teacher, 49*(3), 1–14.

Cazden, C. (1988) *Classroom discourse: The language of teaching and learning.* Portsmouth, NH: Heinemann.

Cazden, C. (2002) *Classroom discourse: The language of teaching and learning* (2nd Edn). Portsmouth, NH: Heinemann.

Children's Lit. Listserv (1995) Retrieved October 23, 2010 from: http://www.fairrosa.info/disc/goosebumps.html.

Christensen, L. (2000) *Reading, writing, and rising up: Teaching about social justice and the power of the written word.* Milwaukee, WI: Rethinking Schools.

Christensen, L. (2009) *Teaching for joy and justice: Re-imagining the language arts classroom.* Milwaukee, WI: Rethinking Schools.

Clyde, J.A. (2003) Stepping inside the story world: The subtext strategy—A tool for connecting and comprehending. *The Reading Teacher, 57*(2), 150–160.

Clyde, J.A., Barber, S., Hogue, S., & Wasz. L. (2006) *Breakthrough to meaning: Helping your kids become better readers, writers, and thinkers.* Portsmouth, NH: Heinemann.

Collins, H.T., Czarra, F., & Smith, A. (1988) Guidelines for global and international studies education. *Social Education, 62*(1), 311–317.

Comber, B. (2001) Negotiating critical literacies. *School Talk, 6*(3), 1–3.

Copenhaver, J. (2001) Running out of time: Rushed read-alouds in a primary classroom. *Language Arts, 79*(2), 148–158.

Criscuola, M.M. (1994) Read, discuss, reread: Insights from the Junior Great Books program. *Educational Leadership, 51*(1), 58–61.

Croce, K., Martens, P., Martens, R., & Maderazo, C. (2009) Students developing as meaning-makers of the pictorial and written texts in picturebooks (pp. 156-170). In K. Leander, D. Rowe, D. Dickinson, M. Hundley, R. Jimenez, & V. Risko (Eds.), *58th Yearbook of the National Reading Conference.* Oak Creak, WI: National Reading Conference.

Cunningham, A. & Shagoury, R. (2005) The sweet work of reading: Kindergartners explore reading comprehension using a surprisingly complex array of strategies. *Educational Leadership, 63*(2), 53–57.

Damico, J.S. (2005) Evoking heads and hearts: Exploring issues of social justice through poetry. *Language Arts, 83*, 137–146.

Damico, J.S. (2010) *Critical web reader:* http//cwr.indiana.edu.

Daniels, H. (1994) *Literature circles: Voice and choice in the student-centered classroom.* York, ME: Stenhouse.

Daniels, H. (2002) *Literature circles: Voice and choice in book clubs and reading groups.* York, ME: Stenhouse.

Delbridge, K. (2008) What we know about the nature of adolescent reading (pp. 158–175). In S. Kucer (Ed.), *What research REALLY says about teaching and learning to read.* Urbana, IL: National Council of Teachers of English.

Diakiw, J.Y. (1990) Children's literature and global education: Understanding the developing world. *The Reading Teacher, 43*(1), 296–300.

DiCesare, K. (2008) Organizing book baskets: Letting kids in on the plan (pp. 40–46). In K. Szymusiak, F. Sibberson, and L. Koch (Eds.), *Beyond leveled books: Supporting early and transitional readers in grades K-5* (2nd Edn). Portland, ME: Stenhouse.

Doyle, B. & Bramwell, W. (2006) Promoting emergent literacy and social-emotional learning through dialogic reading. *The Reading Teacher, 59*(6), 554–564.

Doyle. R.P. (2010) *Think for yourself and let others do the same: Books challenged or banned in 2009–2010.* Retrieved October 13, 2010, from: http://www.ala.org/ala/issuesadvocacy/banned/bannedbooksweek/ideasandresources/free_downloads/2010banned.pdf.

Duncan-Andrade, J. & Morrell, E. (2000) *Using hip-hop culture as a bridge to canonical poetry texts in an urban secondary English classroom.* Paper presented at the annual meeting of the American Educational Research Association, New Orleans, LA.

Edmiston, B. (1993) Going up the beanstalk: Discovering giant responsibilities for responding to literature through drama (pp. 16–27). In K. Holland, R. Hungerford, & S. Ernst (Eds.), *Journeying: Children responding to literature.* Portsmouth, NH: Heinemann.

Edmiston, B. & Enciso, P. (2002) Reflections and refractions on meaning: Dialogic approaches to classroom drama and reading (pp. 868–880). In J. Flood, D. Lapp, J. Squire, & J. Jensen (Eds.), *The handbook on research and teaching in the language arts.* New York: Simon & Schuster.

Ellsworth, E. (2005) *Places of learning: Media, architecture, pedagogy.* New York: Taylor & Francis.

Enciso, P. (2011) Storytelling in critical literacy pedagogy (pp. 8–22). In H. Janks & V. Vasquez (Eds.), *Critical literacy revisited: Writing as critique for English teaching.* New York: Taylor & Francis.

Ernst, S. (1995) Gender issues in books for children and young adults. In S. Lehr (Ed.). *Battling dragons: Issues and controversy in children's literature.* Portsmouth, NH: Heinemann.

Fader, D. (1981) *Hooked on books.* New York: Berkley.

Fairclough, N. (1989) *Language and power.* Toronto: Pearson.

Fairclough, N. (1995) *Critical discourse analysis: The critical study of language.* London: Longman.

Fletcher, R. (2005) The author study: Knowing a writer from the inside out. In. S. Frost & F. Sibberson (Eds.), *School Talk, 10,* 1–3.

Fox, K.R. (2006) Using author studies in children's literature to explore social justice issues. *The Social Studies, 97*(6), 251–256.

Franzak, J.K. (2006) Zoom: A review of the literature on marginalized adolescent readers, literacy theory, and policy implications. *Review of Educational Research, 76*(2), 209–248.

Freedman, L. & Johnson, H. (2001) Who's protecting whom? *I Hadn't Meant to Tell You This,* a case in point in confronting self-censorship in the choice of young adult literature. *Journal of Adolescent & Adult Literacy, 44*(1), 356–369.

Freire, P. (1970) *Pedagogy of the oppressed.* South Hadley, MA: Bergin & Garvey.

Fresch, E.T. (2004) *Connecting children past and present.* Portsmouth, NH: Heinemann.

Frost, S. & Sibberson, F. (2005) Author studies, *School Talk, 10,* 1–3.

Gallo, D.R. (1994) Censorship of young adult literature (pp. 115-122). In J.S. Simmons (Ed.), *Censorship, a threat to reading, learning and thinking.* Newark, DE: International Reading Association.

Gambrell, L. & Palmer, B. (1992) Children's metacognitive knowledge about reading and writing in literature-based and conventional classrooms (pp. 217–223). *41st Yearbook of the National Reading Conference.* Chicago: National Reading Conference.

Gee, J. (1996) *Social linguistics and literacy: Ideology in discourse* (2nd Edn). New York: Taylor & Francis.

Gee, J. (1999) *An introduction to discourse analysis: Theory and method.* New York: Routledge.

Gee, J. (2004) *Situated language and learning: A critique of traditional schooling.* New York: Taylor & Francis.

Gertz, C. (1973) *The interpretation of cultures.* New York: Basic Books.

Goodman, K. (1990) Expert interview. In J.C. Harste & E. Juerwicz (Host & Director), *Visions of literacy* (Videotape series). Portsmouth, NH: Heinemann.

Goodman, K. (1996) *On reading.* Portsmouth, NH: Heinemann.

Goodman, K., Goodman, Y., & Burke, C. (1978) Reading for life: The psycholinguistic base (pp. 2–29). In E. Hunter-Grundin & H. Grundin (Eds.), *Reading: Implementing the Bullock Report.* London: Woodcock Educational.

Goodman, Y. (1978) Kidwatching: An alternative to testing. *Journal of the National Elementary School Principals, 57*(4), 22–27.

Goodman, Y. & Burke, C. (1972) Reading miscue inventory. New York: Macmillan.

Hansen, J. & Vasquez, V. (2002) Genre study. *School Talk, 7*(1), 1–6.

Harris, T. & Hodges, R. (1995) *The literacy dictionary.* Newark, DE: International Reading Association.

Harste, J.C. (1978) *Navajo School Evaluation Report: Wingate Language Arts Program—Grades 5–8* (mimeographed). Bloomington, IN: Division of Teacher Education, Indiana University.

Harste, J. (2008a) Visual Literacy (pp. 52–59). In Mitzi Lewison, Christine Leland, & Jerome Harste, *Creating critical classrooms.* Mahwah, NJ: Erlbaum.

Harste, J. (2008b) Uncertainty and the teaching of reading and writing. In Mitzi Lewison, Christine Leland, & Jerome Harste, *Creating critical classrooms.* Mahwah, NJ: Erlbaum.

Harste, J. (2011) Seamlessly art (pp. 5-8). In R.J. Meyer & K.F. Whitmore (Eds.), *Reclaiming reading.* Mahwah, NJ: Erlbaum.

Harste, J., Breau, A., Leland, C., Lewison, M., & Ociepka, A., Vasquez, V. (2000) Supporting critical conversations in classrooms (pp. 506–554). In K.M. Pierce (Ed.), *Adventuring with books*: A booklist for pre-K–grade 6 (12th Edn). Urbana, IL: National Council of Teachers of English.

Harste, J., Leland, C. H., & Jackson, C. (2002) Little Red Riding Hood goes to college: Inviting the language of critique in teacher education (pp. 253–272). In Diane L. Schallert, Colleen M. Fairbanks, Jo Worthy, Beth Maloch, & James V. Hoffman (Eds.), *Linking literacies of yesterday and today with literacies of tomorrow* (51st Yearbook of the National Reading Conference). Oak Creek, WI: NRC.

Harste, J., & Short, K., w/ Burke, C. (1988) *Creating classrooms for authors: The reading-writing connection.* Portsmouth, NH: Heinemann.

Harste, J. & Vasquez, V. (1998) The work we do: Journal as audit trail. *Language Arts, 75*(1), 266–276.

Harste, J., Woodward, V., & Burke, C. (1984) *Language stories and literacy lessons.* Portsmouth, NH: Heinemann.

Harvey, S. (1998) *Nonfiction matters: Reading, writing, and research in grades 3–8.* York, ME: Stenhouse.

Hasslett, D. (2009) A remixed model of the reading/writing process: The semiotic scaffolds of visual texts. Presentation at the National Reading Conference, Albuquerque, NM.

Hawkins, B. (2008) Professional development: Paradigms, possibilities for change, and praxis (pp. 250–271). In S. Kucer (Ed.), *What research REALLY says about teaching and learning to read.* Urbana, IL: National Council of Teachers of English.

Heater, D. (2000) Does cosmopolitan thinking have a future? *Review of International Studies, 26*(1), 179–197.

Heath, S.B. (1982) What no bedtime story means: Narrative skills at home and school. *Language in Society, 11*(1), 49–76.

Heath, S.B. (1983) *Ways with words.* Portsmouth, NH: Heinemann.

Heffernan, L. (2000) Critical literacy and writer's workshop. Presentation at the Indiana Teachers of Writing Annual Conference, Indianapolis, IN.

Heffernan, L. & Lewison, M. (2000) Making real world issues our business: Critical literacy in a third-grade classroom. *Primary Voices, 9*(2), 15–21.

Heffernan, L. & Lewison, M. (2009) Keep your eyes on the prize: Critical stance in the middle school classroom. *Voices from the Middle, 17*(1), 19–27.

Hillegass, M.M. (2005) Early childhood author studies. In. S. Frost & F. Sibberson (Eds.), *School Talk, 10,* 1–3.

Hirsch, E.D. (2010) *The making of Americans: Democracy in our schools.* Cambridge, MA: Yale University Press.

Holdaway, D. (1999) *Foundations of literacy (K–6).* Portsmouth, NH: Heinemann.

Howard, E.F. (1991) Authentic multicultural literature for children: Cultural perspectives (pp. 142–164). In M. Lindgren (Ed.), *The multicolored mirror: Cultural substance in literature for children and young adults.* Fort Atkinson, WI: Highsmith Press.

Huck, C. (1966) *Good books for all children.* Columbus, OH: Ohio State University Press.

Huck, C. & Kerstetter, K. (1987) Developing readers (pp. 15–19). In B. Cullinan (Ed.), *Children's literature in the reading program.* Newark, DE: International Reading Association.

Hull, G. & Avila, J. (2008) Narrative and digital storytelling. *New literacies: A professional development wiki for educators.* Developed under the aegis of the Improving Teacher Quality Project (ITQP), a federally funded partnership between Montclair State University and East Orange School District, New Jersey.

Hull, G. & Avila, J. (2010) NewLits.org: https://newlits.wikispaces.com/Narrative+and+digital+story telling.

Hutchins, R.M. (1952) *Great books of the western world* (54 Volume Set). New York: Encyclopedia Britannica.

Indiana Library Federation (2008) *Young Hoosier book award.* Retrieved February 14, 2009, from http://www.ilfonline.org/Programs/yhba/yh-baprogram.htm.

Jackson, T. & Boutte, G. (2009) Liberation literature: Positive cultural messages in children's and young adult literature at Freedom Schools. *Language Arts, 87*(2), 108–116.

Janks, H. (2005) Deconstruction and reconstruction: Diversity as a productive resource. *Discourse, 26*(1), 31–45.

Janks, H. (2010) *Language and power.* New York: Routledge.

Jenkins, C.B. (2006) "Did I tell you that you are the best writer in the world?": Author studies in the elementary classroom. *Journal of Children's Literature, 32*(1), 64–78.

Joels, R.W. (1999) Weaving world understanding: The importance of translations in international children's literature. *Children's Literature in Education, 30*(1), 65–83.

Kawabata, A. & Vandergrift, K.E. (1998) History into myth: The anatomy of a picture book. *Bookbird, 36*(2), 6–12.

Kelly, E. (1955) Teaching current issues in the school (pp. 59–70). In R. Elsworth & O. Sand (Eds.), *Improving the social studies curriculum.* Washington, DC: National Council for the Social Studies.

Kidd, K. (2007) Prizing children's literature: the case of Newbery gold. *Children's Literature*, *35*(2), 166–190.

Kincheloe, J. (2007) Critical pedagogy in the twenty-first century (pp. 9–42). In P. McLaren & J, Kincheloe (Eds.), *Critical pedagogy: Where are we now?* New York: Peter Lang.

Knobel, M. & Lankshear, C. (2008) Remix: The art and craft of endless hybridization. *Journal of Adolescent & Adult Literacy*, *52*(1), 22–33.

Knobel, M. & Lankshear, C. (2009) Wikis, digital literacies, and professional growth. *Journal of Adolescent & Adult Literacy*, *52*(7), 631–634.

Kooy, M. (2003) Riding the coattails of Harry Potter: Readings, relational learning, and revelation in book clubs. *Journal of Adolescent & Adult Literacy*, *74*(2), 136–145.

Koshewa, A. (1992) *Voice and choice.* In J. C. Harste & E. Juerwicz, *Visions of literacy* (Videotape series). Portsmouth, NH: Heinemann.

Krashen, S. (2004) *The power of reading: Insights from the research.* NY: Libraries Unlimited.

Krashen, S. (2006) Free reading. *School Library Journal*, *52*(9), 42–45. Retrieved March 23, 2009 from the Wilson Web.

Krashen, S. (n.d.). *88 generalizations about free voluntary reading.* Retrieved May 16, 2009 from: http://www.sdkrashen.com/handouts/88Generalizations/index.html.

Kress, G. (2003) *Literacy in the new media age.* London: Routledge.

Kucer, S. (2008) *What research REALLY says about teaching and learning to read.* Urbana, IL: National Council of Teachers of English.

Labbo, L.D. (2006) The social semiotics of early literacy learning and computer technologies. *Journal of Reading Education*, *45*(1), 89–93.

Lakoff, G. (2004) *Don't think of an elephant: Know your values and frame the debate.* White River Junction, VT: Chelsea Green.

Laman, T.T. (2006) Changing our minds/changing the world: The power of a question. *Language Arts*, *83*(1), 203–214.

Landt, S.M. (2006) Multicultural literature and young adolescents: A kaleidoscope of opportunity. *Journal of Adolescent & Adult Literacy*, *49*(1), 890–897.

Lankshear, C. & Knobel, M. (2006) *New literacies* (2nd Edn). Oxford: Open University Press.

Lankshear, C. & McLaren, P.L. (1993) Preface (pp. i–iv). In C. Lankshear & P.L. McLaren (Eds.), *Critical literacy, Politics, praxis, and the postmodern.* New York: State University of New York Press.

Lee, M. (2010) Between two languages and two worlds: Identity of Korean early study-abroad undergraduates in the U.S. Doctoral Dissertation, Indiana University.

Lehman, B. (2007) *Children's literature and learning: Literary study across the curriculum.* New York: Teachers College Press.

Lehr, S. (1995) Books under fire: Issues of censorship in children's literature (pp. 1–2). In S. Lehr (Ed.), *Battling dragons, issues and controversy in children's literature.* Portsmouth, NH: Heinemann.

Leland, C.H. & Fitzpatrick, R. (1993) Cross-age interaction builds enthusiasm for reading and writing. *The Reading Teacher*, *47*(4), 292–301.

Leland, C.H. & Harste, J.C. (1994) Multiple ways of knowing: Curriculum in a new key. *Language Arts*, *71*(5), 337–345.

Leland, C.H. & Harste, J. (1995) Stretching our definition of literacy. *Indiana Reading Quarterly*, *27*(4), 21–25.

Leland, C., Harste, J., & Clouse, L. (in press) It's no big deal: Seeing and not seeing stereotypes.

Leland, C.H., & Harste, J.C., with Davis, A., Haas, C., McDaniel, K., Parsons, M., & Strawmyer, M. (2003) "It made me hurt inside": Exploring tough social issues through critical literacy. *The Journal of Reading Education*, *28*(2), 7–15.

Leland, C., & Harste, J., with Huber, K. (2005) Out of the box: Critical literacy in a first-grade classroom. *Language Arts*, *82*(5), 257–268.

Leland, C., Harste, J., Ociepka, A., Lewison, M., & Vasquez, V. (1999) Exploring critical literacy: You can hear a pin drop. *Language Arts*, *77*(1), 70–77.

Leland, C., Ociepka, A., & Kuonen, K. (2012) Reading from different interpretive stances: In search of a critical perspective. *Journal of Adolescent and Adult Literacy*.

Lewis, C. (2000) Critical issues: Limits of identification: The personal, pleasurable, and critical in reader response. *Journal of Literacy Research*, *32*(2), 253–266.

Lewison, M., Leland, C., Flint, A.S., & Möller, K.J. (2002) Dangerous discourses: Controversial books to support engagement, diversity, and democracy. *The New Advocate*, *15*(3), 215–226.

Lewison, M., Leland, C., & Harste, J.C. (2000) "Not in my classroom!" The case for using multi-view social issues books with children. *The Australian Journal of Language and Literacy*, 23(1), 8–20.

Lewison, M., Leland, C., & Harste, J.C. (2008) *Creating critical classrooms: K-8 reading and writing with an edge*. Mahwah, NJ: Lawrence Erlbaum.

Lo, D.E. (2001) Borrowed voices: Using literature to teach global perspectives to middle school students. *The Clearing House*, 75(1), 84–87.

Louie, B.Y. (2006) Guiding principles for teaching multicultural literature. *The Reading Teacher*, 59(1), 438–448.

Low, W. (2007) Chinatown. In *Trophies* (Grade 2). Orlando, FL: Harcourt.

Luke, A. & Freebody, P. (1997) Shaping the social practices of reading (pp. 185–225). In S. Muspratt, A. Luke, & P. Freebody (Eds.), *Constructing critical literacies*. Cresskill, NJ: Hampton Press.

MacGinitie, W.H. (1983) The power of uncertainty. *Journal of Reading*, 26(8), 677–683.

Manning, A. (2010) Postcards of the mind. *Graduate Program in Literacy*. Education, Mount Saint Vincent University.

Manzo, K.K. (2005) Social studies losing out to reading, math. *Education Week*, March 16, 40.

Martens, R., Martens, P., Croce, K., & Maderazo, C. (2010) Reading illustrations: Helping readers use pictorial text to construct meaning in picturebooks (pp. 187–210). In P. Albers & J. Sanders (Eds.), *Literacies, the arts & multimodality*. Urbana, IL: National Council of Teachers of English.

Martin, B. (1987) The making of a reader: A personal narrative (pp. 15–19). In B. Cullinan (Ed.), *Children's literature in the reading program*. Newark, DE: International Reading Association.

Martin, G. (2007) The poverty of critical pedagogy (pp. 337–353). In P. McLaren & J. Kincheloe (Eds.), *Critical pedagogy: Where are we now?* New York: Peter Lang.

McClure, A. (1995) Censorship of children's books. In S. Lehr (Ed.), *Battling dragons, issues and controversy in children's literature* (pp. 3–30). Portsmouth, NH: Heinemann.

McGill-Franzen, A. & Botzakis, S. (2009) Series books, graphic novels, comics, and magazines: Unauthorized texts, authorized literacy practices (pp. 110–117). In E. Hiebert (Ed.), *Reading more, reading better*. New York: Guilford Press.

Medina, C.L. (2004) Drama wor(l)ds: Exploration of Latina/o realistic fiction. *Language Arts*, 81(4), 272–282.

Mee, M. (2007) Enough about you, let's talk about me: Student voice in the classroom. *Middle Ground*, 10(1), 37–38.

Meier, T. (2008) *Black communications and learning to read: Building on children's linguistic and cultural strengths*. New York: Erlbaum.

Miller, C. & Saxton, J. (2004) *Into the story: Language in action through drama*. Portsmouth, NH: Heinemann.

Miller, D. (2009) *The book whisperer: Awakening the inner reader in every child*. New York: Jossey-Bass.

Miscevic, N. (1999) Close strangers: Nationalism, proximity and cosmopolitanism. *Studies in East European Thought*, 51(1), 109–125.

Moje, E., Young, J., Readence, J., & Moore, D. (2000) Reinventing adolescent literacy for new times: Perennial and millennial issues. *Journal of Adolescent & Adult Literacy*, 43(1), 400–410.

Mooney, M.E. (1990) *Reading to, with, and by children*. Katonah, NY: Richard C. Owen.

Moskowitz, M. (Director) (2002) *Stone Reader* (DVD). New York: JET Film, LLC.

Mueller, S. (2005) *Everyday literacy: Environmental print activities for children 3 to 8*. Silver Springs, MD: Gryphon House.

Myers, M. (1996) *Changing our minds*. Urbana, IL: National Council of Teachers of English.

Nagy, W., Herman, P., & Anderson, R. (1985) Learning words from context. *Reading Research Quarterly*, 20(2), 233–53.

National Council of Teachers of English (NCTE) (1981) *Guidelines on the student's right to read: http://www.ncte.org/positions/statements/righttoreadguideline*.

National Council of Teachers of English (NCTE) (2004) *Guidelines for dealing with censorship of nonprint and multimedia materials*: http://www.ncte.org/positions/statements/censorshipofnonprint.

National Council of Teachers of English (NCTE) (2004) *Guidelines for dealing with the censorship of nonprint materials*: http://www.ncte.org/postions/statements/censorshipofnonprint.

National Council of Teachers of English (NCTE) (2008) *Rationales for teaching challenged books*: http://www.ncte.org/action/anticensorship/rationals.

Nieto, S. (1999) *The light in their eyes: Creating multicultural learning communities*. New York: Teachers College Press.

Nilsen, A.P. & Donelson, K.L. (2009) *Literature for today's young adults* (8th Edn). New York: Pearson.

Nixon, J.L. (1995) *Writing with teachers: Mystery writing.* Retrieved September 1, 2011, from: http://teacher.scholastic.com/writewit/mystery/.

Norton-Meier, L.A. (2009) In defense of crappy literature: When the book is bad but the literary thinking is rich! *Language Arts, 86*(1), 188–195.

O'Brien, T. & Sullivan, M. (2008) *Afghan dreams: Young voices of Afghanistan.* New York: Bloomsbury.

O'Neill, C. (1995) *Drama worlds: A framework for process drama.* Portsmouth, NH: Heinemann.

Peterson, R. & Eeds, M. (1990) *Grand conversations.* New York: Scholastic.

Petrie, M., Moran, R., & Lutkus, A. (2005) *National Assessment of Education Progress (NAEP) 2004 trends in academic progress: Three decades of student performance in reading and mathematics.* Washington, DC: US Department of Education, Institute of Education Sciences.

Pierce, K.M. (1996) Getting started: Establishing a reading/writing classroom (pp. 151–169). In K. Short, J. Harste, & C. Burke. *Creating classrooms for authors and inquirers.* Portsmouth, NH: Heinemann.

Pierce, K.M. (1999) "I am a level 3 reader": Children's perceptions of themselves as readers. *New Advocate, 12*(4), 359–375.

Poonam, A., Martens, P., Wilson, G., Altwerger, B., Jin, L., Laster, B., & Lang, D. (2005) Reclaiming literacy instruction: Evidence in support of literature-based programs. *Language Arts, 83*(1), 63–72.

Porter, C. (1998) Student-created units: Choice, collaboration, and connection (pp. 121–135). In. K.G. Short & K.M. Pierce (Eds.) *Talking about Books: Literature discussion groups in K-8 classrooms.* Portsmouth, NH: Heinemann.

Read-Write-Think (2011) *Website.* Hosted by the International Reading Association and the National Council of Teachers of English: http://www.readwritethink.org/classroom-resources/lesson-plans/stop-signs-mcdonald-cheerios-949.html.

Rhodes, L. (1983) I can read! Predictable books as resources for reading and writing instruction. *The Reading Teacher, 34*(5), 511–518.

Rizvi, F. (2006) Epistemic virtues and cosmopolitan learning. *The Australian Educational Researcher, 35*(1), 17–35.

Robb, L. (1992) Books in the classroom: Controversial novels. *Horn Book Magazine, 68*(1), 1–4.

Rosenblatt, L. (1987) *The reader, the text, the poem.* Carbondale, IL: Southern Illinois University Press.

Said, E.W. (1978) *Orientalism.* New York: Vintage.

Sanders, J. & Albers, P. (2010) Multimodal literacies: An introduction (pp. 1–25). In P. Albers & J. Sanders (Eds.), *Literacies, the arts & multimodality.* Urbana, IL: National Council of Teachers of English.

Saskatoon Public Schools (2004–09) *Picture books and illustrator studies*: http://olc.spsd.sk.ca/DE/pd/instr/strats/picturebooks/index.html.

Serebrin, W. & Broderick, P. (2009) Process drama (pp. 10–27). In D. Stephens & J. Harste (Eds.), *Come Monday morning.* Columbia, SC: Department of Instruction and Teacher Education, University of South Carolina.

Shannon, P. (2002) The myths of reading aloud. *The Dragon Lode, 20*(2), 6–11.

Sharp, C. & Martinez, M. (2010) Exploring mystery in fifth grade: A journey of discovery. *Voices from the Middle, 17*(1), 19–28.

Shor, I. (1999) What is critical literacy? (pp. 1–25). In I. Shor & C. Pari (Eds), *Critical literacy in action: Writing words, changing worlds.* Portsmouth, NH: Heinemann.

Short, K.G. (2009a) Critically reading the word and the world building understanding through literature. *Bluebird: A Journal of International Children's Literature, 47*(2), 1–10.

Short, K.G. (2009b) *Cultural x-rays.* In D. Stephens & J. Harste (Eds.), *Come Monday morning.* Columbia, SC: Department of Instruction and Teacher Education, University of South Carolina.

Short, K.G. & Fox, D.L. (2004) The complexity of cultural authenticity in children's literature: A critical view (pp. 373–384), *53rd Yearbook of the National Reading Conference.* Chicago, IL: National Reading Conference.

Short, K., & Harste, J., with Burke, C. (1996) *Creating classrooms for authors and inquirers.* Portsmouth, NH: Heinemann.

Short, K. & Pierce, K.M. (1998) *Talking about books: Literature discussion groups in K-8 classrooms.* Portsmouth, NH: Heinemann.

Siegel, M.G. (1984) Reading as signification. Unpublished doctoral dissertation, Indiana University, Bloomington.

Siegel, M.G. (1995) More than words: The generative power of transmediation for learning. *Canadian Journal of Education, 20*(4), 455–475.

Siemens, L. (1996) "Walking through the time of kids": Going places with poetry. *Language Arts, 73*(1), 234–240.

Silvers, P., Shorey, M. & Crafton, L. (2010) Critical literacy in a primary multiliteracies classroom: The hurricane group. *Journal of Early Childhood Literacy, 10*(1), 379–409.

Sims Bishop, R. (1992) Multicultural literature for children, making informed choices (pp. 109–123). In V.J. Harris (Ed.), *Teaching multicultural literature in grades K-8.* Norwood, MA: Christopher Gordon.

Smith, F. (1981) Demonstrations, engagement and sensitivity: The choice between people and programs. *Language Arts, 58*(2), 634–642.

Smith, F. (1982) *Writing and the writer.* New York: Holt.

Smith, F. (1983) Reading like a writer. *Language Arts, 60*(1), 558–567.

Smith, F. (1988) *Joining the literacy club: Further essays into education.* Portsmouth, NH: Heinemann.

Smith, K. (1995) Bringing children and literature together in the elementary classroom. *Primary Voices K-6, 3*(2), 22–30.

Smolkin, L.B. & Suina, J.H. (1997) Artistic triumph or multicultural failure?: Multiple perspectives on a "multicultural" award-winning book. *The New Advocate, 4*(1), 307–322.

Stan, S. (1999) Going global: World literature for American children. *Theory into Practice, 38*(1), 168–177.

Staples, S.F. (1996) Why Johnny can't read: Censorship in American libraries. *The Alan Review, 23*(1), 1–3.

Steinberg, S. & Kinchloe, J. (Eds.) (1997). *Kinderculture: The corporate construction of childhood.* Boulder, CO: Westview Press.

Stockton, F. (1982) *The lady and the tiger. The Century, 25*(1), 83–86.

Street, B. (1995) *Social literacies: Critical approaches to literacy, development, ethnography and education.* Boston, MA: Addison Wesley.

Suhor, C. (1984) Towards a semiotics-based curriculum. *Journal of Curriculum Studies, 16*(3), 247–257.

Sumara, D. (2002) *Why reading literature in school still matters: Imagination, interpretation, insight.* Mahwah, NJ: Erlbaum.

Szymusiak, K. & Sibberson, F. (2001) *Beyond leveled books: Supporting transitional readers in grades 2–5.* Portland, ME: Stenhouse.

Taxel, J. (1986) The black experience in children's fiction: Controversies surrounding award winning books. *Curriculum Inquiry, 16*(1), 245–281.

Taylor, R.H. (2000) Indian in the cupboard: A case study in perspective. *Journal of Qualitative Studies in Education, 13*(1), 371–385.

Thomson, P. (2002) *Schooling the rustbelt kids: Making the difference in changing times.* Crows Nest, New South Wales: Allen & Unwin.

Tomlinson, C. (1995) Justifying violence in children's literature (pp. 39–50). In S. Lehr (Ed.), *Battling dragons, issues and controversy in children's literature.* Portsmouth, NH: Heinemann.

Trelease, J. (1982) *The read-aloud handbook* (1st Edn). Toronto: Penguin.

Trelease, J. (2006) *The read-aloud handbook* (6th Edn). Toronto: Penguin.

Van Allen, R. (1976) *Language experience in communication.* Boston, MA: Houghton Mifflin.

Van Sluys, K. (2005) *What if and why? Literacy invitations for multilingual classrooms.* Portsmouth, NH: Heinemann.

Van Sluys, K. (2008) Writing respect (pp. 25–27). In M. Lewison, C. Leland, & J.C. Harste, *Creating critical classrooms: K-8 reading and writing with an edge.* Mahwah, NJ: Erlbaum.

Vasquez, V. (2004) *Negotiating critical literacies with young children.* Mahwah, NJ: Erlbaum.

Vasquez, V. (2010) *Getting beyond "I like the book."* Newark, DE: International Reading Association.

Vasquez, V. (2011) What do we mean by literacy now? Critical curricular implications. Global Conversations in Literacy Research, Sponsored by Georgia State University and the National Council of Teachers of English.

Villaume, S. & Worden, T. (1993) Developing literate voices: The challenge of whole language. *Language Arts, 70*(6), 462–468.

Walkerdine, V. (1984) Someday my prince will come (pp. 162–184). In A. McRobbie & M. Nava (Eds.), *Gender and generation.* London: Macmillan.

Watson, D. & Davis, S. (1988) Readers and texts in a fifth-grade classroom (pp. 59–67). In B. Nelms (Ed.), *Literature in the classroom: Readers, texts, and contexts*. Urbana, IL: National Council of Teachers of English.

Weaver, C. (1994) *Reading process and practice: From socio-psycholinguistics to whole language*. Portsmouth, NH: Heinemann.

Wells, G. (1986) *The meaning makers: Children learning language and using language to learn*. Portsmouth, NH: Heinemann.

Wenger, E. (1998) *Communities of practice: Learning, meaning, and identity*. Boston, MA: Cambridge University Press.

Whelan, D.L. (2009a) A dirty little secret: Self-censorship is rampant and lethal. *School Library Journal*, *55*(2), 26–30.

Whelan, D.L. (2009b) *SLJ self-censorship survey*: http://www.schoollibraryjournal.com/article/CA6633729.html.

Whitin, P. (1996) *Sketching stories, stretching minds: Responding visually to literature*. Portsmouth, NH: Heinemann.

Will, H. (1986) Junior Great Books: Toward a broader definition of the more able learner. *Teachers of Gifted, Talented, and Creative Children*, *9*(1), 6–7.

Wilson, G.P., Martens, P., & Arya, P. (2005) Accountability for reading and readers: What the numbers don't tell. *The Reading Teacher*, *58*(7), 622–631.

Wohlwend, K. (2009) Damsels in discourse: Girls consuming and producing identity texts through Disney Princess play. *Reading Research Quarterly*, *44*(1), 57–83.

Wood Ray, K. (1999) *Wondrous words: Writers and writing in the elementary classroom*. Urbana, IL: National Council of Teachers of English.

Yokota, J. (1993) Issues in selecting multicultural children's literature. *Language Arts*, *70*(1), 156–167.

Zinn, H. (2003) *A people's history of the United States: 1492 to present*. New York: HarperCollins.

Index

access to literacy: via art 126–131; overview 12–13, 19, 22, 31, 91, 100, 128–129, 136, 165, 173; as a result of access to materials 153; as a result of censorship 173–174; as a result of emergent literacy practices 38–42

Adams, P. 49, 203

adolescents: focused studies 12, 110–113, 121–122, 175, 187, 191–193; graphic novels 24–25, 27, 42–43, 68–69, 112, 118, 155, 192, 209, 215; language study 48, 88, 91–92, 94, 104, 143–151, 158, 181, 184–185, 188–189, 192, 197–200, 211; literature study 90–97; novels for teens 42–43, 209; reading aloud 23–24; using authentic multicultural literature 62–65; using international literature 65–71; using risky or troublesome texts 151–152, 166–169; working with 42

Adomat, D. 96, 209

aesthetic stance 67, 96, 133, 171, 187

agency 4, 90, 150–151, 153, 177, 189

Albers, P. 127–128, 133, 137, 171, 209, 215–216

Allard, H. 167–168, 203

Allington, R. 26, 209

Altman, L. 31, 203

Altwerger, B. 29, 57, 210, 216

Alvarez, C. 205

American Indian Youth Literature Award 65

American Library Association 9–10, 42, 162–163, 165, 167, 170, 174, 209

Américas Book Award 65

analytical stance 133, 154, 187

Andersen, B. 205

Anderson, R. 20, 215

Angel, C. 207

annotations, children's literature and other resources (see www.routledge.com/cw/leland)

anomalies, 13, 91, 103

Anzaldua, G. 31, 74, 203

Aral, T. 204

Aristophane 43, 203

Aronson, M. 171, 209

Art Trading Cards 125–126, 139–140

Arya P. 29, 210, 218

Asch, F. 45, 203

assessment: am I creating passionate readers? 10–11; am I effectively using social issue, multicultural, and international literature? 76–77; are focused studies going well? 121; identifying what good readers do 41–42; inviting students' assessment via 'three pluses & a wish'

200–201; is literature study going well? 101; is my classroom library and reading program adequate? 175; keeping track via book logs 100; sharing what was learned via a learning wall 111, 120–121, 190–192; useful resources for assessing culturally authentic literature 65; using an audit trail to assess focused studies 120–121; using 'picture this' to reflect on learning 193, 197; using a sketchbook to document the influence of the arts on your literacy program 70, 138, 193, 197; we know language study is happening when . . . 155–156; we know we are doing a good job of teaching reading with literature when . . . 54

Association for Indiana Media Educators 169

Au, K. 40–41, 117, 210

authentic multicultural literature: characteristics of 63–65; criteria for selection 64

author studies: author websites 120; authors wall of fame 180–181; dimensions of 115; in early childhood education 116; examples of 113–116; small group author studies 115

Author Wall of Fame 180

Avila, J. 54, 213

Aylesworth, J. 148, 156–157, 203

Backer, M. 206

Baildon, M. 158, 210

Ballentine, D. 61–62, 210

Balouch, K. 204

Banana Slug String Band 49, 210

Banks, L. 64, 203

banned books 10, 161–163, 165, 170, 174–176, 191, 210

Banting, E. 69, 203

Banyai, I. 153, 203

Bargiel, S. 72, 210

Barnes, D. 6, 210

Bartholomew Steen, S. 139, 180, 203

Barwell, Y. 76, 203

basal reading programs 4–6, 12, 38, 40, 97–98, 172

Bates, C. 209

Beck, I. 19, 72, 210

Becoming a Text Analyst 88, 91, 94, 181–182

Beers, K. 6, 210

Begler, E. 67, 210

Bellairs, J. 26, 203

Benson, K. 69, 203

Berger, B. 45

Berghoff, B. 110, 112, 210

Berkowitz, S. 119, 210

Bernstein, S. 175, 210

Big Books 182–183

Bird, M. 110, 210–211

Black, R. 54, 137, 210

Blackall, S. 203

Blake, Q. 122, 204

Bleich, D. 133, 187, 210

Book and Periodical Council of Canada 175

book annotations and other resources (see www.routledge.com/cw/leland)

book awards: award winning books 169, 171–172; complicating book awards 169–172; consequences of book awards 171–172; controversies around 170–171; listing of book awards 65; stereotypes in award winners 171

Book Brochures 77–78, 183

book discussions: 30-second informal book talks 167; Buddy Reading 42, 120, 182–183, 191; as conversations 18; discussion questions for small groups 39; importance of 11; investigating a fairy tale text set 89–90; and lack of time 29–30; literature circles 87–88, 98, 100–101, 107, 183, 190–191, 193, 196, 200, 211; not all books are equal 168–169; partner reading 87, 97, 172, 191, 193; selection of books 27; text sets as support 88–90; understanding positioning 27–28

book talks (30-second) 167

Booth, C. 174, 203

Bourdieu, P. 73, 210

Boutte, G. 53, 213

Brabham, E. 51, 210

Bradbury, R. 165, 203

Bradby, M. 127, 203

Bramwell, W. 19, 211

Breathed, B. 158, 203

Breau, A. 60, 212

Brewster, J. 66, 210

Bridges, S. 184, 203

Broderick, P. 131, 195, 216

Brooks, R. 17, 66, 208

Brown, K. 207

Brown, R. 205

Browne, A. 13, 27, 61, 72, 129, 132, 134, 150, 158, 171, 203

Brozo, W. 57, 210

Bruner, J. 7, 210

Brunner, B. 163, 210

Bruzas, S. 47

buddy reading 42, 120, 182–183, 191

bullying 13, 20, 27–28, 61–62, 75, 88, 132, 134

Bunting, E. 31, 84, 98, 126, 148, 156, 176, 184, 203–204, 210

Burke, C. 21–22, 43, 46, 48, 64, 83, 111, 136, 186, 195, 197, 210, 212–213, 216

Cairns, S. 163, 210

Caldecott Book Award 170–171

Calkins, L. 7, 62, 210 195, 197, 210, 212–213, 216

Cambourne, B. 22, 41–42, 210

Carle, E. 23, 51, 122, 204

Carter G. Woodson Book Award 65

Cazden, C. 30, 152, 211

Celenza, A. 49, 130, 204

censorship: Jim Trelease on censorship 174–175; overview 13–14; resources to help teachers 163; self-censorship in classrooms 163–164, 173, 175, 177, 212, 218; self-censorship in libraries 164–165; self-censorship paradox 164; as a threat to democracy 162–166; trashy books 167–168; troublesome books 167–169

Center for Inquiry in Indianapolis 30, 56, 130, 133

challenged and banned books, 10, 160–163, 165

chapter principles: the arts as access 128–131; the arts and critical literacy 132–135; author studies 110–116; censorship threatens democracy 162–166; creating a 'readerly identity' 21–25; creating readers 11–12; creating readers who are savvy consumers of text 12–13; creating readers who know how to unpack text 13–14; a critical–transactive model of reading 42–48; drama 131–132; enjoy, dig deeply, take action 1, 3–4; focused studies 110–113; frames and stereotypes 147–149; genre studies 116–118; good books lead to good conversations 18–21; no apologies for having fun 25–26; not all emergent literacy programs are equal 38–42; reading and writing go together 48–51, 114, 217; reading is a social event 86–88; reasons for literature study, goals and strategies 90–97; social issue books open up new curricular spaces 60–63; text sets 88–90; troublesome books have potential 166–169; using authentic multicultural literature 62–65; using international literature 65–71; on the value of multiple perspectives 144–147

Chart-A-Conversation 91, 93, 183

Chayka, D. 208

Chbosky, S. 163, 204

Children's Lit. Listserv 167, 211

children's literature: definition 5

Chin, C. 75, 204

Choi, Y. 66, 204

choosing books: importance of 10; overview 12; problems with leveling 51

Christensen, L. 88, 199, 211

Christie, G. 205, 207

Cisneros, S. 9, 204

Clouse, L. 87, 214

Clyde, J. 92, 104, 197, 211

Cogan, K. 207

Cohen, B. 84, 204

Cohn, D. 74, 135, 204

Cole, B. 203

Cole, H. 204–205, 207

Coleman, E. 76, 135, 204

Coles, R. 135, 204

collaboration 130, 157, 216

Collier, B. 125, 204–206

Collier, C. 23, 204

Collier, J. 23, 204

Collier, J. 23, 204

Collins, H. 67, 211

Collins, S. 137, 204

Colon, R. 206

Comber, B. 7, 151, 211

commercial influences 29, 185, 201

communication potential 94, 125, 127, 136, 138

conceptual frameworks: conditions of learning 41; critical literacy 7–9; critical transactional reading model 42–48; how reading works 42–48; inquiry cycle 12, 14, 23, 30, 52, 56, 91, 93, 104, 107–123, 130, 133, 138, 149, 154, 171–172, 177, 190, 192–193, 210, 216–217; reading as meaning-making 44

connecting kids with writers: the allure of authors 113; via author study 114–115; via illustrator study 121–122, 187; via multiple response 114–115

Conscience Circle 91, 94, 183, 194–195

controversial books 10, 62, 72, 161–162, 166–169, 172, 175–176, 214

Cooney, B. 149, 156, 204

Cooper, F. 206

Copenhaver, J. 29–30, 34, 211

Coretta Scott King Award 65

Cormier, R. 113, 204

Couch, G. 204

Counter-Narratives 183, 185

Cowley, J. 168, 204

Crafton, L. 123, 217

crappy literature 169, 177, 216

Creating Critical Classrooms 7, 132, 153, 199

Criscuola, M. 147, 211
critical discourse analysis (CDA) 48, 91, 94, 147, 150, 184–185, 188, 212–213, 218
critical lens 6–7, 13–14, 22, 115, 118, 133, 143, 169, 185, 187, 212
critical perspective 6, 19, 22, 47, 94, 149, 153, 214
critical stance: disrupting the commonplace 132–133, 152–153; interrogating multiple viewpoints 9, 132–133; overview 7, 9, 14, 23, 47, 132–133, 177, 199, 213; seeing things in a sociopolitical context 9, 60, 63, 132, 134; taking social action 9, 13–14, 134–135
Croce, K. 5, 129, 211, 215
Cronin, D. 129, 204
cross-age reading 24–25
cross-cultural studies 66–67, 80
Crutcher, C. 24, 98, 204
Cruz, R. 208
Cullinan, B. 213, 215
cultural capital 73
cultural models 4, 147, 149, 154, 185
Cultural X-Rays 91, 95–96, 183–184, 216
Cunningham, A. 57, 211
Cutler, J. 136, 204
Czarra, F. 67, 211

Damico, J. 123, 158, 210–211
Damin, C. 27
Daniels, H. 87, 211
Darrow, W. 166, 171, 204
Davis, A. 104, 214
Davis, S. 98–99, 218
Dayton, B. 43, 204
De Brunhoff, J. 176, 204
de Dios, A. 204
de Groat, D. 205
De Hann, L. 125, 204
de Jesus, E. 207
De Paola, T. 27, 204
decodable text 22, 51
Deconstructing Fairy Tales 32–33, 184
Delbridge, K. 148, 211
Denton, T. 37, 204
Deraney, M. 204
Developing A Miscue Ear 47, 55–57, 184
Diakiw, J. 66, 211
dialogic reading 19, 211
Diaz, D. 122, 204
DiCamillo, K. 20, 204
DiCesare, K. 51, 211
Dickinson, D. 211
Dillon, D. 130, 204
Dillon, L. 130, 204

Discourse Analysis For Kids 48, 91, 94, 147, 184–185
discourses 61, 147, 156, 185, 214
Disney princess text set 88
diversity 12, 59–80, 93, 126, 174, 213–214
Donelson, K. 166, 216
Doppert, M. 205
Dorris, M. 107, 110, 204
Doyle, B. 19, 211
Draw And Write In Role 185
Drop Everything And Read (DEAR) time 26
dual language books 74–75
Duburke, R. 43, 206
Duncan-Andrade, J. 154, 211
Dunrea, O. 19, 204
Dunston, P. 209
Dykes, T. 207

early reading: big books 182–183; environmental print books 185–186, 191; learning to read 5, 27, 38, 40–41, 45, 50, 54, 57, 127, 211, 213–214; little books 48, 91, 95, 191, 193; not all emergent literacy programs are equal 38–42; nursery rhymes 48–49, 182, 193; predictable books 100; supporting literacy learning 38–42; using reading to support writing and vice versa 21, 49–50, 114
Edgar Book Award 170
Edmiston, B. 97, 131, 193, 211
Edwards, R. 75, 204
Eeds, M. 19, 86, 216
Egawa, K. 110, 210
elements of literature: characterization 7, 168; characters 5, 7, 17, 19–23, 104, 143–147, 149, 154–157, 168, 171, 174, 182, 184–188, 190, 197–199; literary analysis 114; plot 7, 22, 39, 90, 94–95, 117, 169, 182; resolution 94; setting 7, 90, 94, 117, 174, 186–187, 194; symbolization 7, 179, 185, 202; theme 7, 12–13, 49, 51, 66–67, 72, 74, 97, 103, 110, 114–116, 136, 154, 162, 169, 174, 186, 200
Ellsworth, E. 131, 212
Elsworth, R. 213
Emancipatory Fairy Tales 90, 183, 185–186, 202
emergent literacy 5, 27, 38–42, 45, 50, 54, 57, 127, 211, 213–214
Enciso, P. 131, 193, 211–212
Environmental Print Books 48, 185–186, 191
Ernst, S. 78, 211–212

fables 118
Face to Face project 134
Fader, D. 10, 212

Fairbanks, C. 212
Fairclough, N. 47, 144, 150, 188–189, 212
fairy tales 4, 32–33, 89–90, 118, 168, 183–186
Fancher, L. 206
fantasy 117, 143
Farr, R. 210
fiction 117–118
Fierstein, H. 27, 204
Figueredo, D. 84, 204
Fischer, P. 37–38
Fitzpatrick, R. 24, 214
Fleischman, P. 95, 204
Fletcher, R. 114–115, 123, 212
Flint, A. 1, 61, 214
Flood, J. 211
Flores, E. 205
focused studies: artifacts 111, 120, 137, 155, 197;
    conceptually related texts and media
    112; culminating experiences and
    celebrations 109, 112, 120, 194, 196,
    199; devices for organizing and sharing
    111; examples, Columbus, Hurricane
    Katrina 107–109, 118–119; exploring
    critical issues 112; focusing questions
    110–111; illustrator study 121–122, 187;
    initiating experiences 111; key issues in
    implementation 118–119; kids in history
    109–112; learning center invitations 111;
    mini-inquiries 175, 191; mini-inquiry
    books 110, 192–193; overview 12;
    planning to plan 111; small group work
    112–113; twenty-four hour 110, 119
folktales 74, 118, 120, 129, 143
Ford, G. 204
Fox, D. 63–64, 216
Fox, K. 180, 212
Fox, M. 31, 37, 51, 167, 204
Frames & Stereotypes 149, 154, 156–157, 186
Franzak, J. 153–154, 212
Freebody, P. 47, 88, 115, 158, 181, 215
Freedman, L. 163–164, 212
Freire, P. 64, 68, 212
Fresch, E. 109, 212
Frost, H. 24, 204
Frost, S. 123, 212–213
Fullerton, S. 209

Gaiman, N. 24, 204
Gallo, D. 72, 212
Gambrell, L. 52, 209, 212
Garden, N. 93, 95, 150, 204
Gardiner, J. 10, 204
Gee, J. 146–147, 184, 212
generativeness 125, 127, 131, 133, 135, 197, 201, 217

genre studies: fables 118; fairy tales 4, 32–33,
    89–90, 118, 168, 183–186; fantasy
    117, 143; fiction 117–118; folktales 74,
    118, 120, 129, 143; genres of literature
    117–118; historical fiction 23, 27, 64,
    107, 109–110, 118; memoirs 118; mystery
    117, 216; nonfiction 23, 29, 37, 65–66,
    95, 107–110, 118, 213; nursery rhymes
    48–49, 182, 193; picture books 23, 27, 37,
    42, 45, 79, 109, 118, 129, 136, 156, 185,
    216; poetry 1, 46, 51, 113, 116–117, 123,
    127, 130, 154, 204, 211, 217; rationale for
    116–118; science fiction 117
Gertz, C. 183, 212
Geter, T. 204
Gilliland, J. 31, 205
Gillis, V. 209
Giovanni, N. 49, 130, 204
Gollub, M. 130, 205
Gomi, T. 167, 205
Gonzalez, M. 206
Gonzalez, R. 74, 205–206
Goodman, K. 10, 43, 50, 52, 212
Goodman, Y. 43, 46, 56, 212
Goss, J. 23, 50, 205
Graffiti Board 186–187
grammar (see syntax)
graphic novels 24–25, 27, 42–43, 68–69, 112, 118,
    155, 192, 209, 215
graphophonemics 45
Grimes, N. 154, 205
Grundin, H. 212
guided reading 88
Guillory, R. 43, 205

Haas, C. 104, 214
Hague, M. 205
Hakim, J. 109, 205
Hal Leonard Corporation 49, 205
Hall of Shame 59–60
Hanke, K. 205
Hannah, J. 84, 130, 205, 208
Hannon, L. 161–162
Hansen, J. 117, 212
Hargreaves, G. 204
Harper, L. 205
Harris, T. 4–5, 64–65, 212, 217
Harris, V. 65, 217
Harste, J. 1, 4, 7, 21–23, 46, 48, 50, 60–62, 64,
    72–73, 80, 83, 87, 92, 104, 110–111,
    127–128, 133, 136–137, 140, 158, 186,
    188, 190, 195–196, 200–202, 205,
    209–210, 212–217
Hartung, S. 206

Harvey, S. 27, 87, 213
Haskins, J. 69, 203
Hasslett, D. 129, 213
Hawkins, B. 130, 213
Headley, K. 209
Hearne, B. 126, 205
Heater, D. 72, 213
Heath, S. 39–40, 213
Heffernan, L. 70, 177, 213
Heide, F. 31, 205
Helakoski, L. 133, 205
Henkes, K. 51, 72, 122, 205
Herman, P. 20, 215
Herron, C. 176, 205
Herzog, A. 130, 205
Hesse, K. 154, 205
Hicks, F. 43, 205
Hiebert, E. 209, 215
Hill, E. 50, 205
Hill, L. 61–62, 210
Hill, L. C. 126, 205
Hillegass, M. 116, 119, 123, 213
Himler, R. 204, 210
Hirsch, E. 6, 213
historical fiction 23, 27, 64, 107, 109–110, 118
Hoban, L. 207
Hoban, T. 48, 205, 207
Hodges, R. 4–5, 212
Hoffman, J. 84
Hoffman, M. 84, 205
Hogrogian, N. 143, 156–158, 205
Holdaway, D. 182, 213
Holiday, B. 71, 108, 130, 184, 205–206
Holland, K. 211
homosexuality 61, 92, 125–127, 152, 164, 173
Hoonan, B. 110, 210
Hoose, P. 32, 109, 205
Hornbook Fanfare 163
Hoshino, F. 205
Hot Seat 187, 194–195
Howard, E. 63, 108, 213
Huber, K. 92, 158, 188, 214
Huck, C. 6, 23, 213
Hull, G. 54, 213
Hundley, M. 211
Hungerford, R. 211
Hunter, R. 205
Hunter-Grundin, E. 212
Hurd, T. 49, 205
Hutchins, P. 6, 49, 205, 213

I-R-E questions 30
I-Statement Charts 91, 96, 134, 188
identities 126–127

Illustrator Study 121–122, 187
implemenation issues: access issues due to censorship 173–174; allowing book choice 51; avoiding controversy, the fallacy of 72; book selection 27; but do we want kids to challenge and talk back? 151–152; but I'm not an artist 135–136; but what about the skills? 52; curricular mandates 71–72; decodable texts 51–52; district mandates 172–173; how do I insure groups are working? 98–99; I don't have the time 28–30, 118–119, 135; keeping track of progress 98; language study challenges the status quo 153; leveled books 51; my district requires me to use a basal 98; the discourse of testing 29; what data to collect 99–100; where do I get language study materials? 153
Indiana Library Federation 169
Ink Shedding 187, 196
Innocenti, R. 206
inquiry (see focused studies)
integrated reading curriculum 53
international literature: authenticity issues in 67–68; international graphic novels 68–69
Interpretive Stances 133, 187–188, 214
invitations (see also literature response strategies): art trading cards 125–126, 139–140; book brochures 77–78, 183; character maps 96; deconstructing fairy tales 32–33, 184; frames & stereotypes 149, 154, 156–157, 186; graphic organizers 70; illustrator study 121–122; Kids in History Museum 109; making connections 85–86; mini-inquiries into challenged or banned books 175–176; sample book log 100; six-box graphic organizer 102–103; through the cracks 138–139, 201
Isadora, R. 130, 205
Iwaoka, H. 43, 205

Jackson, C. 4, 212
Jackson, E. 90, 205
Jackson, T. 53, 213
James, S. 203
Jane Addams Book Award 65
Janks, H. 4, 94, 147, 150, 212–213
Jenkins, C. 114–115, 213
Jensen, J. 211
Jimenez, F. 154, 205, 211
Jimenez, R. 211
Jin, L. 29, 57, 210, 216

Joels, R. 67, 213
Johnson, H. 163–164, 206, 212
Johnson, S. 206
Johnston, T. 136, 205
Joosse, B. 64, 92, 205
journals 53, 107, 111
Juerwicz, E. 212, 214
junior great books 140–141

Kaplan, W. 135, 205
Kawabata, A. 78–79, 213
Kelly, E. 71, 213
Kerstetter, K. 23, 213
Key Ideas 87, 188, 196
Khan, R. 69–70, 205
Kidd, K. 172, 214
Kim, S. 43, 95, 188, 205, 207
Kincheloe, J. 152, 214–215
Kinchloe, J. 88, 217
Kitamura, S. 206
Kitchel, J. 204
Knobel, M. 7, 137, 155, 214
Koblitz, D. 72, 210
Koch, L. 211
Kooy, M. 24, 214
Korky, P. 136, 207
Koshewa, A. 10, 214
Krashen, S. 10, 26, 29–30, 34, 214
Kress, G. 11, 214
Kubler, A. 49, 205
Kucer, S. 50, 144, 158, 211, 213–214
Kuonen, K. 17, 133, 214
Kurusa 135, 205

Labbo, L. 128, 214
Lagarrigue, J. 208
Lakoff, G. 147, 214
Laman, T. 1, 62, 114, 214
Landt, S. 63–65, 214
Lang, D. 57, 210, 216
language and power 151, 212–213
Language at Work 48, 150, 188–189
language experience approach 50, 217
language study: becoming a text analyst 88, 91, 94, 181; developing a miscue ear 47, 55–57, 184; discourse analysis for kids 48, 91, 94, 147, 184–185; examining frames in multiple texts 148–149; language at work 48, 150, 188–189; producing counter-narratives 149; questions to support readers unpacking texts 158; reading against the frame 147–148; recognizing frames 147–149, 154; recognizing stereotypes 147–149; subtext strategy 91–92, 104, 197–198, 211; target, perpetrator, ally, bystander 192, 199–200; unpacking frames 149, 154; unpacking implicit messages in texts 151; unpacking multiple perspectives 144–146; unpacking texts 143–144, 150–151

Lankshear, C. 7, 60, 137, 155, 214
Lapp, D. 211
Larner, C. 9
Laster, B. 29, 57, 210, 216
Layman, J. 43, 205
Leander, K. 211
learning to read 5, 27, 38, 40–41, 45, 50, 54, 57, 127, 211, 213–214
Learning Wall 111, 120–121, 190–192
Lears, L. 59, 205
Lee, H. 163, 205
Lee, M. 72, 214
Lee-Tai, A. 75, 205
Lehman, B. 87, 214
Lehr, S. 72, 212, 214–215, 217
Leland, C. 1, 4, 7, 14, 24, 60–62, 72–73, 80, 87, 92, 104, 116, 127–128, 132–133, 140, 158, 170–171, 173, 187–188, 195, 201, 212, 214–215, 217
Lester, H. 28, 109, 205
Leveled Books 51
Lewin, B. 122, 204
Lewin, T. 204, 207
Lewis, C. 96, 214
Lewison, M. 1, 7, 32, 59–62, 71–73, 80, 90, 93, 95, 132–133, 140, 151, 153, 169–170, 177, 185, 187, 192, 212–215, 217
Libby, V. 110, 210
Lindgren, M. 213
lingering in text 12–13, 93, 114, 128, 138, 143–160
linguistically and culturally diverse students: access issues 173–174; choosing books 73–75; how the arts support 136–137; on the importance of read alouds 30–31; language study 153–154; supporting literature discussions 100; teaching reading with literature 52–54
Lionni, L. 72, 130, 205
Literature Circles 87–88, 98, 100–101, 107, 183, 190–191, 193, 196, 200, 211
Literature Logs 186, 190–191
Literature Response Little Books 91, 95, 191, 193
literature response strategies: art trading cards 179–180; chart-a-conversation 91, 93, 183; cultural x-rays 91, 95–96, 183–184, 216; graffiti board 186–187; i-statement charts 91, 96, 134, 188; illustrator study

121–122, 187; ink shedding 187, 196;
interpretive stances 133, 187–188, 214;
key ideas 87, 188–189; literature circles
87–88, 98, 100–101, 107, 183, 190–191,
193, 196, 200, 211; literature logs 186,
190–191; little books 91, 95, 191, 193;
musical conversation 130, 192, 202;
one observation, one connection, one
question, one surprise 192; one–page
stapleless books 176, 192–193; overview
14; patterns & surprises 87, 91, 193, 196;
postcards of the mind 193, 197, 215;
quotable quotes 87, 91, 138, 188, 190, 193,
195–196; roles in literature circles 87,
190–191, 196; save the last word for me
91, 100, 196; say something 87, 190, 193,
196; six-box literature response strategy
91, 102–103, 197; sketch to stretch 128,
138, 190, 197, 202; sketchbooks 70,
138, 193, 197; subtext strategy 91–92,
104, 197–198, 211; taking inventory 87,
190, 198–199; target, perpetrator, ally,
bystander 192, 199–200; three pluses & a
wish 200–201; transmediation 127, 131,
133, 197, 201, 217; what if 90, 153, 186,
202; written conversation 91, 94, 98, 130,
192, 196, 201
literature study: goals for 90–97; sample
    engagements 91
Little Books 48, 91, 95, 191, 193
Lo, D. 66, 215
Lobel, A. 44, 205
Lofts, P. 204
London, J. 130, 205
Lopez De Mariscal, B. 74, 205
Lorbiecki, M. 134, 205
Louie, B. 63, 80, 215
Low, W. 98, 205, 215
Lowry, L. 94, 205
Luke, A. 47, 88, 115, 158, 181, 215
Lutkus, A. 25, 216
Lyga, B. 177, 205

McClure, A. 166, 215
McCourt, F. 120
McDaniel, K. 104, 214
McDermott, G. 170, 206
McEwan, I. 176, 206
McGill–Franzen, A. 24, 215
MacGinitie, W. 153, 215
McGovern, A. 126, 206
McGuffee, M. 135, 206
MacHale, D. 10, 206
McKean, D. 204

McKeown, M. 19, 210
Mackler, C. 163, 206
McLaren, P. 60, 214–215
McNaughton, C. 130, 206
McPhail, D. 94, 131, 195, 206, 208
McRobbie, A. 217
Madden, M. 43, 203
Maderazo, C. 129, 211, 215
Maloch, B. 212
Manning, A. 197, 215
mantras: dig deeply 1, 3, 13, 114, 118, 125, 143, 149,
        162; enjoy 1, 3, 9, 11–14, 18–19, 21, 25–26,
        37, 129, 135, 172, 190; take action 1, 3–4,
        13, 19, 61, 109, 132, 135, 165
Manzo, K. 71, 215
Marin, G. 74, 206
Marshall, J. 4, 176, 203, 206
Martchenko, M. 206
Martens, P. 1, 5, 29, 57, 129, 210–211, 215–216,
        218
Martens, R. 5, 129, 211, 215
Martin, B. 21, 23, 134, 147, 174, 206, 215
Martinez, A. 74, 118, 206, 216
Mazellan, R. 205
meaning-making: a conceptual frame 44;
        through different fonts 129; through
        music and dance 129–130; open-ended
        questions 20; opening up new curricular
        spaces 60–62; overview 5, 122, 125–126,
        188
Medina, C. 97, 193, 215
Mee, M. 147, 215
Meier, T. 18, 22, 168–169, 177, 215–216
Mendez, C. 203
Mennonno, A. 83–86
metaphorical stance 19, 133, 187
Meyer, R. 140, 212
Meyer, S. 24, 163, 206
Milich, Z. 48, 206
Miller, C. 131, 215
Miller, D. 10, 215
Mills, H. 200
Mini-Inquiry Books 110, 192–193
Minor, W. 203
Miscevic, N. 72, 215
miscue analysis 46–48
Mitumasa, A. 122, 204
Mohammed, K. 69–70, 208
Moje, E. 144, 154, 215
Möller, K. 61, 205
Mooney, M. 166, 215
Moore, D. 144, 154, 163, 215
Moore, M. 203
Mora, P. 31, 74, 206

Moran, R. 25, 216
Morrell, E. 154, 211
Mortenson, G. 69, 206
Moser, B. 206
Moskowitz, M. 114, 215
Moss, L. 49, 206
Mueller, S. 48, 215
multicultural literature 60, 62–71, 215:
    guiding principles for teaching
    multicultural literature 215;
    importance of 65–71
multimodal responses to literature: art trading
    cards 125–126, 139–140; digital
    storytelling 54, 213; draw and write
    in role 185; highlighting social action
    134–135; highlighting the sociopolitical
    134; hip-hop 154, 211; illustrator
    study 121–122, 187; interpretive
    dance 130–131; music and reading 49;
    musical conversation 130, 192, 202;
    process drama 131–132, 193–195; role
    playing 193; transmediation 127, 131,
    133, 197, 201, 217; using art to disrupt
    the commonplace 132–133; using art
    to interrogate multiple viewpoints
    133–134; using art to support taking a
    critical stance 132–135; using clay 127;
    zentangles 139–140, 180–181, 202
multimodality 12, 113, 125–140
multiple ways of knowing: alternative ways of
    knowing 118, 123, 140, 171, 180, 210; art
    125–126, 132–135, 139–140, 180–181,
    202; clay 127; dance 13, 19, 111, 125–127,
    129–131, 133, 136, 201; drama 131–132,
    193–195; interpretive dance 130–131;
    music 13, 49, 54, 109, 111, 113, 125–130,
    133–134, 136–139, 154, 192, 195, 198,
    201–202; remix 137, 155, 213–214; role
    playing 193; transmediation 127, 131,
    133, 197, 201, 217
Munsch, R. 28, 206
Munsinger, L. 205
Musical Conversation 130, 192, 202
Myers, C. 75, 206
Myers, M. 11, 215
Myers, W. 130, 206
Myracle, L. 163, 206
mystery 117, 216

Nagy, W. 20, 215
National Assessment of Educational Progress 25
National Book Award 162
National Book Award for Children's Literature
    162

National Council of Teachers of English 48, 165,
    172, 176, 210–218
National Council of Teachers of English Standing
    Committee Against Censorship 173
National Exhibition of Children's Art 136, 206
Nava, M. 217
Naylor, P. 167, 206
Nelms, B. 218
Neri, G. 43, 206
new literacies 137, 155, 209–210, 213–214
new technologies 117, 120, 127, 135, 137–138
Newbery Book Award 162, 167, 170
Newbery Honor Book Prize 162
Nieto, S. 61, 216
Nijland, S. 125, 204
Nilsen, A. 166, 216
Nixon, J. 117, 216
Noiset, M. 204
Norton-Meier, L. 168–169, 177, 216
notable social studies trade books 65
novels for teens 42–43, 209

O'Brien, T. 67, 69, 206, 216
O'Connor, A. 72, 210
O'Keefe 200
O'Malley, K. 205
O'Neill, C. 131, 193, 216
Ociepka, A. 60, 72, 80, 133, 212, 214
Olivera, F. 206
Olson, G. 179, 206
One Observation, One Connection, One Question,
    One Surprise 192
One-Page Stapleless Books 176, 192–193
Oxenbury, H. 207

Paek, M. 207
Pak, S. 206
Paladino, C. 135, 206
Palmer, B. 52, 212
Panahi, H. 130, 206
Paolini, C. 10, 206
Pari, C. 216
Park, L. 67, 206
Parker, R. 205
Parnell, P. 163, 176, 207
Parsons, M. 20, 104, 214
Parsons, T. 20
Partner Reading 87, 97, 172, 191, 193
Paterson, K. 10, 162–163, 206
patterned books 22–23, 51, 193, 216
Patterns & Surprises 87, 91, 193, 196
Pedersen, J. 204
Perez, A. 84, 206
Peters, J. 24, 206

Peterson, R. 19, 86, 216

Petrie, M. 25, 216

philosophical stance 133, 187

Phong, A. 207

Picoult, J. 163, 206

picture books 23, 27, 37, 42, 45, 79, 109, 118, 129, 136, 156, 185, 216

Picture This 193, 197

Pierce, K. 1, 52, 72, 87–88, 118, 210, 212, 216

Pilkey, D. 167, 206

Pinkney, B. 122

Pinkney, J. 122, 205

Poetry 27, 46, 51, 113, 116–117, 123, 127, 130, 154, 204, 211, 217

Polacco, P. 135, 149, 156, 206

Poonam, A. 57, 216

Popp, K. 205

Porter, C. 113–114, 216

Postcards of the Mind 193, 197, 215

pragmatics 42–43, 45–46

predictable books 22–23, 50–51, 193, 216

Priceman, M. 206

Prinz Book Award 170

Process Drama: components of 91, 94, 96, 131–132, 135, 183, 185, 187, 191, 193–195, 216–217; conscience circle 91, 94, 183, 193–195; draw and write in role 185, 193–195; hot seat 187, 193–195; mantle of the expert 19–195; mock courtroom dramatizations 131, 193; sculpting 194–195, 197; soundscape 132, 193–195, 197; student in role 132–133, 193–195, 197; tableau 131–132, 193–195, 198; tapping in 132, 193–195, 199; teacher in role 195, 200

professional development: collaborative kidwatching 56; creating a focused study 122–123; developing a miscue ear 47, 55–57, 184; gender issues and children's literature 78; getting comfortable with art 139–140; questioning authenticity 78–79; studying self-censorship 176–177; supporting reading aloud 33–34

Pura Belpré Award 65

Push Pop Press 120

quality conversations 18–21, 24, 27–30, 42, 60–62, 76–77, 80, 86, 88–90, 140, 166–169

Quotable Quotes 87, 91, 138, 188, 195–196

Raczka, C. 134, 139, 206

Ramsey, M. 199, 206, 208

Ransome, J. 204, 208

Rappaport, D. 134, 206

Raschka, C. 23, 122, 207

Rawls, W. 21, 207

Rayo, R. 206

read-write-think 48, 216

Readence, J. 144, 154, 215

readerly identity 21–25

reading: the basics 9; a critical transactive view 14–15; differences between approaches 5–7; and fun 25–26; recommended social practices 46; as social 86–88

reading aloud: as an advertisement for books 17; and drama 20–21; how frequently? 21; importance of 18; key issues 26–30; with older readers 23–24 preparing for 20; variations of 22; and vocabulary growth 20; to young readers 22–23

Recorvits, H. 84, 207

Reinier, R. 73

Relin, D. 69, 206

research: on the achievement of children in literature rich classrooms 29; on book discussion and comprehension 10; on early literacy 48; on the effects of time constraints and mandates 29–30; on how the arts expand communication 128; on how the availability of multiple ways of representation expands communication potential 94, 125, 127–128, 136, 138; on how book awards perpetuate stereotypes 171; on how reading supports achievement 17; on the importance of book discussions 19; on the importance of language study 150–151; on the importance of using multicultural literature 62; on the integration of art and reading instruction 129; on literate homes 18; on the multiple perspectives Native Americans hold on book awards 170; on play 88; on preferred ways of responding to text 167; on the reading process 42–46; on the teaching of history in our schools 71; on the use of controversial books 62; on the use of culturally authentic books 65; on the value of free reading 30; on the value of inviting multiple perspectives 128–129; on the value of literature based reading instruction 52, 57; on the value of sustained silent reading 26, 34, 167; on vocabulary growth 20

Rethinking Schools 199, 211

Revel-Wood, M. 53

Reynolds, P. 135, 204, 206–207

Rhodes, L. 23, 216
Richardson, G. 210
Richardson, J. 163, 176, 207
Risko, V. 211
risky texts 10, 19, 62, 72, 161–162, 166–169, 172, 175–176, 214
Ritz, K. 205
Rivera, D. 74, 206
Rizvi, F. 72, 216
Robb, L. 162, 216
Robinson, A. 125, 204, 207
Robles, A. 75, 207
Rock, H. 107–110
Rockwell, A. 207
Rohmer, H. 74, 207
Roles in Literature Circles 87, 190–191, 196
Rosen, M. 49, 207
Rosenblatt, L. 14, 144, 216
Roth, S. 69, 206
Rowe, D. 211
Rowley, L. 110, 143–144, 149–150, 210
Rowling, J. 9–10, 24, 161, 170, 207
Ryan, P. 76, 207
Rylant, C. 149, 157, 207

Said, E. 60, 216
Salinger, J. 163, 207
Sam, J. 207
Sanchez, A. 152, 203–204, 207
Sanchez, E. 203–204
Sand, O. 213
Sanders, J. 128, 215–216
Saskatoon Public Schools 122, 216
Satrapi, M. 68, 207
Save the Last Word for Me 91, 100, 196
Saxton, J. 131, 215
Say Something 87, 190, 193, 196
Say, A. 184, 207
Schallert, D. 212
Schulman, J. 207
science fiction 117
Scieszka, J. 100, 207
Sculpting 194–195, 197
semiotics 127, 131, 133, 197, 201, 214, 217
Sendak, M. 176, 183, 207
Serebrin, W. 131, 195, 216
Seuss, Dr. 158, 176, 207
Shagoury, R. 57, 211
Shannon, D. 31, 207–208
Shannon, P. 27–28, 151, 158, 216
Sharp, C. 118, 216
Sharra, S. 67–68, 207
Shattil, W. 208
Shiga, J. 43, 207

Shin, S. 66, 75, 207
Shor, I. 69, 216
Shorey, M. 110, 112, 118, 123, 217
Short, K. 21, 63–64, 66–68, 71, 80, 83, 87, 91, 94–95, 118, 136, 183, 186, 195, 213, 216
Shwartz, O. 207
Sibberson, F. 52, 123, 211–212, 217
Sibert Award 171
Siegel, M. 127, 136, 217
Siemens, L. 116–117, 217
Sign Systems 111, 126–127, 133, 139–140, 201–202
Silvers, P. 110, 112–113, 118, 123, 217
Simmons, J. 212
Sims Bishop, R. 63–64, 217
Six-Box Literature Response Strategy 91, 102–103, 197
Sketch to Stretch 128, 138, 190, 197, 201
Sketchbooks 70, 138, 193, 197
Smith, A. 67, 211
Smith, F. 5, 21–22, 73, 114, 217
Smith, K. 7, 104, 217
Smith, L. 207
Smith, P. 93, 183
Smolkin, L. 170–171, 217
social issue books: avoiding controversy, the fallacy of 72; characteristics of 60–61, 80; research using 62, 133–134
social issues: banning books 10, 74, 161–163, 165, 170, 174–176, 191, 209–211; bullying 13, 20, 27–28, 61–62, 75, 88, 132, 134; classism 164; diversity 12, 59–80, 93, 126, 174, 213–214; drugs 134; equity 47, 127, 135, 149; gangs 126, 134; gender identification 62, 164, 173; homelessness 88, 126, 134; homophobia 61, 93, 125–127, 134, 152, 167; homosexuality 61, 152, 164, 173; immigration 66, 69, 74, 83–84, 88, 126; name-calling 62, 83; physical abuse 173; racism 62, 72, 126, 134, 163–164, 171, 173, 199; sexual abuse 62, 164; slavery 76, 109, 130, 207; verbal abuse 61, 173; violence 31, 66–77, 108, 126, 43, 145, 148, 153, 161, 164, 173, 217
Socratic seminars 146–147
Soentpiet, C. 203
Sollman, C. 138–139, 207
Soundscape 132, 193–195, 197
Spalding, J. 137, 207
Spiegelman, A. 68, 207
Spinelli, E. 31, 207
Spinelli, J. 168, 207
Spiteri, L. 135
Squire, J. 211
Stamaty, M. 69, 207

Stan, S. 66–68, 70, 90, 217
Staples, S. 162–163, 217
Stecker, P. 209
Steig, W. 72, 128, 176, 207
Steinberg, S. 88, 217
Stephens, D. 216
stereotypes, unexamined in children's literature
Stinchecum, A. 205
Stine, R. 167, 207
Stockton, F. 133, 207, 217
story mapping 91, 94, 111, 190
strategies (see invitations & literature response
        strategies)
Strauss, G. 199, 206
Strawmyer, M. 104, 214
Street, B. 136, 217
Strickler, D. 210
Student in Role 132–133, 195, 197
Subtext Strategy 91–92, 104, 197–198, 211
suggestions for further reading: on censorship 177;
        on choosing books 80; on conducting
        focused studies 123; on the importance
        of read alouds 34; on language study
        158; on multimodal responses to
        literature 140; on teaching reading
        with literature 57; on ways to support
        literature discussions 103–104
Suhor, C. 127, 201, 217
Suina, J. 170–171, 217
Sullivan, E. 206
Sullivan, M. 67, 69, 216
Sumara, D. 13, 151, 217
sustained silent reading 26, 34, 167
Swiatkowska, G. 207
Sydney Taylor Award 65
Sylvada, P. 204
syntax 45
Szymusiak, K. 52, 211, 217

Tableau 131–132, 193–195, 198
Taking Inventory 87, 190, 198–199
Tal, E. 75, 207
talking back to text: counter narratives 183,
        185; deconstructing fairy tales 32–33,
        184; emancipatory fairy tales 90, 183,
        185–186, 202; overview 28–29, 146, 148,
        151–152, 185
Tan, S. 69, 207
Tapping In 132, 193–195, 199
Target, Perpetator, Ally, Bystander 192, 199–200
Taxel, J. 171, 217
Taylor, R. 64–65, 217
Taylor, S. 205
Teacher in Role 195, 200

teacher study groups 56, 107, 122, 152, 176
teaching reading with literature: key issues in
        implemantation 51–52; overview 12;
        research support 17, 19, 29, 34, 52, 57, 62,
        128–129
technology extensions and electronic resources:
        author interviews 75–76; Banned Books
        Week website 174; blogs 135, 137–138;
        censor and children's lit website 174;
        critical web reader 154–155; fan fiction
        137; frequently challenged books
        webpage 174; iMovies 120, 137; NewLits.
        org 155; online read alouds 31, 76; pop
        culture remixes 137–138; for support in
        conducting focused studies 120; video
        on assigning roles to support literature
        discussion 100–101
Telgemeier, R. 43, 207
Tennapel, D. 43, 207
Text Sets (see www.routledge.com/cw/leland
        for additional topics and text sets):
        Afghanistan text set 69; creating and
        using 1, 12, 88, 90, 98, 100, 104, 112,
        133, 171, 190, 200; Disney princess text
        set 88; immigration 84; novels for teens
        42–43, 209
textbooks 23, 26, 37, 46, 57, 65, 68, 88, 107–110,
        119, 174
texts: are never neutral 27, 47, 88, 144, 172; have
        designs on you 4, 7, 11, 24, 27–28, 33, 47,
        60, 88–90, 97, 148, 154, 156–157, 186;
        lingering in 12–13, 93, 114, 128, 138,
        143, 160; talking back to 32–33, 90,
        183–185, 201
texts are never innocent 151
Thomas, M. 174
Thomas, V. 136, 207
Thomas, V. M. 130, 207
Thomson, P. 73, 217
Thomson, S. 206
Three Pluses & a Wish 200–201
Through the Cracks 56, 138–140, 201
Tomás Rivera Award 65
Tomlinson, C. 57, 65, 210, 217
totally tangled 139–140
touchstone texts 62, 114
trade books: definition 4–5
Tran, T. 75, 207
Transmediation 127, 131, 133, 197, 201–202
trashy books 167–168
Trelease, J. 3, 18, 34, 174, 217
troublesome books 166–169
Tsuchiya, Y. 78–79, 207
Tugeau, J. 204

Turner, J. 110, 210
Tweit, S. 148, 156, 208

unpacking fairy tales 4, 32–33, 89–90, 118, 168,
    183–186
unpacking frames 149, 154
unpacking implicit messages in texts 17, 47, 88,
    144, 151, 172
unpacking multiple perspectives 4, 9, 12, 21, 42,
    62, 72, 87–88, 91, 94, 98, 101, 110, 117,
    125, 128, 134, 143–146, 150–152, 170,
    183, 188, 200, 217
unpacking texts 143–144, 150–151

Van Allen, R. 50, 217
Van Sluys, K. 73, 153, 217
Vasquez, V. 14, 60, 72, 80, 111, 117, 120, 133, 137,
    140, 209, 212–214, 217
Villaume, S. 51, 99, 210, 217
Viorst, J. 23, 208
virtual school bay 73
visual discourse analysis (VDA) 122, 127–128, 131,
    137, 140, 171

Wackerly, A. 61–62
Walker, A. 163, 208
Walkerdine, V. 88, 217
Ward, D. 204
Watson, D. 98, 218
Wattenberg, J. 147, 156, 208
Weaver, C. 50, 218
Weber, V. 69–70, 208
Weing, D. 43, 208
Weisner, D. 129, 208
Wells, G. 17, 218
Wenger, E. 110, 218
What If 90, 153, 186, 202

Whelan, D. 164, 173–174, 177, 218
Whitin, P. 127–128, 218
Whitmore, K. 140, 212
Wild, M. 17, 129, 148, 156, 208
Wiles, D. 102, 208
Will, H. 144, 218
Willard, N. 45, 208
Williams, K. 69–70, 208
Wilson, G. 29, 57, 210, 216, 218
Wilson, N. 92, 208
Wilson, R. 207
Wilton, N. 204
Winger, S. 204
Winter, J. 69, 208
Wohlwend, K. 88–89, 218
Wolf, B. 203, 208
Wolf, S. 72, 210
Wolff, V. 95, 208
Wood, A. 14, 23, 208
Wood, D. 208
Wood, R. 62, 114, 218
Woodson, J. 27, 61, 65, 154, 163, 208
Woodward, V. 22, 48, 64, 213
Worden, T. 99, 217
Worthy, J. 212
writing and reading 48–51, 114, 154, 158, 202,
    210–218
Written Conversation 91, 94, 98, 130, 192, 196, 201

Yang, B. 84, 208
Yashima, T. 125, 208
Yokota, J. 63–64, 218
Yolen, J. 108, 208

Zentangles 139–140, 180–181, 202
Zimmerman, F. 69, 208
Zinn, H. 108, 218